THE ENGLISH ON THE DELAWARE

The map on the endpapers of this volume, America Septentrionalis, *is the first English map naming Delaware Bay, although the name is incorrectly placed above the present Chesapeake Bay. It was engraved by R. Elstracke from drawings supplied by Henry Briggs, and first appeared in* Hakluytus Posthumus or Purchas His Pilgrims, *by Samuel Purchas (1625), accompanying a treatise on the northwest passage written by Briggs. The map is reproduced by courtesy of the Henry E. Huntington Library and Art Gallery.*

The English
on the Delaware:
1610-1682

C. A. WESLAGER

RUTGERS UNIVERSITY PRESS

NEW BRUNSWICK, NEW JERSEY

Second Printing 1969

Other Books by C. A. Weslager

Delaware's Forgotten Folk, 1943

Delaware's Buried Past, 1944

Delaware's Forgotten River, 1947

The Nanticoke Indians, 1948

Brandywine Springs, 1949

*Indian Place-Names in Delaware
(with* A. R. Dunlap*), 1950*

Red Men on the Brandywine, 1953

The Richardsons of Delaware, 1957

*Dutch Explorers, Traders, and Settlers
in the Delaware Valley (with* A. R. Dunlap*), 1961*

The Garrett Snuff Fortune, 1965

Foreword

~~~~~~

This volume is intended as a companion study to my *Dutch Explorers, Traders and Settlers in the Delaware Valley* (University of Pennsylvania Press, 1961). The role of the English on the Delaware has never before been treated separately and independently. In his *Swedish Settlements On The Delaware,* Dr. Amandus Johnson covered many phases of early English explorations and settlement, but the information he developed is interspersed throughout two volumes dealing primarily with the Swedes, and is purposely subordinate to the main topic—and it does not go beyond 1656. Other authors refer to the English incompletely, to be sure, as an incidental part of the histories of New Netherland, New York, New Jersey, Pennsylvania, and Delaware. A separate and complete account has long been needed to enable the student to see in full perspective the sequence of historic events in the Delaware Valley from the English point of view in contrast to the part played by the Dutch and Swedes.

Since English institutions and language ultimately replaced the Dutch and Swedish cultures, the significance of the present study is self-evident. Inasmuch as Maryland, Virginia, New York, New Jersey, Delaware, and New England were all involved in English activity on the Delaware, I have brought together scattered references from the historical literature of those areas, some of which are already familiar. However, my interpretation of these data will be found to differ in many respects from beliefs now generally held which no longer have validity in the light of information now available.

For example, the paucity of information in England about the Delaware River prior to Thomas Yong's voyage in 1634 (whereas it was well known to the Dutch) has not been recognized in other sources. This is a key point in my interpretation of how the Dutch came to settle the Delaware Valley well in advance of the English. The buffer zone created by James I in his grant to the Virginia Company, which included the entire Delaware drainage system, is mentioned in passing in many historical accounts. What is brought forth for the first time in this volume is how this buffer zone had far-reaching influence in the 17th-century English colonization efforts along the Delaware affecting Lord Baltimore, Sir Edmund Plowden, and the Duke of York, as well as the Puritans of New Haven.

The efforts of New Haven to colonize the Delaware has never been treated fully, and by piecing together the references in Swedish sources and the citations from the New Haven court records, the story can now be given with a continuity that it has heretofore lacked. Some historians may be surprised to learn, as I was when I first encountered the documentation, that New Haven seriously intended moving the seat of its government from Connecticut to the Delaware River. This information parallels in importance the documentation in the Dutch volume previously cited that the

West India Company originally intended Burlington Island in the Delaware River as the seat of the New Netherland. Also of significance is the voyage of Thomas Dermer who has not previously been clearly identified as the probable English "discoverer" of the Delaware River.

The attempts of the Massachusetts merchants to reach the mythical Lake Laconia via the Delaware River is also brought into focus. This permits interpretation of the Aspinwall expedition which was thwarted by the concerted action of the Swedes and Dutch, who never knew the real reasons for Aspinwall's effort to penetrate the headwaters of the Delaware.

Among the documents given in the Appendix, and upon which portions of the text are based, those appearing for the first time in print include Governor Berkeley's letter of 1642 to Governor Printz; Elizabeth Luter's letter, c. 1646; Governor Eaton's letter to Governor Rising, June 6, 1654; the letter sent by Charles I to Jamestown, c. 1642, relating to the English illegally seated on the Delaware; and the instructions to the Dutch squadron prior to the recapture of the New Netherland from the English. The latter adds measurably to our knowledge of events during the short period when the Dutch seized their former American colonies from the Duke of York's officers.

The reader may be annoyed by the number of direct quotations I have incorporated in the text instead of paraphrasing the references cited. I have done this deliberately to reinforce interpretations that might otherwise be open to doubt if quotations from primary sources were obscured by words of my choice. Although I hope that this volume will hold excitement for the average reader interested in history, it is by no means the kind of book that can or should be read at one sitting, and the direct quotations of necessity will slow down the reading time.

Grateful appreciation for assistance and advice is due a number of individuals and institutions, and special thanks is hereby accorded to Dr. A. R. Dunlap, Arthur G. Volkman, Clifford Lewis III, Edward Carter II, William B. Marye, Dr. Albright Zimmerman, the Enoch Pratt Free Library, the Historical Society of Delaware, the Historical Society of Pennsylvania, Salem County (N.J.) Historical Society, the Wilmington Institute Free Library, the Morris Library of the University of Delaware, the New York Public Library, the Newberry Library, the Royal Archives at Stockholm, the Massachusetts Historical Society, the Virginia State Library, the Connecticut State Library, and the Henry E. Huntington Library and Art Gallery.

C . A . W .

Hockessin, Delaware
August 1, 1966

Contents

Important Dates in English Chronology on the Delaware

The differences between the old and new style calendars are well known to historians, but are worth repeating since, throughout this volume, I have used the dates as they appear in the source material without attempting to reconcile the old style with the new. The Julian or old style began the Roman calendar year in March, but in 1582 Pope Gregory XIII abolished the Julian system substituting the Gregorian or present calendar in which January became the first month. In the 17th century the Dutch used the Gregorian system, or new style, which was 10 days ahead of the Julian, or old style, which continued in use by the Swedes and English. The English began their year on March 25, and both years were often given for dates between January 1 and March 24; for example, March 24, 1639/40, which was followed by March 25, 1640. The Gregorian system was adopted by law in England in 1751, after which January became the first month. English Quakers numbered instead of naming the months while the Julian system was in use, designating March as the first month and so on through the year with January becoming the 11th month and February of the following year the 12th month.

April 10, 1606 James I grants charter to Virginia Company, and establishes a buffer zone lying between the 38th and 41st parallels.

August 27, 1610 Captain Samuel Argall anchors in a bay located in the buffer zone, which he later referred to as "the De la Warre bay," named in honor of Sir Thomas West, third Lord de la Warr.

Spring 1620 Thomas Dermer "discovers" the Delaware River.

June 20, 1632 Charter for the Province of Maryland issued to Lord Baltimore, and one of the bounds was that part of Delaware Bay "which lieth under the 40th degree of north latitude."

September 1632 A sloop from Virginia, with six or eight men, sails up the Delaware River and the men are killed by the Indians.

June 21, 1634 Charter for New Albion issued to Sir Edmund Plowden, and one of the bounds was the "north side" of Delaware Bay.

Fall of 1634 Captain Thomas Yong, in search of the northwest passage, explores the river emptying into Delaware Bay, calling it Charles River. Yong seats an English party at *Arrowamex* (Fort Nassau), later removed by the Dutch.

1641–1642 English from New Haven, under command of George Lamberton and Nathaniel Turner, buy lands from the Indians, settle at *Watcessit* on the Varkens Kill (Salem River), and build a trading post on the Schuylkill, which was soon destroyed by the Dutch.

Spring 1643 Sir Edmund Plowden unsuccessfully attempts a settlement in New Albion.

July 10, 1643 Governor Printz tries George Lamberton, finding him guilty of illicitly trading in New Sweden.

June 1644 English Puritans from Boston, under command of William Aspinwall, seek the northwest passage via the Delaware River, but are turned back at Fort Nassau by the Dutch, with considerable loss to the Company they represented.

Fall 1651 Governor Stuyvesant turns back a vessel from New Haven at Manhattan bound for the Delaware with 50 English settlers.

April 19, 1655 New Haven General Court agrees to lend two cannon and ammunition to a party of settlers intending to colonize the Delaware.

September 6, 1659 Colonel Nathaniel Utie, an emissary from Maryland, arrives at New Amstel on the Delaware, notifies the Dutch that they are occupying Lord Baltimore's lands and orders them to depart. Stuyvesant sends Augustine Herrman and Resolved Waldron for discussions; they find *hactenus inculta* phrase in Lord Baltimore's charter.

March 12, 1664 Charles II grants his brother, James, Duke of York, proprietary rights to lands in America.

June 24, 1664 Duke of York conveys lands in New Jersey to Sir John Berkeley and Sir George Carteret.

October 1664 New Amstel surrenders to Sir Robert Carr; name changed to New Castle. Carr's soldiers destroy Plockhoy's Mennonite colony at the Whorekill; the Delaware territory falls under control of the Duke of York.

August 8, 1673 New York, and all the former New Netherland lands, including the Delaware territory, recaptured by a Dutch squadron under command of Cornelis Evertsen and Jacob Binckes.

Christmas Eve 1673 Lord Baltimore's soldiers burn all the houses at the Whorekill to prevent the settlement falling into Dutch hands.

July 1674 New Castle, the Whorekill, and all the Delaware territory returned to the English under the Treaty of Westminster; the King issues a new patent to the Duke of York, June 29, 1674, and his government regains control.

August 24, 1682 Duke of York conveys to William Penn the lands below the southern border of his Province of Pennsylvania extending to the Whorekill, including New Castle. This area becomes the "three lower counties" of Pennsylvania and falls under the jurisdiction of the Penn government.

October 27, 1682 William Penn arrives at New Castle and the former Duke's territory on the Delaware is officially conveyed to him.

Note: The above Chronology does not take into account important events connected with Dutch and Swedish occupancy; cf. my Dutch Explorers, Traders and Settlers in the Delaware Valley, *pp. 11–13. This volume is referred to hereinafter as* Weslager, 1961.

THE ENGLISH ON THE DELAWARE

1

Samuel Argall
"Discovers" Delaware Bay

It was nine o'clock on the morning of August 27, 1610, and
a little sailing vessel flying the English flag, the *Discovery*, a
pinnace of 20 tons burden, dropped anchor in nine fathoms
of water. Her commander, Captain Samuel Argall, "a good
Marriner, and a very civill Gentleman," wrote that the place
where she anchored was "in a very great Bay," which did not
then have a European name, but which we now call Delaware Bay.

Unknown to Argall, his countryman, Henry Hudson, in
the employ of the Dutch East India Company, had anchored
in the same nameless bay one year before to the month.
Hudson, who was searching for a westward water passage
from Holland to the riches of the Orient, found the part of
the bay where he anchored too shoaly for his yacht, the *Half
Moon,* to navigate. Not having a shallop to precede him
safely farther up the bay (and convinced by the outward flow
of the current that the passage he sought was elsewhere), he
steered out to sea again, sailing up the coast to New England, and later into the river that now bears his name. Hud-

son lost the opportunity of making the discovery that the shoaly bay (sufficiently deep for larger vessels than his, in many parts) was at the mouth of a large river, which at the time of his voyage was not yet shown on Dutch or English maps. Thus Hudson never saw the Delaware River.

Captain Argall had a shallop with the *Discovery* small enough to have maneuvered through the shoals of the bay into the mouth of the river, but the exploration of uncharted bays and rivers was not the objective of his voyage. Thus he too lost the opportunity of having his name remembered in history as the first white man to explore the Delaware River. This event thus awaited the coming several years later of adventurous Dutch navigators in the employ of the New Netherland Company, one of the predecessors of the Dutch West India Company.

Argall had set sail from Jamestown three months before, in company with Sir George Somers, a former member of Parliament, and an admiral who had commanded capital ships in the English navy and had led many attacks against the Spanish. The English settlers at Jamestown had undergone a terrible winter; they were again facing food shortages, accompanied by the ever-present threat of massacre by Powhatan's warriors. To prepare for another long winter that lay ahead, Somers proposed a voyage to the Bermudas in order to "fetch six moneths provision of Flesh and Fish, and some live Hoggs to store our Colony againe." [1] Somers knew whereof he spoke, having spent several months in Bermuda the previous year, en route from England to Virginia, after a storm had battered the *Sea Venture,* forcing her crew and passengers to make a landing on those then uninhabited islands.

Somers' proposal was readily accepted by the other members of the Council, and on June 19, 1610, two vessels started down the James River to seek provisions for the col-

ony. Argall was aboard the *Discovery*, the smallest of three
ships that, under command of John Ratcliffe, had brought
the first settlers from England to Jamestown in 1607. Somers
commanded the second pinnace, the *Patience,* which set the
course. The latter vessel, 29 feet long, made of cedar, had
been built in Bermuda by Somers, using some of the materials from the wrecked *Sea Venture.* She had been constructed "by his owne direction, and partly with his owne
hands, that had not in her any iron but only one bolt in her
keele." [2] The story of the voyage of the two craft has fortu-
nately been preserved in a journal written by Argall on
which the following account is based and from which the
passages in quotation marks are taken.[3]

At the outset, the weather, for the most part, was fair and
the seas smooth, although the vessels encountered rain when
they came to anchor at Cape Henry to take on more ballast
before heading out to sea. On the 11th of July, when they
were well out of sight of land, a gale blew up from the south-
east, and continued that night and for the following several
days. The winds increased in intensity and by the 16th day
the two ships were fighting a raging storm. Winds bent the
masts, and rough seas lashed the sides of the *Discovery* until
it seemed she would be beaten apart. At the height of the
storm she was driven alongside the *Patience,* which still held
the lead, almost colliding with her. Above the noise of wind
and rain, Sir George shouted across the storm-tossed waves
to Argall that they must change course or be swept under.
He commanded Argall to head northwest with him in the
direction of Cape Cod, and his orders were immediately
obeyed. The storm continued, but aided by "some tide or
current that did set northward," they arrived almost a week
later off the New England coast and out of the storm center.

There they faced another weather hazard that enveloped
them without warning—a pea-soup fog. By "hallowing and

making a noyse to another, all the night we kept company." After the fog lifted, they began to fish to replenish their stores, and Argall's crew took "neere one hundred Cods and a couple of Hollybuts." Somers sent word to Argall to set sail again and follow him to the River of Sagadohoc (present Kennebec River) where a short-lived English settlement had existed three years before. Scarcely had they lifted anchor than a curtain of fog again rolled down between the two vessels. The fog continued for three or four days so thick that "we could not see a Cables length from our ship." Argall's efforts to contact Somers by hallowing into the fog, and shooting a small cannon from the deck of the *Discovery* proved futile.

When the fog lifted, the *Patience* had vanished. A shape on the horizon that resembled her from a distance turned out to be a small, rocky, uninhabited island. There Argall went ashore and killed three seals with his sword, and the crew found the meat nourishing. He landed at other small islands, fished and cruised in New England waters, searching randomly for the *Patience,* until August 20. Then, convinced that Somers was lost, he decided to return to Jamestown alone, taking back the fish he had caught as provisions for the colonists. Unknown to Argall, Somers had survived the storms, refreshed himself on the Maine coast, and then steered toward Bermuda, arriving there safely. Unfortunately, he never returned to Virginia; while in Bermuda, "overtoiling himself, on the surfeit, died [November 9, 1611]," [4] after overindulging in roast pig.

Argall's voyage down the Atlantic coast on his return to Virginia, which took a full week, was uneventful and the weather more or less favorable, although an intermittent shifting of winds made it difficult for the *Discovery* to hold to her course. When she came to anchor in the aforementioned "very great Bay," the seas were calm and the winds had died down. She lay at anchor all day, and Algonkian Indians from villages on the bayshore paddled out in their log dugouts to visit the vessel with the white wings—still a curiosity to them. They showed the typical hospitality of the coastal Algonkian peoples toward visitors, and Argall found them "very kind and promised me that the next day in the morning they would bring me greate store of Corne." [5] He knew that corn would be as valuable to the settlers in James-town as the cargo of cod and seal meat that he had aboard. But that night, about nine o'clock, the wind began to blow, shifting from southwest to east-northeast. It was an oppor-tunity not to be lost even at the sacrifice of the corn, and Argall weighed anchor and shaped his course for Cape Charles, arriving there on August 31. Then he continued to Jamestown.

In his journal he made reference to falling among "a great many of shoales, about twelve leagues to the Southward of Cape La Warre." This appears to be the first record of an English name applied to a physical feature in Delaware Bay, and it is reasonable to assume that Argall is responsible for its application. There are two prominent capes, one on either side of the bay, Cape May on the east and Cape Hen-lopen on the west. The historian Scharf made the assump-tion that Argall's Cape La Warre was present Cape May, [6] and some other writers have followed this identification. A careful reading of Argall's account leads me to conclude that he gave the name La Warre to present Cape Henlopen. This seems the most plausible explanation for his statement that, "This Bay lyeth in Westerly thirtie leagues, And the Souther[n] Cape of it lyeth South South-east and North North-west, . . ."

Two years later—June of 1613—Argall wrote a letter to Nicholas Hawes recounting certain of his adventures in Vir-ginia, and in this letter he used the words, "the De la Warre

Bay." [7] This was the first recorded use of an English name for the bay, and the quotation is generally interpreted to mean that the bay took its English name from the cape which was named first. This would classify the second use as a "shift" name, but this is by no means a certainty—Argall may have named both the bay and cape at the time of his visit. He was the first Englishman to record both names, and must be given credit for having first applied them, sup-posedly in honor of his superior, Sir Thomas West, the third Lord De la Warre, then "Lord Governor & Captaine General" of the Virginia colony. De la Warre, who was a member of the superior council of the Virginia Company, arrived at Jamestown only nine days before Somers and Argall departed on the relief voyage to the Bermudas. De la Warre's arrival was a dramatic one, for the 60 miserable survivors at Jamestown (all that were left of some 500 seated there) had deserted the settlement, and had boarded a vessel for Newfoundland when they learned that De la Warre was coming up the James River with men and provisions for their relief. Jamestown was reoccupied and hope renewed; thus, Virginia's claim to the first permanent English settlement in America can be said to be due to the timely arrival of De la Warre.

Paradoxically, this Oxford-educated royalist, and a privy councilor to James I, whose name would later be contracted to "Delaware," and used not only for the bay and cape but for the river, the Indians living on its shores,[8] and a state that became one of the 13 colonies rebelling against the English monarchy, never saw any of these places.[9] De la Warre played no direct role in either exploring or settling the valley of the waterway that still bears his name; indeed, after his dramatic arrival at Jamestown, his participation in the colony was short-lived. The climate of Virginia did not agree with him; he developed "a hot and violent Ague," which was later followed by the "Flux," then the "Crampe." He was also beset with scurvy and a recurrence of gout with which he was previously afflicted. A regimen of bloodletting prescribed by his physician, Dr. Lawrence Bohun, who accompanied him to Virginia, gave him but temporary relief, and except for his youth—he was then only 33—he probably would not have survived.

He left Jamestown on March 28, 1611 (less than a year after his arrival), intending to indulge in the health baths on the Island of Nevis in the West Indies, where George Percy and others in the first Virginia expedition had bathed. Adverse winds took his vessel off course, and he landed in the "Westerne Islands" where a diet of oranges and lemons relieved his scurvy, but did little to correct his other debilities, the cure for them "which by counsell I was perswaded to seeke in the naturall Ayre of my Countrey, and so I came for England." [10] He remained in England until he was apparently cured, publishing a "Short Relation" of his New World experiences, after which he decided to return to Virginia. On June 7, 1618, during a return voyage, he died on board ship.

As for Argall, who was later knighted, there is no record that he ever returned for a second visit to the "very great Bay" which he had named. After his return to Virginia from the voyage, he engaged in the Indian trade for the benefit of the colony—he kidnapped Pocahontas and used her as hostage to effect the freedom of a party of Englishmen held prisoner by Powhatan. In 1617, he became Deputy-Governor of Virginia, holding the position for two years. The grave and persistent problems of holding that settlement together and in improving his own fortune monopolized his attention, leaving no time for further exploration. Thus, the Englishman who named Delaware Bay, and his superior for whom it was named, had nothing to do with settling and developing the territory of the bay and river. In fact, neither of them knew that the river existed.[11]

2

The Jamestown Settlement and Thomas Dermer

It seems almost incredible, yet it is true, that from the time Jamestown was settled in May of 1607 until Captain Argall's voyage of August 1610, the English did not become conscious of the existence of Delaware Bay. Moreover, in 1610, and for some years to follow, they had little or no specific knowledge of the river that emptied into the bay. The so-called "Velasco Map" of 1611 is the earliest English map extant on which the mouth of Delaware Bay is shown, without a name, although the river is not delineated.

The circumstances surrounding the preservation of a contemporary copy of this map are interesting and unusual because of the underlying intrigue. Although of English origin, it is called the Velasco Map because Don Alonzo de Velasco, appointed by the court of Spain in 1610 as ambassador to England, secretly obtained a copy of the original and sent it by special courier with a coded letter to his monarch, Philip III. Velasco and his predecessor, Don Pedro de Zuñiga (also spelled Cuñiga), who successively represented Spain at the English court during the period from 1606 to

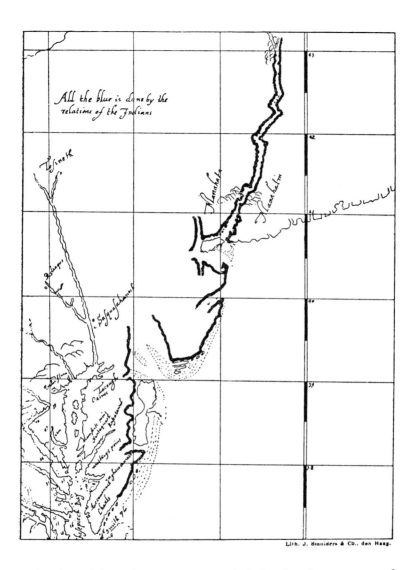

All the blue is done by the relations of the Indians

Lith. J. Smulders & Co., den Haag.

Portion of the Velasco Map (1610–1611) showing the yet unnamed Delaware Bay between the 39th and 40th parallels. The Delaware River, still unknown in England, is not shown. The original map, colored by hand, is now in the General Archives of Simancas. It measures 81 x 111 centimeters.

1613, served not only as diplomats but as espionage agents, obtaining information from many sources and reporting it in code to the Spanish king. They even had an unidentified informant on the Council of Virginia who reported to them what had occurred in the closed council meetings, information they promptly communicated, also in cipher, to Philip III.

Spain claimed the Virginia territory where the English were seated, as well as other parts of the New World, and both Velasco and de Zuñiga urged the Spanish king to remove the English colonists by force of arms if necessary. Every item of information about the progress the English were making had important military and political significance in Spain. But Philip III, who was well-meaning but weak, hesitated to take military action against England even though his council of state strenuously recommended that he do so. Virginia constituted a peril to Spanish commerce in the Americas, but Philip underestimated the menace and considered England wasting money on a worthless region.

Probably by bribing English officials, the Spanish ambassadors were able to get copies of confidential letters, reports, and journals relating to Virginia, as well as secret maps and charts, soon after they were received in London. For example, as early as September 10, 1608, de Zuñiga forwarded to Spain a plan of Virginia and a drawing of the English fort at Sagadahoc. To appreciate fully the efficiency of this intelligence the reader must realize that the English closely guarded their manuscript maps of America (as did both the Spanish and Dutch), and the details of Virginia geography constituted valuable new information hitherto unavailable in Europe. Any member of the Virginia Company who disclosed such information was breaking his oath to keep secret all matters revealed to him, but nevertheless there were leaks in high places.

It is uncertain who made the original of the Velasco Map, but in his letter to Philip III dated March 2, 1611 (old style), Don Alonzo reported that it was drawn by a surveyor, sent to Virginia the year before for that specific purpose, who had returned to England.[1] The map, which is in color, incorporated data attributable to earlier surveys by Captain John Smith, Robert Tyndall, Isaac Madison, Nathaniel Powell, and other English explorers and cartographers. It also contained entries not found on earlier English maps. It was a coalescence of information then available in England about America from Newfoundland to Cape Fear. The delineation of the North Carolina coast appears to have been taken from John White's drawings and surveys, whereas the area of the Great Lakes and the upper tributaries of the Chesapeake are shown in blue to indicate that this information was obtained from Indian informants. Since the Delaware River was not yet discovered, it is, of course, absent from the map. Only the mouth of the bay—discovered by Henry Hudson in 1609 and by Samuel Argall in 1610—is shown immediately above the 39th parallel.

The Velasco Map was not yet in existence when the first English expedition was sent to Virginia. Although there was a substantial body of information on hand in London regarding the coasts of the New World, the latitude and longitude, and the winds and currents, the leaders of the Jamestown venture sorely lacked specific data about the inland waterways along the Atlantic seaboard. Even Chesapeake Bay was known only vaguely, chiefly from the reports of Indians interrogated by Sir Walter Raleigh's agents as they worked out from Roanoke Island. Before the landing at Jamestown, next to nothing was known in England about the extent of Chesapeake Bay, how far its tributaries reached, nor the identities of the Indian tribes living along its banks.

The very first aim of the Jamestown settlers was to locate

a site for a permanent fortification, not only to provide security against the Indians but to defend the colonists against possible attack from the ships and soldiers of Spain, and to give England a foothold in the New World. Virginia was founded upon many different hopes for profitable undertakings—some of them commercial and some industrial. The contemporary records, for instance, disclose an interest in mining, not just for gold, but for copper and iron as well. Profit, and exploitation of other natural resources of the country, were expected. The accounts and papers of this period also suggest that Virginia was being settled for the glory of God, the honor of the King, the welfare of England, the advancement of the Company, and to carry the word of God to the natives.

There was still another important objective, and the instructions to the first expedition directed that the colony be seated on a navigable river, with this important reminder:

> . . . *if you happen to discover divers portable rivers, and mongst them any one that hath two main branches, if the difference be not great make choice of that which bendeth toward the North-West, for that way you shall soonest find the other sea.*[2]

The "other sea" was, of course, the Pacific Ocean, or the "South Sea," as the English termed it, whose waters would reach to the shores of China and the ivory, spices, silks, and other riches of the Orient. The vain hope that trade with the Indies could be established via a water passage through the American land mass was held not only in England but by the other leading maritime nations of Europe. If a new and practicable route to China could be found in America, a colony located close to the route along which the goods to the Orient moved would find a ready market for any products it raised. Also it would protect the route against other nations. The instructions to the leaders of the Virginia colony went on to say:

> *You must observe whether the river on which you plant doth spring out of mountains or out of lakes; if it be out of any lake, the passage to the other sea will be the more easy, and it is like enough that out of the same lake you will find some spring which runs the contrary way toward the East India Sea . . .*[3]

A belief that came to be associated with the northwest passage was that the major rivers of northeastern America possessed a common source in a great lake somewhere in the interior of the continent. This myth persisted in England for many years. Later it was believed that the shores of the lake teemed with beaver, and the quest for beaver pelts replaced the search for the western sea, and notable attempts were made by English traders to find the lake at a very early date.[4] In addition to the Laconia Company, there was even formed in England in 1612 a North West Passage Company, supported by men of wealth and rank.

In order to determine how far the James River was navigable, or if it offered either a passage to the sea or the mysterious Lake Laconia, an exploring party was sent upstream as far as the falls of the river in May of 1607.

The task of exploration was first assigned to Captain Christopher Newport and Captain Anthony Gosnold, but later it was primarily planned and carried out by Captain John Smith over a period of approximately two years. In November and December of 1607, while exploring the Chickahominy River, Smith was captured by the chief Opechancanough, brother of Powhatan. There then followed the much publicized incident of his rescue from death by Pocohontas, the daughter of Powhatan. Not until 1608 did Smith find time to sail to the upper reaches of the Chesapeake and to identify the rivers emptying into it, as well as the Indian settlements on its tributaries. By the fall of 1608, he had completed his explorations of both sides of the Chesapeake, as far as its head, including its inlets, creeks, and the rivers as far as the fall line.

Although it was the quest for knowledge of the surrounding land, the natural resources, and areas of Indian occupation that principally prompted the explorations, Smith always had uppermost in his mind the hope of being the first to discover the water passage to the Orient. From Indian informants living near Jamestown he received the encouraging information that "our Bay stretched to the South Sea," although wise old Powhatan later contradicted this by telling the doughty English captain, "But for any salt water beyond the mountaines, the relations you have had from my people are false." [5]

There is no way of knowing whether Powhatan's assurance that no ocean lay immediately beyond the Appalachians caused Smith to change his views, but his successors persisted in the quest for the passage. About 1621, Lieutenant Marmaduke Parkinson made a discovery that caused considerable excitement among the gentlemen backers of the Virginia colony. Exploring the headwaters of the Potomac, he saw a China box in possession of the Indians, which he described as being made of "braided Palmito, painted without, and lined on the inside with blue Taffata after the China or East India fashion." [6]

When Parkinson inquired where the box, or casket, came from, a Potomac Indian king told him that he had obtained it from a tribe living in the mountains to the southwest, who had obtained it from a people called the *Acana Echinac,* living 30 days journey from the Potomac River. Further inquiry brought forth the information that the *Acana Echi-nac* people lived four days from the sea and ships came into the river where they were seated. Discovery of the area, Parkinson was assured, would "bring forth a most rich trade to Cathay, China, Japan, and those other of the East Indies to the inestimable benefit of this Kingdome."

When Alexander Whitaker wrote his "Good Newes From Virginia" in 1612, he noted that the Indians reported a sea west of the mountains. This body of water, he said, "we commonly call a South Sea, but in respect to our habitation is a West Sea for there the sun setteth from us." [7]

Although Smith failed to find a water route to the Pacific, he acquired a wealth of information about the Virginia tidewater area and its native occupants through his quest for the northwest passage. This and other information appears on the famous map which bears his name, the most carefully detailed and most accurate map of Virginia during the first 100 years of her existence. It was widely copied by many European cartographers and influenced scores of others. But even in its mature 10th edition (containing additions made between 1612, when it was engraved by William Hole and first printed in England, and 1632, when the plates were revised for the last time), Smith's map does not show Delaware Bay as a recognizable estuary separate from the ocean. It is also apparent from his map that Smith's knowledge of the present New Jersey seacoast was inexact in contrast to his amazing accuracy in portraying the Chesapeake system.

There is no reason to censure Smith for failing to find and explore the bay that Henry Hudson "discovered" two years after Jamestown was founded and Argall "discovered" the next year. Smith was chiefly concerned with mapping the immediate area encompassed by the Virginia settlement, and with exploring the streams that coursed northwesterly from the Chesapeake in hope of finding a route to the Orient.

Smith was probably convinced at the outset of his travels that the passage to the Indies did not lie east of Chesapeake Bay, because the Atlantic Ocean (called "The Virginia Sea" on his map) was in that direction. Moreover, in view of the hardships and difficulties that he faced while in Virginia, the exploration of the Chesapeake and its tributaries was in itself a major project. About the beginning of September 1609, he was so severely injured that he was not expected to live, and in October he returned to England, there to recover sufficiently to write a complete version of a *Relation* pertaining to Virginia, which was published at Oxford in 1612, along with Hole's engraving of Smith's map.

Henry Hudson knew, of course, when he entered Delaware Bay, that his countrymen were settled in Virginia; in fact, Smith's earliest drawings of Virginia reached the Treasurer and Council of Virginia in London in 1608, before Hudson's departure for Holland, and there is reason to believe Smith sent him a duplicate copy of the drawing. Emanuel Van Meteren, writing in 1610, stated unequivocally that Smith had sent Hudson "letters and maps" from Virginia, on which he indicated "a sea leading into the western ocean, by the north of the southern English colony." [8] When Smith's map was published in 1612, he had eliminated any entries showing the western ocean and theoretical access to it. If, after leaving Delaware Bay, Hudson had elected to sail to Jamestown (instead of northward to the river that now bears his name), he might have carried information to the English about the new estuary he discovered. Why he did not do so is speculative, but it seems logical to assume that he did not want to disclose his presence in American waters nor his mission. He, too, it must be remembered, was in search of the northwest passage, but he was in the employ of the Dutch East India Company, a competitor of the English, a situation not calculated to endear him to his countrymen.

When Hudson was detained in Dartmouth on his return voyage, the English members of the crew, including one of his mates, Robert Juet of Lime-house, who kept a logbook of the voyage, must have talked about their experiences. Whatever logs, charts, or maps Hudson had made in his cabin in the *Half Moon* were certainly exposed to the eyes of English officials before the Dutch saw them, but if Delaware Bay was shown on his map, there is no evidence that it made any impression in London.

It must therefore be assumed that the full awareness in England of the existence of Delaware Bay dates from Argall's voyage of 1610, and the Velasco Map, which was received in London in the latter part of the same year, but even then the English made no attempt to explore it further. The Dutch, on the other hand, following Hudson's 1609 voyage, dispatched a number of sea captains to explore the bay (as well as Hudson River) as commercial companies became interested in the fur trade. One of these skippers, Cornelis Hendricksen, submitted a report to his superiors on August 19, 1616, revealing that he had discovered "certain land, a bay and three rivers situated between 38 and 40 degrees." One of these rivers was the Delaware, a second was the Schuylkill, and a third could have been the Christina. The bay was, of course, Delaware Bay. Accompanying his report was a "Figurative Map" delineating the Delaware River system as he thought it to be.[9] When Hendricksen delivered this map one can assume that the Dutch authorities considered its contents highly secret information. They had good commercial reasons for wanting to keep the geography of the newly discovered river system a secret as long as they could. If the Dutch were aware of the Velasco Map, which is by no means a certainty, it would have revealed to them the limited knowledge of the bay possessed by the English. Furthermore, Captain Smith's map, first published four years before, and well-known to the Dutch and other nations, did not even delineate the bay.[10] Neither map gave the slightest suggestion of the Delaware River, and thus Hendricksen's map, with its descriptive legend, fitted a new and important piece into the geographical jig-saw puzzle of the New World.

Knowledge that a major navigable river had somehow been overlooked by the English, whose colonists were seated immediately west of it within Chesapeake Bay, was an item of valuable cartographical information in Dutch mercantile circles. This was especially so since Hendricksen's report indicated the river was of utmost importance in developing the beaver trade with the Minquas Indians who lived in the country near the headwaters of the stream. Needless to say, Dutch merchants were not eager to make such valuable data available to the English—nor to any other nation.

A manuscript map made in 1631 by Jean Guèrard of Dieppe is an example of how successful the Dutch were in withholding information about the Delaware River from the French.[11] Guèrard's map (undoubtedly influenced by English maps) shows the bay as "dellowor" or "dellamor bay" in indistinct script, but there is no suggestion of a river emptying into it. I am not aware of any other contemporary French or Spanish maps showing the Delaware River by name; yet, by 1631, the Dutch were intimately familiar with the geography of the Delaware River system which was then shown on a number of their manuscript maps. In fact, as the reader will learn in the next chapter, they had already made settlements on the Delaware.

It is important to realize that there was not a free exchange of geographical information between European nations during this period when large parts of the world still remained undiscovered. In both England and Holland, information about new routes and new lands was possessed by commercial institutions seeking financial gain. It is naïve to believe that the principals in the New Netherland Company, and its successor, the West India Company, would carelessly permit data resulting from their explorations to slip through their fingers or knowingly make their manuscript maps available to their competitors. One must not assume that the full body of map information available today on English, Dutch, Spanish, and other charts made during the period of exploration existed in the 17th century as a common pool for the use of all nations. This is definitely not the case.

For example, in July of 1617, an Amsterdam engraver, Willem Jansz, undertook a project to correct and publish certain maps through the inclusion of new data made available by the explorations of Dutch navigators. A resolution was immediately drawn up and passed by the states of Holland and Westfriesland forbidding him to update any globe or printed maps "but to keep himself strictly and specially holden as interdicted, as such is considered for the Public good; on pain of other proceedings being taken, as may be proper, against him, according as shall be determined against one who contemns the Supreme Authority's Commands and hath incurred its indignation." [12]

As circumstances surrounding the Velasco Map indicate, there was cartographical smuggling between nations; maps were also seized as booty in naval warfare; drawings were illegally exchanged in interpersonal contact, as Captain John Smith is believed to have conveyed his first drawings of Virginia to Henry Hudson. Diplomatic representatives also tried to keep their monarchs informed to the best of their abilities, although in an age when communications were slow and difficult it was one thing to uncover new information and another to transmit it quickly to distant points.

For instance, in the year 1621, intelligence from America reached some of the London financial backers of the Virginia colony that the Dutch were planning to send vessels to the New World to settle colonists on land claimed by England. They immediately presented a remonstrance to James I, who, through his Privy Council, directed Sir Dudley Carleton, his ambassador at the Hague, to intercede with the States-General to prevent any attempt at colonization along the Atlantic seaboard. The communication to Carleton read in part:

> Whereas, his Majesty's Subjects have many years since taken possession of the whole precinct, and inhabited some parts of the north of Virginia (by us called New England) of all which countries His Majesty hath in like manner, some yeares since by Patent granted the quiet and full possession unto particular persons, Nevertheless wee understand that the yeare past [i.e. 1620] the Hollanders have entered upon some parte thereof, and have left a Colonie, and given new names to the severall ports appertaining to that part of the Countrie, and are now in readiness to send for their supplie six or eight ships . . .[13]

The truth is that the Dutch had not yet colonized the Atlantic seaboard, although their sea captains had been exploring the Delaware and Hudson waterways, trading with the Indians, and giving Dutch names to the unnamed physical features. Misinformation in England, which exaggerated the situation, resulted from the lack of knowledge of Dutch activities. Carleton was told by Dutch officials to report back to his government that two companies of Amsterdam merchants had been trading for furs between the 40th and 45th degrees of north latitude, but that no colony had been seated nor one intended.[14]

If there had been a free exchange of information between these two then friendly nations, the English would have known that Dutch navigators had been going in and out of

Delaware Bay and river for many years and had named them respectively, the *Zuyt-Baye* and *Zuydt-Revier* because they were the most southerly waterways in the New Netherland. Later the Dutch would call the bay *Nieuw Port May* in honor of the explorer Cornelis Jacobsen May, and, still later, *Godins Bay,* after Samuel Godyn, a patroon of Swanendael. The *Zuydt-Revier* also appeared on a Dutch map as *Willems Revier* in honor of the son of Prince Frederick Henry. The English would also have known that no Dutch colony had yet been seated on the Atlantic seacoast, but without access to Dutch manuscript maps, there was a paucity of information in England about the rivers and harbors in New Netherland.

It would appear that, at long last, it was information reported to London by an English navigator, Thomas Dermer, that awakened anxieties in England in 1621 about Dutch activity in New Netherland and prompted Sir Dudley Carleton's protests at Amsterdam. Dermer seems to have been the first Englishman to enter Delaware River and the first to refer to it by its present name, but unfortunately the details of his voyage are meager. In fact, not much is known about Dermer himself.

Beginning about 1614 or 1615, Dermer was associated with Captain John Smith in ventures in New England waters on behalf of the Plymouth Company, whose principals, including Sir Ferdinando Gorges, were still interested in colonization despite the Sagadahoc failure. Dermer was capable, intelligent, and courageous, and Captain Smith held him in high regard and spoke of him in very favorable terms.[15]

Returning to England from Newfoundland in 1619, Dermer was employed by Sir Ferdinando Gorges and sent to New England as master of a 200-ton vessel owned by Gorges having a crew of 38 men and boys.[16] Accompanying Dermer was the Indian Squanto, who, with 23 other New England "savages," had been abused and taken in captivity to Spain by the English skipper, Captain Thomas Hunt, who intended selling them into slavery. Squanto escaped from Spain on an English vessel bound for Newfoundland, and from there was taken back to England by Dermer under friendly circumstances. Squanto learned the English language and later astonished the Pilgrims when he greeted them in their native tongue.

Dermer's voyage had several objectives: he was directed to find and join Captain Edward Rocraft (Smith refers to him as Rowcroft), another English mariner who had lately departed from England to explore New England waters under Gorges' auspices. After joining Rocraft, Dermer was instructed to attempt to placate the Indians who had become hostile to the English as a result of their mistreatment by Hunt. A plan suggested by Dermer and approved by Gorges, was to employ Squanto to placate the natives and help remove their prejudice against further settlement efforts by the English. Gorges knew that if the Indians continued unfriendly his efforts to trade and colonize would be thwarted. There was a question to be resolved about the location of a valuable mine, which had been reported to Gorges by another Indian taken to England, and, in addition, Dermer was instructed to bring back a cargo of fish and furs.[17] There was also the quest for the northwest passage, to which Gorges was dedicated, and which Dermer was no less intent on finding.

Arriving off the Maine coast, Dermer began to fish and trade, but he could not locate Rocraft, who had recently been there but had departed for Virginia before Dermer's arrival, unaware that the latter was en route. Dermer loaded Gorges' vessel with fish and peltries and then sent her back to England where, according to Captain Smith, the cargo was sold for a handsome price. Dermer and five or six seamen, including Squanto, remained behind, and he provisioned an open pinnace of five tons burden for use in completing his mission.[18] With Squanto's invaluable assistance he made peace with the Indians, and he also made several test diggings and obtained samples of the earth to be sent back to Gorges for examination.[19]

He next explored the coast from Sagadahoc to Martha's Vineyard seeking harbors and bays. Finding no estuary which seemed to provide access to the northwest passage he decided to proceed down the Atlantic coast to Virginia, exploring the coastline as he went. He also hoped to obtain additional provisions in Virginia. From information he obtained from the Indians, Dermer was certain he was on the verge of discovering the long-sought water route to Cathay.

Following his arrival in Virginia, where he was well treated, he wrote a letter dated December 27, 1619, to his friend Samuel Purchas in London recounting the details of his long voyage and dispatched it on a departing ship.[20] In this letter he states that he found the area between Long Island Sound (which Dermer was probably the first Englishman to navigate, although it was well known to the Dutch) and Virginia a "harbourless Coast for ought we could then perceive, wee found no succour till we arrived betwixt Cape Charles and the Maine on the East side the Bay Chestapeake where in a wilde [wide?] Road we anchored." [21]

From this description it would appear that Dermer was unaware of the existence of Delaware Bay when he arrived in Virginia, even though, as he says in his letter to Purchas, "I stood along the coast to seek harbours." Despite hugging the coastline in his open boat, which did not even have a deck, neither he nor the members of his little crew realized as they rounded the coast at present Cape May that they were overlooking a major bay well-known to the Dutch and shown on their maps of New Netherland.

Dermer spent the winter in Virginia, mended his leaking

pinnace, and equipped it with a deck, intent on making further explorations in search of the passage. He left Virginia in the spring of 1620, headed for New England "resolving to accomplish in his journey back to New-England, what in his last Discovery he had omitted." On this voyage he not only found Delaware Bay, but sailed into it, and entered the Delaware River. He also sailed into the Hudson River where he met with a party of Dutch traders, warning them that they were illicitly trading in English territory. The Dutch replied, according to Gorges, that there were no English occupants there and they had no information that the territory belonged to England. It was this intelligence that provoked Gorges' protest to the Crown, and the Crown, in turn, to the States-General through Carleton.

Perhaps Dermer included information about the Hudson or Delaware, or both, in a second letter that he is known to have written, but which, like his journal, is also missing. What happened was that following his arrival off the New England coast he was seriously wounded in an affray with the Indians, and he returned to Virginia to recover from his injuries. There he wrote the second letter to Purchas, who briefly referred to it as follows, although he never published it: ". . . but crossed with divers disasters, hee returned to Virginia, frustrate of accomplishment that yeare, but fuller of confidence, as in a Letter from Virginia he signified to me, where death ended that his designe soone after." [22]

The contents of this missing letter would doubtless add to our knowledge of Dermer's exploration, and some day it may be found. Along with the missing journal Dermer sent to Gorges,[23] the historian would have exact documentation relative to the explorations of the first English "discoverer" of the Delaware River, who died a painful death in Virginia without ever returning to his homeland to make a report in person.

A final, and most tantalizing note about Dermer (because of its brevity) is found in the records of the Virginia Company of London under date of July 10, 1621. After hearing about two voyages made the previous summer, one by Marmaduke Rayner, and the second by Ensign Savage, which need not now detain us, the members listened to:

> *A Third mr Dirmers Discoueries from Cape Charles to Cape Codd vp Delawarr Riuer, and Hudsons Riuer beinge butt 20: or 30 Leagues from our Plantacon and within our lymite in wch Rivers were found divers Ships of Amsterdam and Horne who yearly had there a great and rich Trade for Furrs, wch have moved the Gouernor and Counsell of State in Virginia ernestly to solite and invite the Company to vndertake soe certaine and gainefull a Voyadge mr Chamberlyn likewise informed the Compa: of the great Trade that the Frenchmen had in those pts of Virginia to their infinite gaine wch might wth farr less charge and greater ease be vndertaken by the Company.*[24]

In short, although the Dutch had been aggressively engaged in the fur trade with the Indians within a short distance of Jamestown—and on territory claimed by England—the members of the Virginia council learned about it for the first time from Thomas Dermer's relation. Moreover, the relation refers to the Delaware River by name for the first time in English literature. Was this relation the missing journal which Dermer sent to Sir Ferdinando Gorges? Was it the second letter that Dermer wrote to his friend Purchas whose contents are still unknown? Or was it a third communication written by Dermer, whose whereabouts today is also unknown? In any event, the entry in the records of the Virginia Company of London put the honorable members on notice that there existed a river emptying into the "great Bay" that Captain Argall "discovered" 11 years before and the Dutch had a profitable fur trade there with the Indians!

Dermer must have realized that in his voyage from the Maine coast to Virginia he passed coastal areas known only vaguely, if at all, to English cartographers. In his letter to Purchas, he wrote, "I have drawn a plot of the coast, which I dare not yet to part with for fear of danger; let this therefore serve for confirmation of your hopes till I can better perform my promise and your desire." [25] This was a veiled reference to the northwest water passage to the Orient, which Dermer must have discussed with Purchas who was prepossessed with the quest for the all-water route that would bring riches to England.

After leaving Virginia and entering Delaware Bay and River, as well as the Hudson River, one may assume that Dermer amended his plot of the coast to include the new geographical features even though there is no documentary evidence that he did so. Whatever maps he made are also, regrettably, missing.

When Purchas published the first edition of his famous work in 1625, in which he included Dermer's letter of December 27, 1619, he also reprinted a treatise on the northwest passage written by Henry Briggs, an English mathematician, professor of geometry at Gresham College, and later a professor of astronomy at Oxford.[26] Briggs believed that access to the western ocean was by water via Hudson Bay, or overland across the mountains from Virginia. Accompanying Briggs' treatise was a map engraved by R. Elstracke entitled *America Septentrionalis* based upon drawings supplied by Briggs. The map seems to represent a coalescence of data from contemporary English, Dutch, French, and Spanish charts. Its significance to the present account lies in the entry "De la war bay," the first reference on a published English map to the bay under its present name. The map also shows a waterway suggestive of the

Delaware River, but was undoubtedly intended to represent the Hudson, which is also named for the first time on an English map. Whether Dermer's discoveries had any influence on Briggs is uncertain,[27] although that possibility cannot be disregarded since Purchas, who first published the Briggs Map, was familiar with Dermer's quest for the passage from two letters the latter had written him from Virginia. But there is no evidence that Purchas had access to any maps made by Dermer, which the explorer closely guarded and probably intended only for the eyes of his patron, Sir Ferdinando Gorges.

Stokes was of the opinion that the Briggs Map and a map published in Holland in 1624 in a printed work entitled *Athanasius Inga, West Indische-Spieghel,* which closely resemble each other, were based on an earlier English map containing entries common to both.[28] The *Athanasius Inga* map also has the entry "De la war bay," although the words are placed along present Chesapeake Bay, and no waterway resembling Delaware Bay is recognizable. There can be little doubt that the two maps are closely related, but they may have been drawn—and probably were—without knowledge of any map Dermer may have made.

3
Sir John Harvey "Discovers" the Delaware River

The defeat of the Armada, thought to be invincible, and the overthrow of Spanish sea power during the reign of Queen Elizabeth ended Spain's command of the seas. The way was opened for English trade expansion, and, as time went on, commercial relations were broadened with Russia through the Muscovy Company; the Levant Company was formed for trade in the Eastern Mediterranean; the Eastland Company for trade in the Baltic; the Guinea Company for trade in Western Africa; and the East India Company, destined to become the most important, for commerce in the Orient.

With the accession of James I in 1603, English capital sought profitable investment on an increased scale. Private enterprise, through joint-stock companies, which brought together the resources of groups of investors, provided the finances to promote new enterprises. Students of economic history now fully understand that the exploitation of the resources of the New World was not an undertaking of the governments of the several European nations, but was promulgated by commercial interests which had many similarities to modern business corporations.

The Virginia Company of London, chartered April 10, 1606, was organized with a profit motive for the numerous stockholders, and colonization of the New World was intended to bring the maximum return from their investments.

The Virginia Company, however, represented much more than the commercial interests of the port of London, and its membership included many gentlemen and noblemen of consequence in the kingdom. Some became subscribers for strictly personal motives, whereas others lent their support because of a sense of public responsibility. The effort was looked upon as a public undertaking, its aim to advance the fortunes of England no less than the fortunes of the adventurers themselves.

The Virginia Company was not only provided with adequate finances, but its charter guaranteed settlers sent to the New World, and any children born to them, the rights, freedoms, and privileges enjoyed by Englishmen at home. The powers of government were invested in a royal council of 13 members known as the Virginia Council, having its seat in London. The members were appointed by the King and were sworn to his special service. Thus the Company, although privately financed, was closely controlled by the Crown, and agreed to yield to the government one-fifth of all the gold and silver discovered, as well as one-fifteenth part of the copper. The Company's charter, a royal instrument engrossed with the Great Seal, made other demands on behalf of the Crown which meant that its financial success was advantageous to the King as well as to his enterprising subjects.

So much has been written about the colony that the Virginia Company established at Jamestown that little new remains to be said. It was England's first successful effort to establish a colony in the New World, after several failures, and I dwell on certain aspects of it briefly only to set the stage for what later took place along the Delaware.

The events leading up to the settlement at Jamestown started more than 100 years before with the voyages of John Cabot in 1497 and 1498, which England claimed gave her right to New World lands in the first place. But England was then occupied with problems in the homeland, with France, and other European countries; and, with Spain commanding the seas, she was unable to press her advantage.

Spain took the lead in New World exploration and settlement and held it unchallenged for several decades, extending Spanish claims over the territories that are now Mexico, Central America, Peru, Venezuela, Chile, Cuba, Jamaica, and the Dominican Republic. Spain became "the mistress of the world and the queen of the ocean." But the English did not remain strangers to American waters, and despite Spain's aggressiveness, English vessels pushed their way into northern waters known only superficially, if at all, in Spain. English vessels fished off Newfoundland where landings, and even temporary settlements were made. The exploits of Martin Frobisher, Michael Lok, John Davis, Thomas Cavendish, Sir Francis Drake, Sir John Hawkins, Bartholomew Gosnold, George Weymouth—and many others—made England conscious of the New World and its potentialities.

No serious attempts at colonization were begun until the reign of Queen Elizabeth when the names of two men stand out prominently above all others—Sir Humphrey Gilbert and Sir Walter Raleigh. Sir Humphrey lost his life in 1583 returning from his attempted settlement of St. John's Port, Newfoundland, leaving to Raleigh the task of planting the English flag along the Atlantic seaboard.

Raleigh's royal patent dated March 25, 1584, gave him the

choice of selecting a site for his colony from the whole unoccupied coast of the New World. He made two attempts, in
1584 and again in 1587, and both failed. It was the expedition of 1587 which set sail for the Chesapeake Bay country,
and has come down to us as the "lost colony," which focused
attention in England on Roanoke Island in present eastern
North Carolina.

By 1600, England was readying herself for a concerted
drive to establish colonies in the New World, and the way
had been prepared by Raleigh with the support of Queen
Elizabeth and others of her court. Interest culminated in the
organization of two companies of Virginia adventurers, one
having its headquarters in London and the second in Plymouth. On April 10, 1606, the first Virginia charter passed
under the Great Seal of England. The document recognized
the two companies, each having its own sphere of influence
in America. Each company was known by the name of the
respective city, and the term "Virginia" was used initially to
designate the full sweep of the North American coast that
lay above Spanish Florida. The latter term, incidentally, was
used to encompass an area much larger than the present state
of Florida.

In the original Virginia charter, the adventurers were
granted the rights of exploration, trade, and settlement of
territory "not now actually possessed by any Christian Prince
or People" from the 34th degree of north latitude in the
south to 45 degrees of latitude in the north. The concept was
accepted by the Crown that discovery alone did not give a
nation valid title unless the new territory was actually occupied and settled. Therefore, the provision in the charter that
it applied to lands not "possessed" by others was an important one because no European nation had yet permanently
settled between the 34th and 45th degrees of latitude.

The charter further subdivided the area: The London

Company was granted land between the 34th and 41st degrees, whereas the Plymouth Company's grant was between the 38th and 45th degrees. In terms of modern geography the country lying between Columbia, South Carolina, and Port Chester, New York, was open for the London Company to colonize. The territory from the present Maryland-Virginia line (near Chincoteague Island) to Bangor, Maine, was open for the Plymouth Company to colonize. The territory overlapped by the two grants between the 38th and 41st degrees of north latitude was open for settlement by either company, but the charter provided that neither company could plant a colony within 100 miles of one already begun by the other.

The Crown deliberately left this overlapping area between the 38th and 41st parallels uncommitted as a sort of neutral territory or buffer zone. This area included almost all of Long Island, the present cities of New York and Philadelphia, the northern part of Virginia, and the District of Columbia. Included, of course, were Delaware Bay, Delaware River, and most of the Hudson River system. The Crown never intended that this buffer zone be settled by the Dutch, or any other nation. Its neutrality was intended to apply only to the two English companies. The companies had the legal rights clearly provided in their royal charter engrossed with the Great Seal as justification for their joint ownership, and the charter was dated 1606. The reader should take careful note of this date when the English clearly specified the area of their ownership which included Delaware Bay, which Henry Hudson "discovered" three years later in behalf of the Dutch East India Company. Neither of the two English companies knew there was a bay in the buffer zone; in fact, they knew nothing about its geography, but whatever was there they could claim belonged to them.

Following the issuance of the charter, and while the English were settling Jamestown, not only did Hudson explore along the Atlantic seaboard, but he was followed by other explorers in Dutch employ who made "discoveries" in the neutral zone. On October 11, 1614, the States-General acknowledged the discovery by navigators in the employ of Dutch merchants of land they called "New Netherland, situate in American between New France and Virginia, the seacoasts whereof lie in the Latitude of forty to forty five degrees." [1] This area was definitely within the patent granted to the Plymouth Company eight years previously and included part of the buffer zone which either of the English companies could settle.

In August of 1616, when Hendricksen claimed discovery of the land, three rivers, and a bay between the 38th and 40th degrees, this territory was referred to in official Dutch records as "adjoining the country heretofore discovered by the Petitioners and by them called New Netherland." [2] This latter extension of New Netherland also included land within the buffer zone covered by the Virginia charter, although no Englishmen were yet settled there.

Following the organization of the West India Company in 1621, the Dutch then proceeded to establish settlements within the buffer zone, which was to become the heart of New Netherland. Although Jamestown had been in existence for about 18 years before the first Dutch settlements were made, neither the London Company nor the Plymouth Company had taken any initiative to move into the buffer zone. The Delaware River system lying within the zone continued to remain *terra incognita* to the English, whereas the Dutch came to know it thoroughly.

In a remonstrance written in Holland in 1649, New Netherland was loosely described as being situated "in latitude of 38, 39, 40, 41, 42 degrees thereabouts." [3] This included the territory from the present Maryland-Virginia

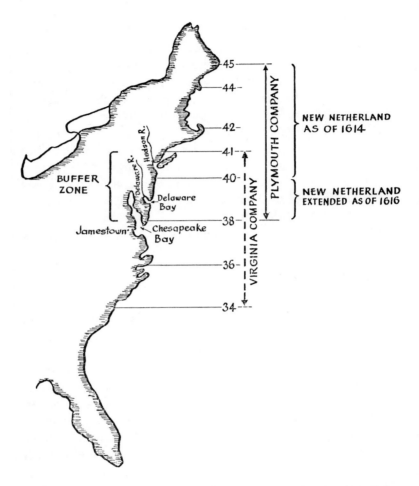

The buffer zone between the 38th and 41st parallels, created by James I, was open for settlement to both the Virginia Company and the Plymouth Company, but neither settled there, permitting the Dutch to concentrate in the area after 1616 when New Netherland was extended.

Line (near Chincoteague Island) to north of Port Chester, New York—in effect, the buffer zone!

The Plymouth grantees, with their prime interest in the area Captain John Smith called New England, established a short-lived colony at Sagadahoc in Maine during August of 1607, only a few weeks after the settlement was made at Jamestown by their countrymen. The Sagadahoc colony was expected to produce great wealth for its backers, since it was intended primarily as a fur-trading post and a base of exploration for precious metals. Of course, there was great hope at Plymouth that the financial return on the initial investments would yield such a profitable return that the undertaking would be expanded into a mature colony. Regrettably, Indian hostility and the severity of Maine's winter weather interfered with the attainment of the first objective, and the glowing reports of Gosnold, Pring, Weymouth, and others concerning the Indian trade were nullified.

The Sagadahoc colony was abandoned in the spring of 1608, and the Plymouth adventurers gave up. This left English occupancy in America concentrated at Jamestown for a decade thereafter until the Pilgrims, followed by the Puritans, appeared on the New England scene to establish their settlements. The persistence of the London adventurers served to tie the name of Virginia to them, and, in time, it came to refer specifically to the settlement on the James River and adjacent lands. But English reluctance to expand beyond Jamestown, even after Argall's and Dermer's voyages, gave the Dutch their opportunity to strengthen their claims by solidifying their position in the valleys of the Delaware and Hudson rivers.

The Dutch West India Company in 1624 placed a small group of Walloon settlers on Burlington Island in the Delaware; in 1626 the West India Company built Fort Nassau at present Gloucester, New Jersey, as a base for the Indian fur trade; in 1631, Dutch patroons founded a whaling colony at Swanendael, near present Lewes, Delaware, later called the Hoerenkil and still later the Whorekill.⁴ The Dutch also built forts or made settlements along the Hudson River, on Long Island, and in Connecticut on a stream they called the "Fresh River." Their largest town, on Manhattan Island, the administrative seat of the colony, also became the commercial center of New Netherland. Dutch penetration of the buffer zone led to a virtual monopoly of the Indian fur trade along the Hudson and Delaware.

The year 1625 saw Virginia under a new king and a new form of government. The charter of the Virginia Company was voided and the colony passed from the jurisdiction of a commercial company to the direct control of Charles I as a royal colony.⁵ The population grew, and separate settlements containing planters and plantations took shape as tobacco became the richest fruit of the land. With the political and economic changes taking place in Virginia, little attention was given to seeking information about Delaware Bay and River, and still no Englishmen moved into the buffer zone.

In 1632, the autocratic Sir John Harvey, then the royal governor of Virginia, dispatched a small sloop with seven or eight men for the purpose of ascertaining if there were a river emptying into Delaware Bay. Whether or not the quest for the water passage to the Orient prompted the mission is not known. The fact is that, at long last, Englishmen from the Virginia colony arrived in the Delaware River, and this is corroborated in a journal written by the Dutch patroon and navigator, David Pieterz. de Vries.

De Vries sailed from Holland on May 24, 1632, in the sloop *De Walvis* accompanied by a small yacht, *Teencoorntgen*. His objective was to reinforce the patroons' colony at Swanendael and to conduct whale fishing in Delaware Bay during the following winter. Arriving at Swanendael he found the remains of the colonists and their livestock amid the ruins of the fort which had been destroyed by the Indians. His food supply growing short, de Vries sailed up the Delaware River in the *Teencoorntgen* to seek corn from the Indians while the crew of *De Walvis* remained behind to try their hand at catching whales. De Vries made contact with several bands of Lenni Lenape Indians at Fort Nassau where the Indians had gathered with their furs awaiting the arrival of Dutch traders from Manhattan Island. He found great unrest among the Indians living along the river because a party of Minquas warriors had killed 90 men of the *Sankikans* and had also slain some of the *Armewamen*. The name *Sankikan* was loosely applied to the area at present Trenton from which the Lenni Lenape living there derived their name. Later I will have something to say about the identity of the *Armewamen* Indians.

De Vries encountered another band of Lenni Lenape living in New Jersey who were more hostile than the others, and the following entry is taken from his journal describing them: "The Indians were from Red Hook otherwise called *Mantes* and had a parcel of English jackets on, which gave me more cause for suspicion, as those were not clothing for them or trading goods." [6]

The *Mantes* (elsewhere referred to as *Mantaes, Mantesses,* etc.) were to become known to the Swedes a few years later as the *Mantesser,* the ending "er" a Swedish plural. De Vries was puzzled about how these *Mantes* came to be wearing jackets of a type worn by Englishmen, and he soon found the answer. An old *Sankikan* squaw told him that the *Mantes* intended to attack his party as "in Count Ernest's River they had seized a shallop with Englishmen and killed the Englishmen."

Not only did de Vries foil the Indians in their attempt to

attack the *Teencoorntgen,* but he was able to arrange a peaceful pow-wow with nine chieftains, representing nine different Lenape communities. He obtained beaver pelts from them in addition to a small quantity of corn which provided food for his hungry crew. The corn was scarce because the Minquas had burned the fields.

After rejoining *De Walvis,* de Vries decided to sail to Virginia in the expectation of obtaining food for his men. On March 11, 1633, he anchored at Jamestown where he was courteously received by Sir John Harvey. According to de Vries, their conversation was along the following lines:

> *He inquired of me where I came from. I answered him from the South Bay of New Netherland. He asked how far it was from their bay. I said thirty [Dutch] miles. He then proceeded with me to his house, where he bid me welcome with a Venice glass of sack, and then brought out his chart and showed me that the South Bay was called by them My Lord Delaware's Bay who had encountered foul weather there some years ago, and finding the place full of shoals thought it was not navigable. They had, therefore, never looked after it since, but it was their King's land and not New Netherland. I answered him that there was a fine river there, that for ten years no Englishmen had been there, and that we for many years had a fort there called Fort Nassau. It was strange to him that he should have such neighbors and have never heard of them.*[7]

If we can believe de Vries—and there seems to be no reason to doubt him—Harvey was not aware that it was Captain Argall, not Lord de La Warre, who first entered Delaware Bay. The map that he showed de Vries depicted Delaware Bay but the Delaware River was absent, and Harvey was unaware of the Dutch activity in the area.

During their conversation, Governor Harvey told de Vries:

> . . . *a sloop was sent there last September, with seven or eight men, to see whether there was a river there, who had not returned, and whether they perished at sea or not he did not know. I told him that we had seen Indians in the South River, who had English jackets on, and had also understood from an Indian, who gave us warning, that the Indians had run down an English sloop there, in which were seven or eight Englishmen. He then remarked they must have been his people; otherwise, they who had been sent to discover the South River would have returned long ago.*[8]

The paradox of an English exploring party sent in 1632 to discover whether or not a river emptied into Delaware Bay is evident. Dutch explorers had been going in and out of the river and bay for almost 20 years; Dutch names had been applied to capes, creeks, bays, and rivers; and Dutch settlements had actually been made at three different sites. One puzzles over the question of why Sir John had not been informed that 12 years before, his countryman Thomas Dermer had written a relation which was read before the Virginia Council in London telling of his discoveries "up Delaware river." Time has obscured the reasons why Dermer's voyage into the river was not given more attention, but the fact remains that the English did not exploit his discoveries.

The net result was that Virginia's royal governor "discovered" the Delaware River through the surprising news he received from a Dutch navigator. He also learned for the first time that he had neighbors he had never met who were trespassing in the buffer zone which was part of the kingdom of England.

4
Thomas Yong "Discovers" the Delaware River

In 1633, Captain Thomas Yong, a 54-year-old Londoner, evidently possessing both wealth and leisure, petitioned Charles I, who succeeded James I, for full power to equip and lead, without expense to the Crown, an expedition to America for the purpose of discovering, occupying, and exploiting uninhabited lands. Yong had the support of a group of Catholic noblemen who were then influential at court, including the prominent Sir Toby Matthew and Lord Baltimore. Yong's elder sister Susanna married Robert Evelyn of the prominent family of Wotton in Surrey, and Yong's nephew, Robert Evelyn, a young man of 17 or 18, served his uncle as his lieutenant on the expedition.

Two letters written before his departure by Yong to Sir Francis Windebank, Secretary of State who had Catholic inclinations, give background details of his plans.[1] These letters refer to Alexander Baker as the cosmographer engaged for the voyage and one Mr. Scott employed as physician. One of the letters makes reference to a certain aspect of the voyage of unusual interest to Charles I, "which remayne private to himself," and that after Yong's party arrived in America the King "expects a speedy and particular account from them" to be carried back by Lieutenant Evelyn in the role of special courier. The obvious inference to be drawn is that the secret phase of the mission was expected to detain Yong in America for an unknown period of time, and Charles I wanted an interim report at the earliest possible moment.

The royal commission issued to Yong in September 1633, under the Great Seal of England, is an interesting and unusual grant of authority. It authorized Yong, at his own expense, to "search, discover and find out what parts are not yet inhabited in Virginia and other parts thereunto adjoining," and to take possession of all lands not yet discovered or then in the possession "of any Christian Prince, Country or State and therein erect our Banners." [2]

Furthermore, Yong was given authority to establish trading posts with exclusive commercial rights in any territories he discovered. He could make such regulations as were necessary for the territory, appoint officers, and establish a civil government. He had the power to meet hostility by force of arms and to slay or pardon an enemy attacker at his own discretion.

Yong could prohibit others from trading or settling in any territory he discovered without first obtaining a license from him. If he found gold, silver, or precious stones he was permitted to retain four-fifths, rendering one-fifth to the Crown. He was also given authority

> to make & set up Factories [*trading houses where factors or agents could be stationed*] in any places he shall discover, and there to fortify with Fortresses and Ordnance, and leave as many of our Subjects with Arms, Munitions or other Provision at the discretion of the said Thomas Yong, as to himself

shall seem needfull, thereby to resist those Nations and Countries that shall attempt by force to expell them from thence and to keep and defend for Us the said Countries, Ports and Places, and to expell, repell and resist all those that shall attempt to pass into any of those Regions, Countries or Passages to be discovered by the said Thomas Young, . . .

I have emphasized a key word buried in the text because it is a veiled reference to the secret matter between Yong and Charles I. As we now know, Yong was in possession of information that convinced him that the long-sought water passage to the Orient was via "the great Bay" that Argall had "discovered." He had settled on his destination before organizing his expedition, and his *Relation* pointedly refers to the fact that it was in "that great Bay wherein I purposed at my departure from England to make triall for the Passage." [3] Although he does not say so, it seems logical to assume that Yong had grounds to believe that a river emptied into the bay, and he reasoned that this river debouched from the great Lake Laconia from which another, but also nameless river, would take him to the South Ocean.

Considerable secrecy surrounded the entire undertaking, Yong having requested of Secretary Windebank "that some verie particular order may be given by his Majestie to my Lord Keeper [of the seals] for the passing and keeping private of these articles from being seene or known by any."

In May of 1634, Yong sailed from England with two fully equipped vessels, reaching Virginia on July 3. The men on one of the vessels had contracted a "pestilential feavor" during the voyage, and 60 of them fell ill and 12 died before they dropped anchor in the James River. Yong remained at Jamestown for about two weeks as the guest of Governor Sir John Harvey, who was deeply impressed by Yong's commission which instructed all of His Majesty's servants to accord him the courtesy "in as absolute manner as any Generall of any Army of ours," and to aid and assist him "in whatsoever shall be needfull for the furthering of his said Voyage and Discoveries." Governor Harvey, who had learned about the South River from de Vries, undoubtedly conveyed this information to Yong, which must have excited the explorer. Perhaps it was Harvey's warning about the reported shoals in the river that caused Yong to construct a small shallop in Virginia. Harvey wrote in a letter to Windebank that he had tried to render every assistance to Yong who "makes great haste to be gone."

On July 20, Yong set sail from Virginia for Lord De la Warre's Bay, taking the newly-built shallop with him, confident of finding the route to the Orient that had brought Thomas Dermer to the identical waterway 20 years before. Strangely enough, there is no indication that Captain Yong was aware of Dermer's voyage. Had Yong known about Dermer or the journals, logs, and manuscript maps of such Dutch skippers as Cornelis Hendricksen, Hendrick Christiaensen, Adriaen Block, David de Vries, Cornelis May, Peter Heyes, and others—all of whom had preceded him in Delaware waters—he may have been less enthused about his prospects.

Yong's *Relation,* intended for the King's eyes, was written aboard his vessel in the Delaware during the period from July 24 to October 20. It is the first complete description of the area in the English language. It is well written, accurate, and extremely important, because it is based upon first-hand observations by a reliable observer. Speaking of the natives, Yong describes his meetings with various Lenni Lenape "kings" and their subjects, enabling the ethnologist to characterize the 17th-century native settlements on either side of the Delaware River as a series of small autonomous communities situated on the navigable streams, each with its own town chief, or "king," and his great men.

Yong also encountered a Minquas warring party from the

Susquehanna who had driven some of the Lenni Lenape from their homes on the western side of the river in the present state of Delaware over to New Jersey, burning their wigwams and destroying their cornfields. This observation corroborates the information recorded by de Vries in his journal two years earlier, and indicates that hostility persisted between the Iroquoian-speaking Minquas and the Algonkian peoples living in the Delaware valley. Although the enmity of these two Indian nations predates the arrival of the whites, the Minquas attacks were intensified with the arrival of the Dutch traders because the Susquehanna chiefs were evidently attempting to eliminate the Lenni Lenape and monopolize trade with the Europeans.

Yong also comments briefly on the trees, fruits, berries, animals, birds, and fish, as well as the climate. He adds that the low grounds were excellent for meadows and were also "full of Beaver and Otter," which would prove of interest to Englishmen in search of furs.

Yong took possession of the country for the King and set up His Majesty's coat of arms upon a tree, and he gave the Delaware River a new name (which he evidently thought was its first)—the Charles River—in honor of the monarch who was to be beheaded 15 years later, and who was termed "a tyrant, traitor, murderer, and public enemy to the good people of this nation."

While he was exploring the river, Yong was surprised by the sudden appearance of a Dutch trading vessel from Manhattan Island. He sent a party to board the vessel and bring the master and merchant trader to him for questioning. Here follows what happened in Yong's words:

When they were come aboard of me, I sent for them into my cabin, and asked them what they made heere, they answered me they came to trade as formerly they had done. I asked them if they had any commission from his Majesty to trade in the River, or no, they answered they had none from the King of England, but from the Governor of new Netherlands they had, to which I replyed that I knew no such Governor, nor no such place as new Netherlands. I told them this Country did belong to the crowne of England, as well by ancient discovery as likewise by possession lawfully taken, and that his Majesty was now pleased to make more ample discovery of this River, and of other places also, where he would erect Collonies, and that I was therefore sent hither with a Royall Commission under the great Seale to take possession heerof.[4]

The Dutchmen asked to see Yong's commission and were visibly impressed by the size of the parchment with the royal seal, and asked for a copy to show their superiors, which Yong refused to give them. However, Yong treated them courteously and civilly because "they were subjects to so ancient allies of my Prince," and he permitted them to stay at anchor for two days and complete their bartering with the natives. The Dutch vessel then departed for Manhattan. Several weeks later, Yong wrote,

Hither also very lately came the Hollanders a second time, sent hither by the Governor of the Dutch plantation [van Twiller] with a Commission to plant and trade heere, but after much discourse to and fro, they have publikely declared, that if the king of England please to owne this River, they will obey, and they humbly desire that he will declare to them their limits in these parts of America, which they will also observe.[5]

The Dutch West India Company might at this time have been persuaded to give up its activity along the Delaware by a show of English force, but this did not occur. While claiming lands the Dutch had planted, the English took no steps to remove them. Neither country wanted to risk straining relations at a time when Spain still presented a common danger.

In seeking the water passage to the Pacific, Yong ran into difficulties in the Delaware River immediately south of present Trenton at what the Dutch called "the falls." Here navigation by sailing vessel was blocked by a series of rocks that extended across the river. However, he sent Evelyn on foot above the falls, and the young lieutenant found that the river was again navigable after a short portage and appeared to run far up into the country. Furthermore, an Indian king informed Yong that he had gone 20 days in a canoe above the falls where he learned from other Indians that

> *this River some five days journey higher issueth from a great Lake, he saith further that four days journey from this River, over certayne mountaines there is a great mediterranean sea and he offereth to goe him self along in person the next sommer with myself or my leiuetennant to shew us the same, he saith further that about two dayes journey above the falls or rocks, the River divides itself into two branches, the one whereof is this wherein wee are, and the other trendeth towards Hudsons River, and that the farther you goe up the River the broader.*[6]

Yong was encouraged with this intelligence about the headwaters of the Delaware, and on October 20, 1634, he wrote a long letter to Sir Francis Windebank to which he attached the original *Relation* he had written. He sent Lieutenant Evelyn to England, by way of Virginia, with these important documents eagerly awaited by the King.

In his letter Yong stated that the following summer he intended to build a vessel to be launched above the falls of the Delaware

> *in which I purpose to go up to the Lake, from whence I hope to find a way that leadeth into that meditarranean Sea, and*

*from the Lake, I judge that it cannot be less than 150 or 200
leagues to the North Ocean, and from thence I purpose to discover the mouths thereof, which discharge themselves both
into the north and South Seas.*[7]

In the meantime, he stated that he intended "to fortefie in
some few places as I goe, and *especially on the River where
I now am,*" and he asked Windebank to intercede with the
King and ask that he be supplied with "some ten or twelve
pieces of Iron ordinaunce."

How long Yong remained upon the Delaware is a question that cannot now be answered, although it seems reasonable to assume that he may have written a sequel to his first
Relation. If so, the account has been lost.

That Yong was instrumental in seating a group of Englishmen on the Delaware is a certainty, and in a deposition
made by James Waye, to which I will make later reference,
occurs this statement, "That as this Deponent hath been informed forty three years since that the first Settlement that
ever was in Delaware River was made by one Peter Holmes
an Englishman near fifty years since brought thither by one
Captain Young at a place called Arrowamex a Little above
Schoolekil." [8]

Waye then went on to say that the English on the Delaware feared an attack by the Indians and asked the Dutch to
take them away.

Again we find in de Vries corroboration of the incident,
occurring in his account written in 1635 during his second
visit to the New Netherland. His explanation of what
prompted the English to leave the Delaware differs from
Waye's version:

*While I was taking my leave of the governor [at Manhattan]
the bark of the Company arrived [from the Delaware] bringing fourteen or fifteen English with them, who had taken*

*Fort Nassau from our people, as our people had no one in it,
and intended to guard it with sloops, but they found that they
must take possession of it again, or else it would be lost to the
English. The arrival of the Englishmen delayed me six days
longer, as Governor Wouter Van Twiller desired that I should
take them to the English Virginias where the English were
expected to assist them. They therefore took their leave of
Wouter Van Twiller, who was governor, and came bag and
baggage aboard my vessel the 8th [of September] we got under
sail with these Englishmen. Their commander was named
Mr. Joris Hooms. [Obviously the aforementioned Peter
Holmes who is also called George Holmes.]*

De Vries arrived at Fort Comfort on September 10 and
landed the Englishmen at "Cicketan," i.e., Kickotank (present Hampton, Va.) "where we found a bark lying with 20
men, bound for the South River to aid them, but our arrival
with their people prostrated their design." [9]

If I interpret the events correctly, what had happened was
that Captain Thomas Yong found Fort Nassau vacant. He
was unaware that the Dutch had not maintained a permanent garrison there, but used it as sort of a market house
where Indians from both sides of the Delaware, as well as
more distant places, came at intervals with their furs to meet
Dutch trading ships from Manhattan. Since it would have
been foolish to build a new fort, he merely took over the
Dutch post, and a small party of Englishmen were placed
there under Holmes' command. Yong then left the Delaware on another mission, no doubt arranging with his
countrymen in Virginia to reinforce the garrison.[10] His explorations above the falls of the Delaware no doubt convinced him that the mysterious lake would have to be
approached via one of the rivers in New England.

After Yong's departure, Dutch vessels arrived in the Delaware for the purpose of continuing their trade with the In-

dians at Fort Nassau, and finding Englishmen living in their fort they seized the intruders and took them back to Manhattan. In addition to Holmes, the name of one of the other contemporary Englishmen, Thomas Hall, is known. Later it was written about him:

> *Thomas Hall came to the South River in 1635 in the employ of an Englishman named Mr. Homs, being the same who intended to take Fort Nassau at that time and rob us of the South River. This Thomas Hall ran away from his master, came to Manhattans, and hired himself as a farmer's man to Jacob van Curlur. Becoming a freeman he has made a tobacco plantation, . . .*[11]

Since Director Van Twiller did not want to provoke trouble with the English, which could have had repercussions in Amsterdam and London, he arranged for de Vries to take the English captives back to Virginia. De Vries did so, arriving in Virginia in time to discourage the Virginia authorities from reinforcing the garrison on the Delaware with a second party of men then preparing to take leave. Thus Fort Nassau remained under Dutch control.

That Captain Yong used Fort Nassau as his headquarters while he was on the Delaware is indicated in a letter written by Lieutenant Evelyn several years later. Referring by name to the several communities of Lenni Lenape Indians in New Jersey, each under the jurisdiction of a separate chief or "king," he writes: "Next is Eriwoneck, a king of forty men *where we sate down.*" [12]

In a 1648 account by Beauchamp Plantagenet also appears a reference to the fort that Yong and Evelyn "begun at Eriwomeck."

The name *Eriwoneck*, like so many Indian proper names, has various spellings depending upon the ear-conditioning of the scribes who recorded it. It was written by the Swedes as *Ermewormahi* or *Arwames,* and by the Dutch as *Arme-wamese* or *Armewanninge,* referring to the Indians living in the area, as well as the area itself that included Newton Creek and Big and Little Timber Creek. It also referred to a specific place within the area where Fort Nassau was built, and the sailor Peter Lourenson stated that the Dutch fort was situated at a place called *Arwamus.*[13] It was here, according to Evelyn, that they "sate down" when he was on the Delaware with his uncle.

The reason Yong decided not to reinforce the garrison probably lies in his failure to find the passage via the Delaware River. His intention was to fortify the route to the Orient, but when he decided his goal lay elsewhere there was no reason to go to the expense of supporting a fort on the Delaware.[14]

Yong's brief sojourn on the Delaware River had little deterring influence on the Dutch, and his own countrymen failed to take advantage of his discoveries. The Dutch continued to remain in control of the land on both sides of the Delaware and to trade freely, and without interference with the Indians, which was the West India Company's chief interest. When he returned to England, Robert Evelyn, as he points out in a letter to Mme. Plowden, turned over a draft of the Delaware River to "M. Daniel, the plotmaker," and the information it contained was then "printed in Captain Powels Map of New England." [15] The latter map maker was probably Captain Nathaniel Powell who was sent to America in 1607 by the Virginia Company. In addition to his drawing of the territory Evelyn delivered the original copy of Yong's *Relation* and carried other documents back to England.[16]

Following Evelyn's return, a map was published by John Daniel in 1639 on which the "Charles River" appears as a tributary to "Dellaware Bay." [17] The information embodied on the map regarding the course of the Delaware may have been copied from the drawing Evelyn turned over to "M. Daniel, the plotmaker." From this time on there could be no doubt that the existence of a river emptying into Delaware Bay was well known in England, and it is shown thereafter on English maps and, in time, the word Delaware supplanted Charles as its name.

To say it was well known does not mean that the English were fully informed about its length and its position in relation to the degrees of latitude. As late as April 2, 1681— almost 50 years after Yong's visit—Conway wrote Lord Baltimore that William Penn's lands (and the italic is mine) "bounded on the East by Delaware River from twelve miles distance northward of New Castle Towne unto the 43th degree of Northern Latitude, *if the said River doth extend so farr Northward,* and if the said River shall not extend so farr Northward, then by the said River so far as it doth extend . . ." [18]

5

The Swedes Come
to the Delaware

〰〰〰〰〰〰〰〰〰〰〰〰〰〰〰〰〰

Sweden was the next nation to turn its attention to the Delaware River valley. If the part the Swedes played has since been exaggerated, it may be partially attributed to an *ex post facto* inflation of the size and importance of their 17th century settlement on the Delaware. I do not mean to belittle their efforts by pointing out that Swedish officialdom, aided by a million or more Americans of Swedish descent, has taken advantage of the opportunity to tighten the bonds of friendship between the two countries by using the first Swedish settlement as the common tie.

As early as 1888, a celebration was held in Minneapolis to commemorate the 250th anniversary of the landing of the first Swedish settlers at the "Rocks" near Wilmington, Delaware. The Swedish-Americans assembled on the occasion sent a cablegram to King Oscar "with affectionate greetings and assurances of filial love for the honored land that fostered them [the Delaware Swedes] and us." [1]

The ceremonies were brought closer home on June 27, 1938, on the occasion of the tercentenary of the Swedish landing at the mouth of the Christina River where the first Swedish expedition built Fort Christina, named for their then child queen. The Crown Prince (later King Gustav VI Adolph) and his son, Prince Gustav Bertil (promptly nicknamed "Bertie" in the American press) sailed up the Delaware to the "Rocks" in company with other Swedish dignitaries, who crossed the Atlantic in the M.S. *Kungsholm*. The President of the United States, Franklin D. Roosevelt, his Secretary of State, Cordell Hull, and other U. S. officials came to Wilmington, where a black granite monument, created by the Swedish sculptor, Carl Milles, was unveiled as a gift of the Swedish people to the American people.

I was present on this occasion and observed that some of the speeches overstated the facts of the 17th-century Swedish occupation. Yet it seemed permissible at a time when emotions were aroused by bands and parades, the exhibits of Swedish fine art brought from Europe and displayed in American cities, and the special coins and commemorative stamps issued for the event in both countries.

Again in 1963, an older and heavier Prince Bertil came to America for the 325th anniversary of the Swedish colony, and his second visit brought forth another wave of publicity in American newspapers. At a press conference in Wilmington, the reporters queried the bachelor prince on such subjects as American girls, marriage, and politics, although little was said about the beginning of the first colony. Perhaps the Prince realized that there was little more to be added on this account since I have no doubt that he was familiar with the monumental history of the colony written by the scholarly Amandus Johnson. Five years in preparation, it required three trips to Sweden and represents primary source material of inestimable value.

This work—as well as other writings by the same author—has done much to keep the Swedish contributions alive in

American historical literature. The Swedish Colonial Society, who sponsored Johnson's history, as well as several
other informative volumes dealing with the Swedish colony,
has been active in locating, identifying, and marking historic sites in the Delaware valley connected with the Swedish
occupation. This activity not only has kept American visitors aware of the Swedish background, but it has also
brought distinguished Scandinavian visitors to America, as,
for example, during the Sesquicentennial Commemoration
of American Independence held in Philadelphia in 1926,
which had nothing to do with the first Swedish settlements.
On that occasion a replica of the old Wicaco Block House
was erected, and the Crown Prince and Princess of Sweden
attended its dedication.

The American Swedish Museum in Philadelphia, maintained by the Society, has preserved Swedish traditions
through exhibits of portraits, maps, documents, and other
materials of both American and European origin, some relating to later personalities of Swedish extraction whose contributions to American life and letters, important though
they were, have no direct connection with the early Swedish
settlements.

My comments are in no way intended to be critical, because there is absolutely nothing wrong with this pro-
Swedish implantation which has helped to make Americans
aware of one facet of their heritage even though it may, at
times, glitter unduly. My only concern is to present the
documented facts to arrive at the true objective view that
history demands for an unbiased appraisal of the part that
the Swedes played in the Delaware valley in contrast to the
Dutch and English.

The facts are apparent that the Swedes were latecomers to
the Delaware River. They did, indeed, found a settlement at
Wilmington in March of 1638, which is usually referred to

as the first "permanent" white settlement in the Delaware valley, although this has misleading connotations because it was not the earliest settlement.

The population of New Sweden on the Delaware was pitifully small, even at its peak. In 1644, there were 83 male inhabitants (number of females and children not recorded); in 1648, there were 83 males. In 1647, there were "183 souls with 28 freemen on farms," and in 1653, there were 200 souls, including men, women, and children.[2]

By 1655, when the Dutch seized control, the total population was about 400, and New Sweden's full span of existence had been only for 17 years.

The fact that the colony existed for only a short time, and that its population was small, does not, however, justify underestimating the role of the Swedes, for it was an interesting and dramatic one. While the Dutch, English, Spanish, Portuguese, Italian, and French navigators were charting the waters and exploring the lands of the New World during the 16th and 17th centuries, the might of the army and navy of Gustavus Adolphus, who ascended the Swedish throne in 1611, was directed against Denmark, Russia, Poland, and, in 1630, against Germany. The political problems the King faced in Europe did not allow him to give attention to explorations of the New World even if he were so inclined.

While Gustavus Adolphus was occupied at home with military and political problems, the first settlement on the Delaware was made by the Dutch West India Company on Burlington Island, New Jersey, in 1624. It is true that it was an impermanent colony, because the handful of Walloon settlers were later moved to Manhattan Island. Then, in 1626, the Dutch West India Company built the first fort on the Delaware at present Gloucester, New Jersey, which they called Fort Nassau. This fort was occupied intermittently from 1626 to 1651 when it was abandoned by Peter Stuyvesant and Fort Casimir erected. Nevertheless, Fort Nassau was garrisoned when the Swedes first appeared in the Delaware River. In 1631, Dutch patroons established a whaling colony at Swanendael at the mouth of Delaware Bay, and although it was "impermanent" because of the Indian massacre of the colonists, it, too, predated Swedish occupancy.

As the reader has seen in the previous chapters, Samuel Argall was in Delaware Bay in 1610, Thomas Dermer in 1620, and, in 1635, as a result of Captain Thomas Yong's explorations, the English made an unsuccessful attempt to found a settlement on the Delaware River. This also occurred before the appearance of the Swedes in the New World.

The Swedes arrived in the Delaware after other nations had shown the way, and the Swedish records are crystal clear that it was primarily Dutch know-how that prompted them to send the first expedition to America. The riches Spain garnered in the New World, Portugal's profitable traffic with the East, England's growing foreign trade after the defeat of the Spanish Armada, and Holland's enrichment with her enlarged mercantile interests, stirred business interests in Sweden to look toward the New World for profits.

Although Sweden was well advanced in her military and political systems, her industrial and commercial organization was at a low level compared to those of England and Holland, despite the organization of commercial and trading companies. In addition, Sweden was slow to act so far as exploiting the New World was concerned. It required the strong and persistent influence of a Dutch business executive, Willem Usselinx, one of the prime movers in the formation of the Dutch West India Company, to persuade the Swedish authorities to organize a commercial company to exploit the resources of faraway lands. Other non-Swedes later furthered the plan, including Samuel Blommaert, a former director of the Dutch West India Company and a patroon of the Swanendael colony, and Peter Spiring Silfverkrona (born Spiring in Holland and enobled as Silfverkrona in Sweden). A third—Peter Minuit—was neither a Swede nor Dutchman, but of French descent. He was an ex-governor of the Dutch colony in the New World, and after leaving the employ of the Dutch West India Company he sold his services to the Swedes.

These three—and Klas Fleming, an admiral in the Swedish navy and a Finn by birth—were the principals in forming the New Sweden Company which was given exclusive right to trade on the Delaware River for 20 years. In addition to the Swedish stockholders in the company, the financial backers included Adam Bessels, Isaac von dem Waeter, Gillies von Brugge, Jaris Hoeffnaegel, and Huygens van Arnheim—all Dutchmen.

When plans were made final in Sweden for an expedition to America, two ships were outfitted—the *Kalmar Nyckel* ("Key of Kalmar") and the *Fogel Grip* ("Bird Griffin"). Their crews consisted principally of Dutch sailors. A Dutchman, Jan Hindrickson van de Waeeter, was appointed skipper of the *Kalmar Nyckel,* and Adrian Joransen commanded the *Fogel Grip.* Henry Huygen, a Dutchman, was appointed commissary for the new colony—and Peter Minuit was placed in charge of the expedition, which set sail for America in December of 1637. Secrecy surrounded the preparation for the voyage, because the Swedish company did not want the news to leak out to the Dutch West India Company that its destination was territory that the Dutch considered part of their New Netherland.

Peter Minuit was the best choice the sponsors of the Swedish expedition could have made to direct their first thrust into the Dutch New World. From 1626 to 1632 he had been the governor of New Netherland with his administrative office on Manhattan Island, and he probably knew more about New Netherland than any living person. He had been a member of the early Dutch expedition to the Delaware; he was well schooled in Dutch business practices; he had issued the patents to the patroons for the Swanendael colony; he had been party to the building of Fort Nassau. Minuit also had long experience in the Indian trade and knew exactly what type of European merchandise—duffels, axes, hatchets, mirrors, chains, finger rings, combs, etc.—was in greatest demand, what tribes supplied the best pelts, and at what time of the year trading was most advantageous. He knew the weaknesses and strengths of the Dutch West India Company, since he had been privy to the instructions issued to their officials in New Netherland. Minuit had seen confidential reports from directors and patroons, as well as personal correspondence, and maps, not intended for the eyes of persons outside the company.

It is well known that in his new role Minuit was apprehensive of running afoul of Dutch territorial interests, but a document dated 1684, recently brought to light, indicates that he was also concerned about encountering English interference.[3] In this document, several old Swedes depose that after sailing up the Delaware Minuit anchored his two vessels in the Christina for six weeks and three days in the expectation of English protest. Receiving none, he summoned the local Indian sachems, including the old Lenni Lenape chief Mattahorn, to establish friendly relations prior to building Fort Christina on the stream he first called the Elb and later renamed after Sweden's child queen. He took five of the chiefs aboard the *Kalmar Nyckel,* and for certain trade goods "bought from them as much of the Adjacent Land as they could shoot over with a Cannon bullet from

Christina."[4] The deeds covering his purchase are now lost, but it is surmised he acquired land in approximately equal amounts from Bombay Hook (present Duck Creek) as far north as the Schuylkill, stretching westward indefinitely. After the parchments, officially engrossed with the totemic marks of the chiefs, were in his possession, Minuit went ashore and erected a pole with the coat of arms of Sweden upon it, formally naming the territory New Sweden. He knew better than anyone in his party that he was trespassing on the territory of the New Netherland, but he also knew that the Dutch West India Company had been more or less indifferent about compensating the Indians for the site he had chosen, and there were no Indian deeds in the company's files covering specific lands between Duck Creek and the Schuylkill. This omission, incidentally, Governor Peter Stuyvesant belatedly attempted to correct when friction later developed between him and the Swedish interlopers.

Minuit also knew that England claimed the land along the Delaware as part of Virginia, for on his return to Holland from the New Netherland six years before on the *Eendracht* the English authorities had detained the vessel in Plymouth. Minuit was arrested "for having traded in countries under the King of Great Britain's jurisdiction" without authority, and the cargo of peltries aboard the *Eendracht* was used as evidence against him.[5] During the period of the vessel's detention in England, diplomatic correspondence was exchanged between the two governments in which the English made reference to the Virginia charter of 1606. As a central figure in this controversy, Minuit was familiar with English claims and was apprehensive of further personal involvement with the English, even though amicable relations then existed between England and Sweden, by whom he was now employed.

Intelligence soon reached the garrison at Fort Nassau, a

few miles up the Delaware River, that there were intruders in their territory. The Dutch petty officer in charge sailed down to warn the newcomers not to pass the fort, and one can imagine his surprise to find that their leader was none other than the former ranking Dutch official in New Netherland. Minuit blithely replied that "his Queen [!] had as much right there as the company."

When he left Dutch employ, Minuit was succeeded by Wouter van Twiller, and the latter in 1637 by Willem Kieft, who was occupying Minuit's former administrative post on Manhattan Island when the two Swedish vessels anchored in the Christina. Kieft, receiving a report from Fort Nassau by special messenger, promptly sent a written warning to Minuit reminding him he was trespassing on Dutch territory "sealed with our blood," [6] referring to the Swanendael massacre. Minuit knew more about this and what had gone on before than Kieft. He also had reason to believe that the West India Company would not go beyond the use of threats to deter him from settling a Swedish force on the Delaware, first, because of their limited strength in New Netherland, and second, because Holland and Sweden were friendly powers and Kieft would not want to provoke an incident. Minuit continued with the erection of Fort Christina, and, at the same time, began to trade with the Indians for beaver pelts, giving more merchandise than the Dutch traders at Fort Nassau, which added insult to the injury he was causing his former employers.

*   *   *   *

It was no will-o'-the-wisp northwest passage or elusive inland Lake Laconia that awakened Swedish interest in the Delaware valley. Like the Dutch, the Swedes, who invested in the New Sweden Company, were seeking a profitable return, and the Delaware River area was second to none among American rivers in terms of the business opportunities offered by its natural resources. The Dutch trader that Captain Yong took aboard his vessel told him that if he were ruling the West India Company he would have made the Delaware River the seat of the colony instead of the island at the mouth of the Hudson.[7] He was apparently unaware that 10 years earlier the Dutch provisional governor, Willem Verhulst, was instructed by the directors of the company to make "High Island" (present Burlington Island) the seat of the New Netherland, although circumstances later caused a shift of the population to Manhattan Island.[8]

Despite its shoals, the Delaware was navigable by large sailing vessels from Cape Henlopen as far north as present Trenton, although an experienced skipper, or pilot, was required to bring a vessel into the bay and up the river. A major, navigable river, like the Delaware, was a highly valuable asset in an age when international movement of people and goods was largely by water. Its many tributaries, like the Maurice, Christina, Salem, Big Timber, Chester, Schuylkill, and other rivers and creeks, permitted deep penetration by sailing vessel of the land on both sides of the main stream. Many of the creeks, like the Brandywine, Shellpot, Little Mill, Cobbs, Darby, Red Clay, and others, were ideal for turning water-powered mills, an important resource to both Dutch and Swedes, in whose homelands the windmills, subject to the vagaries of the weather, served industry where water power was unavailable.

The rivers and creeks teemed with edible fish—shad, sturgeon, rock, bass, pike, trout, perch, catfish, eels—and an abundance of lesser fish. The bay waters yielded oysters, conchs, clams, and crabs, and it was the appearance of whales, the reader will recall, that prompted the Dutch patroons to establish a whaling colony at Swanendael on the bayshore.

Except for the marshes lying open and treeless, and the

fields cleared by the Indians for their crops, the area was covered with an expanse of timberland as far as the eye could see. Oaks, tulip trees, beeches, chestnuts, walnuts, hickories, maples, buttonwoods, and ash—just to mention a few—were plentiful. Pines of several varieties, including Virginia and loblolly, stood straight and slim, and cypress and cedar grew thick in the fastland around the marshes. The trees provided a variety of lumber, useful for ships' masts, barrel staves, planks, and clapboards—another important commodity for peoples living in the low countries where trees were scarce and most of the lumber used for building construction was imported.

The ground was deep with the humus made rich by rotted leaves that had fallen for unknown centuries, and when the land was cleared of trees to make farm fields, the same kinds of crops raised in Europe thrived in American soil. In addition, the land produced the indigenous American plants— corn, tobacco, pumpkins, squash, beans, and others—which the Indians taught the white farmers to plant and raise. The temperate climate of the Delaware River Valley was conducive to agriculture and the development of self-supporting farm communities.

At first, the outlook for mining seemed promising to both Dutch and Swedes, who, like the English in Virginia and New England, sent out parties to prospect for mineral deposits. But the rumors of gold and silver mines proved to be without foundation, nor were copper deposits found suitable for commercial development. Nonetheless the land yielded a natural resource equal in demand to precious metals in the economy of the 17th-century European nations—fur-bearing animals. Bears, wolves, panthers, and wildcats infested the American forests, and elk and deer roamed through them. Foxes, raccoons, opossums, minks, weasels, skunks, rabbits, and squirrels were plentiful. Beavers, otters, and muskrats thrived in countless numbers in the marshes and streams.

Throughout Europe, furs were in demand for both men's and women's clothing, for no fabric could equal the warmth and glistening beauty of natural furs. Persons of importance wore furs to display their rank and wealth, and kings and princes set the style with their robes of priceless white ermine. Fur coats, muffs, wraps, and gloves—and fur-trimmed cloth garments—were all in vogue, and the consuming demand was for beaver pelts used in the manufacture of hats. But it was not material for milady's bonnet, with its ribbons, feathers, artificial flowers and fruit, that drove the fur traders to risk their lives in the American wilderness. In this instance, it was the whim of a segment of Europe's male population—the desire for hats felted from the velvety soft pelt of the beaver—that dictated the fashion. Underlying the heated national rivalries to monopolize the beaver fur trade with the Indians on the Delaware was the vanity, not of woman, but of man.

Peter Minuit knew that beavers lived and bred in many of the tributaries of the Delaware River, and that the beaver population was even greater, and the furs of higher quality, in the nearby Susquehanna country. He recognized that by building a trading post along the Delaware the local Lenni Lenape Indians would be encouraged to trap the beaver along the Delaware's tributaries and bring them to the post to barter for European merchandise. Furthermore, he was also aware that if the trading post were strategically placed on the terminal point of one of the Indian trails leading down from the Susquehanna, namely, along the present Christina River, or Minquas Kill, he could beat the Dutch in the beaver trade with the Iroquoian-speaking Minquas.

The desire of the whites for beaver pelts was no less than that of the Lenni Lenape and Minquas Indians to possess what they considered priceless merchandise offered by the traders. It was a paradox that, although the Indians dressed in animal skins, they thought less of furs as clothing than they did of the cheap, coarsely-woven wool fabric known as "duffel cloth" or simply "duffels" (named for the town of Duffel near Antwerp), which the traders supplied. This common cloth, which the Swedes called "Holland frieze," was dyed red and blue to suit the preferences of the natives who discontinued wearing their mantles of bear pelts and loin cloths of deerskin in favor of the woven cloth. A contemporary writer refers to this cloth "which they hang upon their shoulders; and half a yard of the same cloth, which being put betwixt their legs and brought up before and behinde, and tied with a Girdle about their middle hangs with a flap on either side." [9]

The Indians learned that the red duffels was so conspicuous that it exposed their position when stalking animals, and they soon demanded darker colors. The Indians also held in high esteem, during their initial contact with the white traders, the glass beads, cheap jewelry, clay smoking pipes, combs, mirrors, jew's-harps, iron pots, steel knives and axes, and other new and wonderful European goods, for which they readily bartered their furs. At first, trade with the Indians consisted of haphazard, itinerant bartering, but later it was regularized as posts were built and seasonal hunting and trapping patterns better understood. Trading took on the aspect of important business with keen competition among the traders representing different nations. "It is easy to think of the Indian trade," Zimmerman wrote, "as a romantic story of men in buckskins and moccasins facing the wilderness, but if one wants to understand the trade he must realize furs and deer skins were simply commodities, subject to the same problems of over-production and erratic markets faced by any other commodities."

As time went on, Indian tastes for European merchandise

changed, and there was a greater demand for firearms, powder and lead, as well as intoxicants. As the Indian began to use guns traded to him by the whites he had an increasing need for powder and lead without which the weapon was useless, and he was less interested in beads and baubles. Conversely, after 1700 the mania in Europe for beaver pelts subsided as new styles of clothing came in vogue, and deer and bear skins increased in demand. Trade with the Indians was subject to these changes occurring both in the European and aboriginal economies. The aboriginal medium of exchange, the wampum or "bead money," played a more important part in trade relations in the early and middle part of the 17th century than it did in a later period when currency was used. At the time of the coming of the Swedes, wampum was essential to conduct the Indian trade; it consisted of two kinds: white and blue-black, the latter being more valuable on an approximate ratio of two to one. The term *sewan* or *sewant* (from an Algonkian word meaning "scattered") was used by the Dutch and Swedes along the Delaware in referring to the wampum beads which the Indian women made from shell, and it was applied to loose beads as well as those on strings. Among the English of New England, the bead money was called *wampum* or *peake* (from the Algonkian word *wampumpeake* meaning a "string of white beads"). In Virginia, the white beads were called *roanoke,* and the dark ones were known as *peake.*

Along the Delaware, wampum was usually used for trading in strings of standard lengths of one fathom, or sometimes in loose, unstrung quantities. A string measuring a fathom in length consisted of three ells; an ell was originally a unit of measure equal to the approximate length of a man's forearm.

The manufacture of wampum beads required a high degree of manual skill, and prior to the introduction of metal tools, the Indian beadmaker cut each bead individually from shell, then drilled and polished it with a stone abrader. In bartering with the natives, the white trader had to have a supply of the bead money, as well as European goods, and the beads were principally obtained from the Indians of the sea-side in New England, New York, and Virginia. The trader exchanged European merchandise for beads and then used the beads to buy furs. The Indians then took the beads to trading posts to be accepted as currency, or they circulated them intertribally. On one occasion, an English trader from Virginia brought 862½ yards of beads to New Sweden to be sold to Indian traders. When these strings were added to those on hand, the traders accumulated 1,771 yards, which they used to buy 675 beaver pelts from the Minquas. At another time, a trader sold the Swedes 1,020 yards of beads at four florins (approximately $4) a yard, or about $2,000. On still another occasion, 449 beaver pelts were purchased from the Minquas for 1,234 three-quarter yards of beads which amounted to more than two yards of beads per pelt, or slightly more than eight florins each. Usually two strings of wampum were worth one beaver pelt, although the rate of exchange varied from time to time.

The Indians also wove the wampum beads into cere-monial belts which were used as mnemonic symbols to record important events, such as the signing of peace treaties or the purchase of lands. Human figures and simple geo-metric designs were often worked into the bead pattern, and each had a special meaning for the Indian trained to read and interpret the designs. Peter Minuit understood the In-dian system of bead currency, and he was an experienced hand at conducting business transactions with both Indians and whites.

In addition to purchasing pelts from the Indians for the return voyage to Sweden, Minuit sent the *Grip* to Jamestown to exchange some of her cargo for tobacco, but the skipper learned that the English Governor Berkeley did not have authority to enter into trade with other nationals unless the homeland approved. Berkeley proposed that the Swedish government notify the King of England that their people were settling a district of the New World and request permission to enter into trade with Virginia. A letter shortly thereafter from Jerome Hawley, treasurer of Virginia, to Sir Francis Windebank, His Majesty's principal secretary, in London carried the news that a new nation had suddenly appeared in the buffer zone. Hawley wrote:

> *The shipp remayned heare about 10 days to refresh wth wood and water . . . bound for Delaware Baye, wch is the confines of Virginia and New England, and there they ptend to make a plantation and to plant tobacco, wch the Dutch do allso already in Hudson River wch is the very next River Northward from Delaware Baye.*[10]

There is not the slightest indication that Hawley knew that the Swedes had selected as the site of their settlement a location on an upstream tributary of the Delaware River, but he recognized that it was not to English interests to have them in "Delaware Bay." He suggested that Windebank discuss the situation with the King, and if it were decided to remove the intruders, "I humbly conceive it may be done by his Matys subjects of these parts making use only of some English shipps that resort heather for trade yearly, and be no charge at all to his Matie."

Hawley's assessment of the situation was correct. There would have been no difficulty for one armed English vessel to oust the intruders, for the settlers that Minuit left at Fort Christina to found the first "permanent" settlement on the Delaware consisted of a commander, Mans Kling, the commissary, Hendrick Huygen, 23 soldiers, some Swedish, some Dutch, and one black slave named Anton. There were no women or children.

Had Minuit lived, he undoubtedly would have played a role of continuing importance in the expansion of Swedish interests, but he never returned from the first expedition. He left Fort Christina in June on the *Kalmar Nyckel* and sailed to 'the island of St. Christopher. While lying at anchor in the harbor he was invited aboard a ship from Rotterdam as the guest of the captain. A sudden storm drove the vessel out to sea, and neither the ship nor the men aboard her, including Minuit, were ever heard of again. Minuit's subordinates took the *Kalmar Nyckel* back to Europe with her cargo of beaver, otter, and bear skins, and the *Fogel Grip* returned later, also with a cargo of peltries.

A second Swedish expedition under command of a Dutchman, Peter Hollender Ridder, who had also entered Swedish service, arrived at Fort Christina in the spring of 1640, bringing additional settlers and livestock. A number of subsequent expeditions followed to reinforce the little colony, and the limits of New Sweden were extended by the purchase of additional lands from the Indians on both sides of the Delaware. Trade was carried on with both the Lenni Lenape and Minquas as long as the Swedes had suitable European merchandise to barter. This was done to the detriment of the Dutch West India Company, because the Swedish traders were more liberal with the Indians and deliberately undersold their Dutch competitors.

Although some writers speak loosely of the "Swedes" in the Delaware valley, something like one-half of the inhabitants of New Sweden were Finns. Most of them came, not directly from Finland, but from Swedish provinces where Finns began to settle starting about 1580. In time, the names of both Finns and Swedes became alike, and it is impossible to separate one from the other on the basis of their recorded names. Although Finland and Sweden were politically united, the Finnish people were of a different ethnic group and maintained their own language, which was unrelated to the Scandinavian tongues.

A reluctance on the part of the Swedes to leave the comforts of their homes and come to America to colonize New Sweden led to forcible recruiting of lawbreakers—poachers, persons guilty of breaking forest ordinances, deserted soldiers, debtors unable to pay—and others who had run afoul of the law. Two of the three Swedish provinces included in this recruiting, Värmland and Dalsland, had a large Finnish element in their population.[11]

Following the death of Gustavus Adolphus, Sweden was ruled by five high officers in the government, headed by the Chancellor Axel Oxenstierna, until the child queen came of age. Under Oxenstierna's influence, and with his strong support, the little Swedish colony on the Delaware seemed to have a promising future. But in 1644 the reins of government were handed over to Queen Christina, and she had little interest in the New World. Sweden's affairs at home demanded attention; the Queen was absorbed in the costly brilliance of her court; Blommaert had left Swedish service; Minuit and Fleming were both dead. New Sweden lacked champions at the Swedish court, and the colony was neglected and left without adequate moral and financial support. The lack of sufficient European merchandise weakened the Swedes in their trade with the Indians and provided an opening for the Dutch and English to exploit commerce to their own advantage.

6
Lord Baltimore
and Sir Edmund Plowden

Prominent among the Roman Catholic noblemen in Protestant England in the early 17th century was Sir George Calvert. Prior to his conversion to Catholicism, Sir George held the important position of secretary of state, but his unpopular religious beliefs caused him to resign this post. To keep him on the Privy Council, the King made him Baron of Baltimore in the Irish peerage.

The new Lord Baltimore became intrigued with the idea of founding a colony of his own in the New World. He purchased a tract of land in Newfoundland, later patented to him by James I as the Province of Avalon. Sir George made a trial at settlement, but he became so disgusted at the end of the second spring "with his intolerable plantation at Newfoundland, where he hath found between eight and nine months of winter," he gave up and sailed south to Virginia.

Visiting in Virginia in 1629–1630, he found the temperate climate there more to his liking, and he was impressed with the economic possibilities of founding a sister colony to Virginia on Chesapeake Bay. Upon his return to England he sought a royal charter for land north of Virginia, between the south bank of the Potomac River and the 40th parallel. His petition was favorably received by the King, but Sir George died before his request had passed the seals.

When the charter was issued June 20, 1632, by Charles I, who succeeded James I (after four different warrants in which various revisions were made), it was assigned to Sir George's 26-year-old son, Cecilius (Cecil) Calvert. This second Lord Baltimore became the first Proprietary of the Province of Maryland, named for the wife of Charles I. The charter delegated the right to the Calverts to hold land in free and common socage as absolute lords and proprietors, yielding to the Crown at Windsor Castle as payment two Indian arrows each Tuesday of Easter week, also one-fifth of any gold or silver ore discovered.

After a series of delays, occasioned by such unfounded rumors that Cecil Calvert intended to establish a Roman Catholic state in America, whereas he actually intended to found a colony where freedom of religion could be practiced, an expedition was finally organized. It comprised 200 colonists, consisting of gentlemen adventurers, with their families; yeomen; artisans; and laborers, some with their families; also indentured and other servants. The expedition sailed from England on November 22, 1633, in two vessels, the *Ark* and the *Dove*, with Cecil's brother, Leonard Calvert, in charge as governor. Cecil remained behind in England to handle important matters relating to the colony.

Thus, five years before Peter Minuit brought the first Swedish expedition into Delaware Bay, the Maryland colonists were established at their capital city, St. Marys, a former townsite of the Yoacomico Indians. The progress and growth of the Province of Maryland has been fully treated in a number of historical accounts, and does not now concern us. What is highly significant to the story of the English on the Delaware is the location of the bounds which the Crown established for the Province of Maryland.

According to the charter, the territory granted to the Calverts was adjacent to Virginia, and extended from the Potomac River across Chesapeake Bay to the Eastern Shore "unto that part of the bay of Delaware on the north, which lieth under the fortieth degree of north latitude." It is noteworthy that Argall's designation "De la Warre Bay" had now become "the bay of Delaware." The anomaly in the description given in Baltimore's charter was that the 40th parallel does not cross Delaware Bay, although neither the Crown nor the Calverts were then aware of that fact.

The 40th parallel, as we now know, does cross the Delaware *River,* which was not named in the Maryland charter for the obvious reason that little was then known in England about the existence of the river. Captain Thomas Yong didn't "discover" it until two years later and Cecil Calvert was evidently unaware of Dermer's voyage. Regardless of the limiting phraseology of the charter, Baltimore later insisted that he owned all the land below the 40th parallel lying along the western side of the Delaware River and Bay, after he learned more about the geography of the area. This land was clearly part of the original buffer zone established by James I, and encompassed the area on the west bank of the river where the Swedes built Fort Christina in 1638, as well as Swanendael, where the patroons placed their ill-fated whaling colony a year before Lord Baltimore's charter was issued. Since Fort Nassau was on the eastern side of the Delaware, it was not included in Baltimore's grant, nor was any other part of the present state of New Jersey. The Crown had other plans for the disposition of that area, which will shortly be evident.

There were two Latin words inserted routinely in the preamble of the Maryland charter, *hactenus inculta* (hitherto uncultivated), which, by a strict interpretation, meant that the Calverts were limited in their possession to those lands not previously planted by white men. Much has been made of the *hactenus inculta* provision, although the Crown included a similar disclaimer in almost all land grants, including George Calvert's Newfoundland tract. Some years later these words would be the nemesis of Lord Baltimore when William Penn proved beyond a shadow of doubt that the Dutch had settled and cultivated the land at Swanendael before the Calverts received their patent. Under an exacting legal interpretation of the charter, Maryland's rights to the western bank of Delaware Bay (and River) could not be supported because of prior Dutch occupancy. This will be discussed in a later chapter.

During the first 20 years of the Maryland settlement, while the Dutch West India Company and the New Sweden Company were jousting to control the Delaware, the Maryland government was forced to concentrate its main colonization effort on Chesapeake Bay and its tributaries. Indeed, there were pressing internal problems for the colony, because the neighboring Virginians distrusted the Catholic members of the Maryland settlement. After all, the land patented to the Calverts had actually been part of the original grant to the London Company before its charters were revoked and the franchise returned to the Crown. Many Virginians looked upon the Calverts as papist interlopers usurping the territory rights of Protestant Virginia.

Then, too, William Claiborne, soldier, merchant, statesman, and planter, former treasurer of the Virginia colony, secretary of state, and member of the Council, had built a well-supplied trading center on Kent Island in the Chesapeake prior to the arrival of the Maryland colonists. Having the financial support of several prominent Londoners, he had seated colonists on Kent Island and was conducting prosperous trade with the Minquas along the Susquehanna. So far as he was concerned, he and his people were residents of Virginia even though Kent Island lay within the bounds of the Maryland charter and belonged to the Calverts. Claiborne was a thorn in the side of the Maryland officials, because he had a royal trading commission from Charles I to explore the bay and exploit the Indian trade, and he refused to yield his rights to a new government which he did not recognize.[1]

There were also Indian troubles, especially with the Nanticoke of the Eastern Shore and the Susquehanna Minquas, to say nothing of the problems of organizing the new government and establishing a militia. There simply was no time or inclination on the part of the Calverts to press eastward in their province and confront the Dutch along the Delaware River. Indeed, with the paucity of information about the Delaware, Leonard Calvert did not then know that he had such close neighbors.

To complicate the whole problem of ownership rights to New World lands, Charles I gave orders on July 24, 1632, less than a month after he granted the Maryland charter, for the issuance of another patent in the same general territory. The petitioner was a contentious Roman Catholic nobleman, Sir Edmund Plowden, a man of zeal, in whose soul burned great aspirations. However, he also possessed the unseemly combination of an unfortunate personality, a violent temper, and a penchant for getting into trouble. His cantankerous nature is illustrated by the 112 known lawsuits in which he was a party from 1620 until his death in 1659. He served time in jail on at least two occasions.

In his first petition to the King, Plowden indicated he intended to settle 300 inhabitants; in the second petition, the number was increased to 500. The colony he conceived was intended "for the making of Wine, saulte and iron, fishing of sturgeon & mullet, and for cattle and corne for the Coloney, and for the yearly building of shipping there with all materials for your Majesty's service." [2]

According to its designated bounds, Sir Edmund's tract was a square plot measuring 120 miles on each side, and it also included certain islands beyond the square. It was called New Albion, and was described as a "county palatine," with Plowden in the role of an Earl Palatine.

The name New Albion, incidentally, was applied previously by Sir Francis Drake, as early as 1579, to parts of the northwestern coast of North America. Sir Edmund Plowden's *new* New Albion included almost all of the present state of New Jersey, and it definitely included the present eastern bank of the Delaware River, where the Dutch were then seated at Fort Nassau. Whether the King intended it also to encompass parts of the present states of Delaware and Maryland is a controversial question because of different interpretations given to the phraseology of the charter and inexact knowledge in England about the geography of the area. For example, as in the case of the Maryland charter, the Delaware River is *not* mentioned in the New Albion charter. The "Gulf of Delaware" is named, but from the text one might conclude that it was an inlet of the sea, and that no major river emptied into it.

Although orders to issue the patent were given in 1632, the charter was not in Plowden's hands until June 21, 1634, due to administrative delays at court, and for political reasons which are not now fully understood. Doubt has been expressed by some historians about the validity of Plowden's charter. It has even been called a forgery and a fake. It is said to have been invalid because the Great Seal of England was not placed upon it. A recent author, for example, observes that on the question of whether or not the Great Seal was affixed "only the existence of the original document could settle this matter."[3] Unfortunately, the original charter vanished about 1698 and hasn't been seen since.

Actually, the charter was issued by Charles I as a valid, legal instrument "signed with our proper hand and sealed with our seal." Thomas Plowden, one of Sir Edmund's sons, who had the charter in his possession for some years following his father's death, makes the following statement in his will proved September 10, 1698, two phrases of which I have emphasized:

> *Item I do give and bequeath unto my son Francis Plowden the letters Pattent and Title with all advantages and profitts thereunto belonging And as it was granted by our late sovereign Lord King Charles the first over England and* under *the Great Seal of England unto my father Sir Edmund Plowden of Wanstead in the county of South'ton now deceased. The Province and County Palatine of New Albion in America and the North Virginia and America which Pattent* is now in the custody of my son in law Andrew Wall of Ludshott *in the said County of South'ton who has these severall years wrongfully detained it to my great loss and hinderance.*[4]

It is certain that the original charter bore the Great Seal of Ireland—not England—despite the statement in Thomas Plowden's will, which, as the reader will note, was made when the charter was no longer in his possession. Since the seal of Ireland was, indeed, a royal seal, Thomas Plowden might have mistaken one for the other. Sir Edmund was in Dublin when he first petitioned the King for his charter, and it was there that he was knighted in 1630. He also held official positions in Ireland under the Earl of Cork and Viscount Loftus, the Lords Justice, and later under the Earl of Strafford, Lord Deputy.

The charter was issued under the Crown of Ireland, and,

upon the authority of the King, was signed by Lord Strafford. This information is given by Plowden himself when, to strengthen his proprietary position, he attempted at a later date to have the charter also confirmed under the Great Seal of England:

"This Patent by warrant from his Majesty out of England to the Lord Deputy in Ireland is duly passed under that Great Seale & herein is made a Province dependent & held by tenure of the Crown and King." [5]

Plowden was unsuccessful in having the Great Seal of England affixed, but the Great Seal of Ireland gave his patent royal sanction.

Since the patent was an Irish grant, Plowden had it properly enrolled in Dublin at the Irish Chancery, and it was no less a binding legal instrument than if it had carried the Great Seal of England. There is no doubt about the attitude of Charles I, and his official position is expressed in a document preserved in the Royal Archives in Stockholm. Therein the King states that the Province of New Albion was granted under "our greate Seale unto our loving Cozen Sr. Edmund Plowden, Kn[igh]t." (See the *Appendix* of this volume for a transcript of the document, now published for the first time.)

Of the many Englishmen who attempted exploitation of Delaware Bay and River prior to 1660, when Lord Baltimore asserted his rights, Sir Edmund Plowden alone had the authorization of a *bona fide* royal charter bearing one of the seals of his monarch. Since the *hactenus inculta* phrase was conspicuously absent from the New Albion charter, Plowden's position in one sense was even stronger than Lord Baltimore's. Under a strict interpretation of the charter the territory granted to him became his exclusive possession regardless of whether or not parts of it had been previously settled and cultivated by other Christian peoples. Perhaps the King and his advisors deliberately omitted the *hactenus inculta* provision in the knowledge that the Dutch were already seated on the territory that became New Albion. Both Lord Baltimore and Sir Edmund received their palatinates with all the rights and privileges enjoyed by "any Bishop of Durham." This clause was the basis of almost unlimited power. In the 14th century, the Bishop of Durham held his fief, the County Palatine of Durham, in northern England as a military bulwark against the Scots, and, although a subject of the King, ruled his territory as a semi-independent kingdom. The Bishop of Durham still wielded tremendous authority when Plowden and Baltimore received their patents, and the references to the Bishop of Durham were highly significant. With Lord Baltimore, Sir Edmund received the most powerful bestowal of authority in North America that the English king could grant.

In passing, it is worthy of comment that the Crown gave no recognition to the Indians as the true owners of lands in America. The *hactenus inculta* phrase in Baltimore's charter, for instance, did not take into consideration that the Indians had previously cultivated lands where the Europeans settled. In fact, most of their important towns were built on sites that the Indians had cleared many years before and which they occupied and cultivated. The English Crown looked on the Indians as a heathen race and treated them as though they had no more rights to the land than the wild animals who roamed the woods. It was this disregard for the Indians' rights, first manifest in land matters, that eventually caused friction and bloodshed.

Since Charles I was heavily in debt, it is probable that Plowden paid well for his charter, but there was nothing unusual about that. In fact, it was the custom of the period, and Plowden was in the enviable position of having a rich wife and a financially burdened king. Mabel Marriner, a wealthy heiress whom he wed, brought to her marriage a considerable income from landed property. In later years, Sir Edmund and his wife did not live happily together and were ultimately separated and divorced, but at the time his charter was drawn up their relations were apparently amicable. At least he was dipping liberally into her fortune, evidently with her consent. Not only did the Crown benefit from whatever cash payments Sir Edmund made, but he held his grant *in capite* of the King's Irish Crown, or by knight service. This form of land tenure, in contrast to the terms of Lord Baltimore's charter, obligated Sir Edmund to assume potential feudal dues should the Crown choose to exercise its right to greater financial gain when New Albion became a paying proposition.

In addition to potential financial benefits, New Albion also gave Charles I both a military and commercial bulwark against the Dutch. With the expansion of Dutch power in New Netherland, a wedge had been driven between Virginia and New England. The King was naturally interested in countering Holland, for English jealousies, aroused by Dutch skill in commercial endeavors, was akin to the opposition in England awakened by Spain's military superiority a century earlier. The Dutch were highly successful in establishing trade in all parts of the world, creating a strong merchant marine, and in making Amsterdam a leading financial center of Europe. In the early part of the 17th century, England had started to contest Dutch commercial superiority, and was doing her utmost to equal or surpass her most formidable rival in trade with the New World. Both the Maryland grant and the New Albion charter furthered his cause.

The issuance of the two charters was a forward step in English colonial expansion. The goods and produce of both New Albion and Maryland would undoubtedly constitute a trade, as well as military, buffer against the Dutch.

Sir Edmund's charter invested him with the same wide

latitude of authority possessed by Lord Baltimore, even though he had his land *in capite,* in contrast to Lord Baltimore's free and common socage. Sir Edmund (like Lord Baltimore) had the right to make laws for his province (with the advice and consent of the freemen settled on it); he had the power to execute the laws; all the judicial power rested in his person. He could build fortifications; declare and make war on land or sea; pursue the enemy beyond his province, and spare or slay prisoners as he saw fit. He could erect manors within New Albion and convey honors by means of titles. For example, he gave his children titles for manors within his province. His sons, Francis and Thomas, were given the titles respectively of Governor and Baron of *Mt. Royal,* and Admiral and Baron of *Roymount.* His daughter, Lady Winefrid, was the Baroness of *Uvedale;* Lady Barbara was Baroness of *Richneck;* and Lady Katherine was Baroness of *Princeport.* None of Sir Edmund's children ever took up permanent residence in America to exercise their manorial rights.

Eight years elapsed between the granting of the charter and Sir Edmund's departure for the New World in August of 1642, with the intention of making the beginning of a settlement. During the interim he had been negotiating with various prominent Englishmen, encouraging them to buy land in his province since he intended to transport to New Albion twice as many men as were in Maryland. He was also engaged in lawsuits with tenants, creditors, debtors, and with his wife about his delinquent alimony payments. He also had something to do with the composing and publication of a colonization tract in 1641 extolling the virtues of New Albion and intended to arouse interest in England and recruit settlers. There was evidently a free flow of information between Captain Thomas Yong, Robert Evelyn, and Sir Edmund (as well as with Cecil Calvert), which was to be expected at a time when the minority of English noblemen who professed Catholicism, or who had strong leanings in that direction, were drawn together to pursue their common interests.

The tract published in 1641 contained a glowing description of the Charles (Delaware) River, signed by several adventurers who had been there, including Thomas Yong. The tract also contained the transcript of a letter Robert Evelyn had written Mabel Plowden describing that part of New Albion that lay on the east side of the Delaware River, including an account of the various Indian bands then occupying what is now the state of New Jersey: [6]

> *If my Lord Palatine will bring with him three hundred men or more, there is no doubt but that he may doe very well and grow rich, for it is a most pure healthful air & such pure wholesome springs, river and waters as are delightful of a Desert, as can be seen, with so many varieties of several flowers, trees and forests for swine. So many fair risings and prospects, all green and verdant; and Maryland a good friend and neighbour, in four & twenty houres ready to comfort and supply. And truly, I beleeve my Lord of Baltimore will be glad of my Lord Palatines Plantation and assistance against any enemy or bad neighbor.*

Perhaps Evelyn's purpose in portraying the beauties of New Albion and the opportunity there for Sir Edmund to prosper was to persuade Mme. Plowden in a subtle way to loosen her purse strings and subsidize her husband's colonial venture. It would not have been beyond the Earl Palatine to encourage his young friend to try to win his wife's support.

Because of the outbreak of the Civil War in England, Plowden's hope of taking a large number of colonists to populate New Albion was not realized. The potential settlers he was able to muster included only a handful of indentured servants and the members of his family, except his oldest son Francis, who remained behind in England to supervise his father's interests. Compared to Lord Baltimore's effort it was an extremely feeble first expedition, and, as fate would have it, also the last.

The captain of the vessel was unfamiliar with Delaware waters, and, not having a pilot, Sir Edmund and his party went first to Virginia instead of sailing into Delaware Bay. In Virginia, Sir Edmund ran short of money and became entangled in more lawsuits. After a number of months had passed, the indentured servants, whose term of service was for New Albion and not Virginia, became impatient with waiting and probably weary of their Earl. Some sought their freedom in the Virginia courts, and a few fled to Maryland. The Virginia courts ordered Plowden either to begin his venture or release the plaintiffs of their bonds.

The testimony of Ann Fletcher, one of the servants, indicates the arrangements Plowden made with some of the potential settlers. She said she was bound to him only from one year to another, and, if at the end of the year she didn't like the country, she was free to return to England, compensating Plowden for her passage to America. She was also to receive a small wage for services rendered Mme. Plowden and her daughters as a waiting maid. The Earl Palatine failed to pay her wages, which was one of the reasons she deserted him in Virginia and fled to Maryland.

Two spinster sisters, Jane and Eleanor Stevens, had contracted to serve Plowden for five years "in New Albion in delaware Bay & were to have 50^s sterling per annum & they to find clothes, etc." [7] They, too, fled to Maryland.

In May 1643, Plowden left Virginia in a bark, one half of which he owned (the other half was owned by a Philip White), with 16 of his people. He intended to make the beginning of a settlement somewhere in New Albion, presumably along the Delaware. The prospective settlers, evidently all indentured servants, represented some of the runaways who had been returned, and others who by now had lost their enthusiasm about living under Plowden's rule. On board the vessel they conspired with the skipper, a Mr. Middeler, who was sympathetic with them. They decided that the only way they could win their freedom from Plowden and return home to England was to kill him; but none of them wanted to commit murder and have their master's blood on their hands. It was decided to seize Plowden and cast him ashore on Smith's Island without food, clothing or guns, and leave him there alone to perish. The island was unoccupied except for wolves and bears and he would have little chance to survive. After Plowden was forcibly taken to the island and set ashore, the vessel prepared to leave. It was then that two loyal pages jumped from the bark into the water and swam to the island to be with their lord and master. The vessel sailed away, leaving Plowden and the two youths marooned and helpless.

The mutineers then proceeded to the Delaware River, arriving on May 6, 1643, at Fort Elfsborg, where they asked the Swedish Governor Printz to arrange to transport them to England. Printz was arranging for their return when one of the servant girls finally told the story of what had occurred. Printz then imprisoned the entire party and returned them to Virginia on the next English vessel that visited New Sweden. In the meantime, another English vessel rescued Plowden and his companions, much weakened by exposure and burned by the sun. He was in Virginia when the faithless members of his party returned from the Delaware. The records state that he pardoned most of them.[8] Plowden remained in Virginia for the next five years, and from 1643 to 1648 his name appears no less than 23 times in the courts of Northampton and York.[9] For a while, he rented a store and residence at Kecoughtan, now Hampton, in Elizabeth County.

Sir Edmund gave passes in Virginia to English vessels, permitting them to trade on the Delaware, but as soon as an English ship arrived in New Sweden, Governor Printz halted it and refused to allow it to proceed up the river. Plowden was a nonentity so far as Printz was concerned, and Sir Edmund suffered the frustration of not being able to enforce his authority over lands that, under English law, belonged to him.

The records are vague about when and under what circumstances Plowden personally inspected his land along the Delaware during his first and only visit to America, although one infers that he did so. During his sojourn in Virginia he lived on the Eastern Shore, and there can be little doubt that he must have taken advantage of the opportunity to examine the resources of nearby New Albion that had been reported by Captain Thomas Yong and Robert Evelyn. Years later, in the land controversies between William Penn and Lord Baltimore, it was recorded on hearsay evidence "that in the year 1642 one Ployden sailed up the Delaware River and did not see any house there at that time . . ." [10] This was an exaggeration, because the Calverts were seeking proof that the Delaware was uncultivated and unoccupied before Maryland was settled in order to take advantage of the *hactenus inculta* disclaimer in their charter. Only a blind man could have overlooked the Swedish log houses and Finnish pörtes built along the Delaware, which were in existence in 1642, as well as the forts and trading posts erected by both Dutch and Swedes. Sir Edmund was neither blind nor foolish—he knew exactly what was happening in his beloved New Albion, and if his resources had permitted him to realize his dreams, the course of Delaware Valley colonial history might have been entirely different.

Before returning to England, Plowden visited Boston and Manhattan Island. Brief notes in the records of both settlements supply bits of information from which inferences can be made. For example, in his journal under date of June 4, 1648, Governor John Winthrop made the following entry:

> *Here arrived [at Boston] one Sir Edmund Plowden who had been in Virginia about seven years. He came first with a patent of a county palatine for Delaware Bay, but wanting a pilot for that place, he went over to Virginia, and there having lost the estate he brought over, and all his people scattered from him, he came hither to return to England for supply, intending to return and plant Delaware, if he could get sufficient strength to dispossess the Swedes.*[11]

After leaving Boston, Plowden went to Manhattan Island where he embarked for England, presumably on a Dutch vessel. The only detail of his sojourn there occurs in the following Dutch record:

> *We must now pass to the South River, called by the English Delaware Bay, first speaking of the boundaries; but in passing we can not omit to say that there has been here, both in the time of Director Kieft and in that of General Stuyvesant [does this mean that Plowden was there twice?], a certain Englishman, who called himself Sir Edward Ploeyden, with the title of Earl Palatine of New Albion, who claimed that the land on the west side of the North River to Virginia [Hudson] was his, by gift of King James of England, but he said he did not wish to have any strife with the Dutch, though he was very much piqued at the Swedish governor, John Prins, at the South River, on account of some affront given him, too long to relate. He said also that when an opportunity should offer he would go there and take possession of the river. In short, according to the claims of the English, it belongs to them, and there is nothing left for the subjects of Their High Mightiness*

—one must have this far, and another that far, but they all argue never to fall short.[12]

This brief note ended Sir Edmund Plowden's first attempt to settle New Albion, and he returned to England disappointed, frustrated, and resentful. He continued to declare his rights to Delaware Valley lands as the only legal owner by virtue of his royal charter bearing the Great Seal of Ireland, and he dedicated himself to the mission of returning to New Albion with settlers to oust the intruders in his province.

When, in 1651, a new "mapp of Virginia," bearing the name of Dominia Virginia Farrer, was engraved and published in England, "Nova Albion" was shown, and alongside the river designated as "Lord Delaware's Bay and River," the cartographer lettered these words, "This River the Lord Ployden hath a pattent of, and calls it New Albion, but the Sweeds are planted on it and have a great Trade of Furrs."

If the map maker possessed all the facts, he might have added that Sir Edmund's countrymen from New Haven in New England were also planted on his New Albion lands, but the significance of that news, the subject of the next chapter, was not yet realized in England.

7

New Haven Settles
on the Delaware

The popular impression that the quest for religious freedom alone brought the Pilgrims and Puritans from the Old World to New England is still widely held, although there were also underlying economic motives. The original decision of the Pilgrims to come to America may have been basically noneconomic, but their venture was financed by a joint stock company representing adventurous gentlemen and merchants headed by Thomas Weston, a London businessman. An agreement between the subscribers and settlers provided that the colony was to be operated for profit as a fishing and fur trading post.[1]

Because the expedition was so poorly equipped, and the Pilgrims so ignorant of the region, their settlement almost met the same fate as Sagadahoc. Due to a pestilence that had reduced the Indian population in the Cape Cod area, the furs obtained the first year and sent to England on the *Fortune* amounted only to two hogsheads of beaver and otter skins. The bulk of the cargo was made up of clapboards, which the colonists had laboriously hewn during the summer. The London sponsors were so sorely disappointed over the initial return on their investment that they did not send supplies for the colonists nor suitable goods for the Indian trade. To keep their families alive, the Pilgrims were diverted by grim necessity from fur trading to corn raising.

In 1624, Edward Winslow took the first surplus of the corn harvest to the Kennebec River where it found a ready market among the Maine tribes who lived primarily by fishing and hunting. He brought back 700 pounds of beaver pelts and other furs, and the successful use of corn in the fur trade gave it a new value as a medium of barter with the northern Indians. It also provided further incentive for agriculture among the Pilgrims, which seemed the most natural occupation for them, since they were mostly farmers and craftsmen of humble birth and occupation.

The Pilgrim leaders also turned their attention to the Connecticut River valley in search of furs, and a small trading post, under command of Lieutenant William Holmes, was built along the river. The efforts by the Pilgrims to develop the fur trade (which included ventures in other areas not relevant to the present story) had a strong influence on the Puritans settled in the nearby Massachusetts Bay Colony. They, too, pressed into Connecticut after French competitors pushed English traders out of Maine, and blocked the trade in Nova Scotia. With this competition from Puritan merchants of Boston, and the trade with the natives disrupted because of a war between the Pequot and Narragansett tribes, the Pilgrims abandoned their trading post on the Connecticut River. By 1640, the Plymouth colony was an important source for agricultural products used in Boston, and fur trading became relegated to a secondary position.

On the other hand, the fur trade was a prime consideration in the founding of the New Haven Colony, which was actually an offshoot of the Massachusetts Bay Colony, although Puritan newcomers from England, not the original colonists, were responsible for New Haven.

It all came about when the monarchy of the early Stuarts was at its lowest ebb, after vain struggles in England to better ecclesiastical, civil, and economic conditions. It was then that the Reverend John Davenport, and Theophilus Eaton, a London merchant, in 1637 led a company of ultra-conservative Puritans from London to Boston, where the Bay Colony was already in existence.[2] Both Eaton and Davenport were contributors to the Bay Colony, although they remained in England when their Puritan brethren originally departed. The party accompanying Eaton and Davenport seven years later, largely recruited from Davenport's parish in the heart of commercial London, numbered about 250 men, women, and children. It was their intention to settle permanently in Massachusetts. After their arrival they found the Bay Colony torn with religious dissension, and conditions no more to their liking than in England. Visualizing a "Kingdom of Christ," with strong commercial overtones, they decided to move to the shores of Long Island Sound to form their own community. They took with them a number of the Puritans previously settled in the Bay Colony sympathetic to their cause. In the spring of 1638 (when Peter Minuit was sailing to America with the first Swedish expedition), they left Boston and pushed on to found a new home where they expected to practice their religion without interference, and, at the same time, carry on profitable mercantile pursuits.

They had no royal patent, legal warrant, commission, nor any other authorization from the Crown to establish a colonial government. In fact, the Dutch had already purchased lands from the Indians on the Connecticut River and established a trading post there before the English came. Nevertheless, they purchased land that suited them from the Indians along the northern shore of Long Island Sound in present Connecticut and on Long Island itself. Then they proceeded to erect their civil government on the uncertain foundation of the Indians' deeds, much the same as the Swedes did along the Delaware. One of the main attractions at the principal site they had chosen in Connecticut was the harbor from which they planned to carry on coastal trade. They started their first plantation at *Quinnipiac* (it was officially named New Haven on September 1, 1640), which expanded into the New Haven Colony. Eventually there came into existence the towns, or "plantations," as they were called, of New Haven, Guilford, Milford, Stamford, and Branford on the mainland, and Southold on Long Island.

Expansion was slow, and in 1640 New Haven was still trading with the Connecticut Indians for food to support the colony. The fur trade did not develop as the founders anticipated, because the coastal beaver population had been depleted by the traders from Plymouth, as well as the aggressive Dutch from Manhattan Island. Furs were vital to the commercial success of New Haven, not for the furs alone, but in order to build up credit for their trade with London. Bills of exchange on London could be purchased with beaver and other pelts, as well as tobacco, sugar, and other American commodities. The funds were then invested in English goods to be transported from London to Boston, and reshipped to New Haven. With their mercantile background, the leading men of New Haven adopted bold plans to make the new plantation an important commercial center. They began trading not only with Boston and London, but with New Amsterdam, Virginia, the Barbados—and finally they decided to seek beaver pelts along the Delaware River.

New Haven must not be regarded as an isolated colony

intent upon its own purposes, unmindful of the other New England settlements, for such is not the case. Close ties existed between all of the English colonies in New England, and in 1643 articles of confederation were drawn up "between the plantations under the Governor of Massachusetts, the Governor of New Plymouth, the Government of Connecticut, and the Government of New Haven to be called 'the United Colonies of New England.' " [3] I will make later reference to this New England Confederation which had an important bearing on the English activities along the Delaware River.

George Lamberton and Nathaniel Turner were two of the prominent members of the New Haven Colony recruited by Davenport from among the Bay Colony Puritans. They both joined the movement from Boston to Connecticut. Lamberton was one of the four New Haven planters whose estates were worth in excess of £1,000 and were exceeded only by those of Theophilus Eaton. Lamberton was a mariner, a shipowner, a man of mind and substance who had a strong influence on the other settlers.

Nathaniel Turner came from England with John Winthrop in 1630, and as a citizen of Lynn, he represented the town in the first General Court of Massachusetts before he removed to *Quinnipiac*. Having had military service as an officer in the Pequot War he was chosen captain at New Haven in 1640 "to have the command and ordering of all martial affairs of this plantation as setting and ordering of watches, excercising the training of soldiers, . . ." [4] Many entries in the New Haven 17th century court records refer to George Lamberton and Captain Nathaniel Turner.

The records do not indicate who initiated what became known as the Delaware Company of New Haven, organized for the purpose of spreading the commercial influence of the colony southward, but Lamberton and Turner were foremost among the promoters of the project. Intelligence about the rich resources of the Delaware—particularly the lucrative beaver trade with the Minquas Indians carried on by Swedes and Dutch along the Schuylkill and Christina— had been obtained by New Haven traders during their voyages to Virginia. Indeed, Lamberton himself may have brought back the information from one of his several voyages.[5]

Although both Lamberton and Turner invested in the Delaware Company, Theophilus Eaton, then the governor of New Haven, had the largest financial interest.[6] Other members of the Company included Stephen Goodyear, John Dane, Thomas Grigson (also spelled Gregson), Richard Malbon, Matthew Gilbert, and John Turner.[7]

Because Lamberton and Turner were in the Delaware River together, and individually, on more than one occasion, there has been considerable confusion about the dates and events of their several voyages. When the Dutch and Swedish contemporary records are carefully compared with entries in the New Haven court records, and with the highly significant James Waye deposition,[8] the story can now be told with reasonable accuracy, although its continuity is still interrupted by missing gaps in the records.

In the spring of 1641, Lamberton and Turner were in the Delaware together in a small sloop, well provided with European merchandise to be used to buy lands from the Indians, and also to exchange for beaver pelts. They had been authorized by the Delaware Company of New Haven to select suitable sites for the proposed colony and to purchase the lands from the Indian owners. The New Haveners were evidently unaware that the English Crown had granted land along Delaware Bay to Sir Edmund Plowden, who, at that very moment, was making final plans in England to bring settlers to seat his Province of New Albion.

The two Englishmen sailed up and down the river, and explored its navigable tributaries, seeking a good location for a colony. As they made contact with the Indians they also bartered for furs, and the Swedish records say that Lamberton and Turner ruined the Indian trade for the Swedes while they were in the river, probably by being more liberal in their dealings with the natives.[9] The Englishmen were doing only what the Dutch earlier complained the Swedes had done to divert the trade to themselves.

James Waye was a member of the Lamberton-Turner party and he states in his deposition that there were 14 Englishmen in the group that purchased land from the Indians in 1641 on the Varkens Kill (Hogs Creek), present Salem Creek, Salem County, New Jersey. One of the Indian names for this location was *Watcessit,* and this was the identical place that Sir Edmund Plowden intended as the seat of New Albion. The Varkens Kill was navigable to shallops for about 30 miles, and vessels of 100 tons could come up the stream as far as the present town of Salem which lies about three-and-a-half miles from the stream's confluence with the Delaware.

The following year, 1642, Waye was also a member of the English party from New Haven who purchased land on the Schuylkill from the Indians for European merchandise worth approximately £40 sterling. The Indian name for this general area was *Wickquacoingh,* usually contracted by the whites to *Wicaco.*

Waye's deposition was unknown to Amandus Johnson when he wrote his *Swedish Settlements* or he would not have written that "Shortly after the purchase at the Varkens Kill, Lamberton and Turner bought certain lands from Mattahorn at the Schuylkill." [10]

Governor John Winthrop is authority for the information that at first the Delaware Indians refused to sell any of their land to the English. Winthrop intimates that the local Indians were familiar with the conflict between the English in New Haven and the Pequot Indians and were suspicious that the English would foment another conflict if allowed to build a town on the Delaware. He states further that a Pequot chief interceded with the Delaware Indians on behalf of Lamberton and Turner, urging them to befriend the English and sell them the requested land. He adds that as a result of the Indian wars in Connecticut this chief had fled to the Delaware River with some of his followers, and was then living with one of the Delaware bands. The Pequot sachem, according to Winthrop, persuaded the Delawares that the English were honest men "whereupon the [Delaware] sachem entertained them and let them have what land they desired." [11]

Winthrop was not familiar with Swedish relations with the Indians, and he overlooked the likelihood that the Delaware chieftains may have been reluctant to sell land to the English at the risk of antagonizing both Dutch and Swedes. Minuit, Jan Jansen, Ridder, and others had already ingratiated themselves with the natives, and the Indians were not inclined to jeopardize their good relations with the whites already seated on the river.

It is now clear that Lamberton and Turner selected not two, as most historians have concluded, but *three* locations as sites for potential English settlements. The first was on the aforementioned Varkens Kill; the second on the Schuylkill River within the city limits of present Philadelphia; and the third, also along the western bank of the river, probably in the region of present New Castle, Delaware.

The plot on the eastern side of the river was owned by Usquata, sachem of "Narrattacus" (*Narraticonck*) and Wehwsett, sachem of "Wattsesinge" (*Watcessit*), and it extended from a small creek called "Chesumquesett" "North-

ward wher the Land of the said Usquata Sayamk of Narrattacus doth begine unto the Seacoast Southward."

The plot on the Schuylkill purchased from the great chief
Mattahorn and several of his lesser chiefs lay along the western shore of the Delaware, extending from a creek called
"Pestacomeco," or "Howsheshocken," north of the Swedish
fort, to a place called "Eccocoeym" (*Wicaco*) which was described as lying on the opposite side of the river from Fort
Nassau.

The third plot, which was on the west bank of the Delaware, extended from a stream called *Tomguncke* to another stream called *Papuq* . . . The latter word is only
fragmentary in the document, and I am unable to recon-
struct the complete form.[12] *Tomguncke* is undoubtedly a
form of *Tamaconcke,* the well-known Indian name for land
at New Castle.[13] There is another reason apart from this
evident linguistic relationship for identifying this plot with
present New Castle; see p. 146 below.

It is next to impossible to fix the boundaries of these three
tracts with certainty in relation to today's geographical features. Moreover, the original Indian deeds in the possession
of Lamberton and Turner have not yet been located, and
the only descriptions of the bounds now available are those
found in the defective Swedish copies of Lamberton's protest made some months after the lands had been purchased.
Yet it is clear that the Delaware Company of New Haven
had resolved to stake out claims on both sides of the Delaware River, irrespective of the interests of the Dutch and
Swedes, and without commission, warrant, or patent from
the English Crown. Lamberton later maintained that none
of the lands he purchased had been previously sold by the
Indians, but he was clearly in error, as subsequent events
will reveal. As they had done at New Haven, the Puritans
were determined to establish their Delaware settlements

strictly on the basis of Indian title deeds. In so doing they were unintentionally committing a serious offense against the Crown and two lordly proprietors. The Varkens Kill was clearly on Sir Edmund Plowden's New Albion grant, and the western bank of the Delaware, where the other two purchases were made, was considered by Lord Baltimore as part of the Province of Maryland to the extent that it lay below the 40th parallel.

Whether any of the Englishmen remained to settle on the Varkens Kill in 1641, after the land was purchased, is uncertain so far as my studies go, although Johnson states on this voyage Lamberton and Turner built a blockhouse on the Varkens Kill. He adds that a second blockhouse was built at *Manaiping* on Province Island in the Schuylkill where Fort Nya Korsholm was later erected by the Swedes.[14] Since it is now certain that the Schuylkill lands were not purchased until 1642, it is extremely unlikely that a blockhouse was erected there in 1641, although it is not impossible that a fort of some kind may have been built on the Varkens Kill. I am unable to illuminate the question as to whether settlers were placed on the Varkens Kill as early as 1641, but it is certain that they were residing there in 1642.

Returning to New Haven, Lamberton and Turner made a report of their progress to other members of the company, and the following entry is found in the records of the General Court of New Haven on the 30th of the 6th month 1641.[15] The General Court of New Haven was equivalent to a town meeting, but only church members admitted as free burgesses could vote. There was also a General Court held in conjunction with the New England Confederation. I have normalized the spelling in this and other General Court entries for purposes of clarity:

Whereas there was a purchase made by some particular persons of sundry plantations in Delaware Bay, at their own charge, for the advancement of public good as in a way of trade, so also for the settling of churches and plantations in those parts, in combination with this. And thereupon it was propounded in the General Court whether plantations should be settled in Delaware Bay, in combination with this town, yea or nay, and upon consideration and debate, it was assented unto by the court and expressed by holding up of hands.

So far as Captain Turner hath reference to the civil state and employed therein, provided that his place be supplied in his absence, the Court hath given free liberty to him to go to Delaware Bay for his own advantage and the public good in settling the affairs thereof.

It is ordered that those to whom the affairs of the town is committed shall dispose of all the affairs of Delaware Bay according to the intent of the agreement for combination with this town in settling plantations and admitting planters to sit down there.

What this entry appears to mean is that, although the original reconnaissance of the Delaware conducted by Lamberton and Turner was a private venture of the Delaware Company, that the New Haven Colony would officially sponsor any settlements made there. Furthermore, even though Captain Turner also had obligations as a civil official at New Haven, the importance of the project justified his going to Delaware, both to satisfy his own private interests in the Indian trade, and to assist in establishing the new colony.

A Dutch document gives April 8, 1641, as the date a party of settlers were subsequently brought from New Haven to the Delaware in a bark owned by Lamberton, under command of Robert Cogswell (also spelled Coxwell). Johnson believes the document is dated incorrectly and, for reasons he gives, should be dated 1642.[16] The vessel stopped en route at Manhattan Island where Governor Kieft, made aware of its mission, sent a protest to the English captain.

> *I, Willem Kieft, . . . make known to you Robert Coghwel*
> *and your associates, [he wrote] not to build or plant on the*
> *South river, lying within the limits of New Netherland, nor*
> *in the lands extending along it, as they lawfully belong to us,*
> *by our possessing the same many years ago, before it was fre-*
> *quented by any Christians, as appears by our forts which we*
> *have on it; the mouth of the river is also sealed with our*
> *blood [the same expression he used in his warning to Minuit]*
> *and the soil itself, most of which has been purchased and*
> *paid for by us.*
>
>   *Unless you will settle under the Lords the States [General]*
> *and the Honble West India Company, and swear allegiance*
> *and become subject to them, as other inhabitants do. Failing*
> *therein, We protest against all damages and losses which may*
> *accrue therefrom, and desire to be holden guiltless thereof, &c.*
>
>   *Robert Coghwel answers: He does not propose to settle*
> *under any government, but to select a place over which the*
> *States General have no authority; and in case such place is not*
> *to be found, he intends to return, or if he settle within the*
> *limits of the States, he will repair under it, and take the*
> *oath.*[17]

With this assurance he was allowed to proceed.

How many settlers came with Cogswell from New Haven is unknown, but Winthrop writing August 24, 1642, says that 20 families had been transported to the Delaware, and the instructions to Printz written the same year indicate that 60 English persons were settled on the river.[18] In any event, by 1642 New Haven people were settled at two places—on the Varkens Kill and on the Schuylkill. The third tract Lamberton and Turner had purchased from the Indians at New Castle was not settled by the New Haven English, apparently to avoid direct conflict with the Swedish authorities living on the western side of the river.

Reports reached Sir Edmund Plowden in London before he sailed for America in August of 1642 that some of his countrymen had seated themselves on his New Albion lands. The Earl furiously petitioned Charles I for relief, complaining also "of the entry and intrusions of certain aliens on His Majesty's dominion and province in Delaware Bay or South River," referring to the Swedes and Dutch. Accordingly, the Crown directed that a communication be sent to the governor and council of Virginia requiring them to give speedy and real assistance to Sir Edmund in repulsing the intruders.[19]

The letter Charles I dispatched to Jamestown reiterated that Swedes and Dutch were unlawfully seated on Sir Edmund Plowden's grant, according to intelligence that had reached him, and that some of his subjects living in New England had also removed to the Delaware without warrant or commission. The latter, he said, were being expelled from his dominion for their illegal act and were thereafter to be declared enemies. Evidently copies of this royal communication were also sent to New England, New Amsterdam, and New Sweden, and a portion of the document sent to the Swedes is still preserved in the Royal Archives at Stockholm. A transcript appears in the Appendix to this volume. Evidently, the date appears on a missing page, but it would seem it was written in late 1641 or early in 1642.

Upon receipt of this and other communications from London, including one from Sir Edmund, Governor Berkeley on March 18, 1642/1643 addressed a letter of protest to "the right worthy Governor of Manatos and to Jno Jackson [Jan Jansen] his Commander in the River and to the righte worthy the Govern'r of the Sweads and to Henrich Hugo [Hendrick Huygen] in Charles or South River." Berkeley pointed out that Sir Edmund Plowden was the "Lord and Governor" of the Province of New Albion which extended from "Delaware bay or South River unto Hudsons River or Manatoes," and that Plowden had acquainted King and

Parliament that intruders had settled on his property. Berkeley stated further that he had been instructed to give speedy assistance to Sir Edmund, and that he was taking this opportunity to warn both Dutch and Swedes not to sell arms or ammunition to the Indians; not to attempt to hinder the passage, residence, or trade of Englishmen on the Delaware; and that all Dutch and Swedes in the area should promptly submit to the authority of Charles I and Sir Edmund Plowden. A transcript of this letter also appears in the Appendix.

Some of the New Haven people settled on the Delaware were primarily interested in the Indian fur trade, but those on the Varkens Kill came for the purpose of agriculture, particularly to raise tobacco. Tobacco by this time was in demand in most European countries, and the New Haven merchants knew that it would prove highly profitable if they could raise their own crops instead of trading for the leaf in Virginia.

The Swedish colonists had already planted a few scattered tobacco fields along the Delaware, under Ridder's direction, but Swedish settlers never raised tobacco in quantity. The first large cargo of 11,878 pounds of tobacco shipped to Sweden on the *Kalmar Nyckel* in 1640 was mainly obtained in Virginia. It was sold in Sweden at a good profit. The backers of the Swedish company were also desirous of growing their own tobacco crops in New Sweden instead of buying tobacco from Virginia planters and traders. Printz was instructed to "pay good and close attention to the cultivation of tobacco and appoint thereto a certain number of laborers, pressing the matter so that that cultivation may increase and more and more continued and extended so that he can send over a good quantity of tobacco on all ships coming hither." [20]

There was, of course, still a demand for beaver pelts, and, with New Haven competing with the Dutch and Swedes, a lively trade ensued with the Lenni Lenape and Minquas Indians. English liberality caused the natives to divert a majority of their beaver pelts to the English post on the Schuylkill. From there the skins were transported to New Haven and thence to Boston or London. Peter Hollender Ridder once more protested that the English were underselling them, as did Jan Jansen, the Dutch commissary at Fort Nassau.

Although they had been competitors in the Indian trade, the Swedes and Dutch managed to live together in reasonable harmony before the arrival of the New Haveners, even though the Dutch West India Company always considered the Swedes interlopers in Dutch territory, as the English considered the Dutch trespassers in the same region. The Swedes took the position under international law that discovery alone did not give a nation title to a new territory unless that nation settled the newly discovered land. They claimed there were no Christian peoples previously living on the lands they settled along the Delaware; they insisted that they had complete territorial rights to places where their people were seated and the Dutch were not. Furthermore, the Swedes could show that they had exhausted Indian title by purchase from the natives. The truth is that the West India Company never had as its aim the colonization of the Delaware Valley as an extension of Dutch culture to the New World. The company was so beset with commercial interests and so eager for financial gain that it weighed every expenditure against the probable return, and it was simply not a good business risk to support a colony on the Delaware River. Their objective was to control the Indian trade, which they did with notable success before the arrival of the Swedes.

With a third rival on the scene, Dutch and Swedes were brought closer to each other, and they temporarily laid

aside their differences and pooled their resources to discourage and block the common competitor. The Dutch took
the first action against the English unilaterally, although
there is no doubt that Ridder, who cooperated fully, was
kept informed. On May 15, 1642, the council at Manhattan
passed a resolution to the effect that since "some Englishmen
have presumed to come into our Southriver obliquely opposite our fort Nassau where they settled down in the Schuylkill without commission from any potentate . . . seriously
injuring the trade of the West India Company . . . we
have resolved to expel them." [21]

On May 22, 1642, Jan Jansen received orders from Governor Kieft that the company's sloops, the *Real* and *St. Martin,* had been sent to reinforce him; that he should move his
garrison aboard the vessels to join the soldiers brought from
Manhattan, and proceed immediately to the English blockhouse on the Schuylkill. There he was to demand to see the
royal commission which gave the English authorization to
settle on Dutch territory, and if they had none, he should
order them to leave, but should not shed any blood. If the
English refused to depart, he should forcibly take them
aboard his vessels, without injury to them or their personal
effects, and bring them to Manhattan. After their departure
he was told to "lay waste the place." [22]

James Waye said of this incident that "the Dutch came in
and burnt our houses or Garrison & carried us away prisoner
to New Haven in New England from whence this Deponent
with the rest of the aforementioned company came from."

A number of years later, Edward Hopkins, describing the
incident in a letter to Governor Stuyvesant said that

> *without any legall protest or warning Monsere Kieft the then
> Dutch Governor sent armed men in 1642 and by force in a
> hostile way burnt their trading house seized and for som time*

detained the goods in it not suffering theire servants soe much
as to take a just Inventory of them; hee there allsoe seized
theire boate and for a while kept theire men Prisoners for
which to this day they can get no satisfaction.[23]

It is known from other contemporary records that the
Englishmen seized at the Schuylkill post were first taken to
Manhattan Island and imprisoned. Later they were returned
to New Haven. This was the end of the English settlement
on the Schuylkill. It might be noted in passing that the site
of Governor Printz's home on Tinicum Island has been
called the location of the first settlement by Europeans
within the bounds of the present state of Pennsylvania,
which is incorrect. The English from New Haven, as I have
shown, were established on the Schuylkill before Governor
Printz arrived in America, although their settlement, like
the Dutch colony at Swanendael, was short-lived.

The records do not explain why the English farmers on
the Varkens Kill—which, incidentally, was probably the first
European settlement in the state of New Jersey—were not
molested by the Dutch. The names of the English planters
at the Varkens Kill "under Swedish jurisdiction" in 1643–
1644 were as follows: [24]

Elias Baily
William Braunveil (?)
Robert Coxwell [Cogswell]
John Erie
Thomas Marod
Mr. Spinning [25]
John Wall [Woollen?]

Probably the reason these Englishmen and their families
were not disturbed was because they were not a factor in the
beaver trade, so important along the Schuylkill. By building

a post on the latter stream the English were able to intercept the Minquas en route from the Susquehanna country to Fort Nassau with their furs. The Dutch West India Company simply could not tolerate this interference in its profitable Indian trade. Since the people on the Varkens Kill had no influence on the beaver trade, the Dutch saw no need to interrupt them, particularly since they were under the watchful eyes of the Swedes.

The Delaware venture, although audacious, had been a profitless one for the New Haven merchants. It was reported their losses were in excess of £1,000.[26] But they were stubborn men, unwilling to give up their plans.

8
Printz Brings
Lamberton to Trial

With the arrival on the Delaware of Johan Printz in 1643, the government of New Sweden was reorganized and systematized. Previously the officers, soldiers and servants were paid by the New Sweden Company, whereas the budget for Printz and his staff was paid by the Crown. Printz was directly responsible to the Swedish government, although he was also obligated to protect the company's interests. The new governor was vested with full administrative and judicial powers, and although he was instructed to rule the colony in the name of Queen Christina, the details of procedure were left to his discretion. In comparison with the power conferred on the governors of neighboring colonies, Printz had far greater authority. He could, in actuality, rule the people and the company's employees to suit his whims. Since the territory was now considered Swedish soil, under the direct jurisdiction and protection of Printz as the Queen's servant, the new governor could speak authoritatively in his relations with other nationals. Printz was an impressive man, weighing in excess of 300 pounds, regal in bearing, autocratic in behavior.

In the instructions issued to him by his superiors on August 15, 1642, before his departure from Stockholm, occurs this passage relating to the English, indicating the Swedish government was reasonably well informed about New Haven's activities:

> *Inasmuch as in the last passed year, 1641, several English families, together with perhaps about sixty persons strong, have settled and begun to build and cultivate the land on the other, namely upon the east side of the above mentioned South River, on a little stream, called Ferken's Kil, so have also the aforesaid subjects of [Her] Roy[al] Maj[esty], and shareholders in the Company, purchased for themselves of some of the wild inhabitants of the country the whole of this eastern side of the river, from the mouth of the aforesaid Great River [Delaware] at Cape May and to a stream called Narraticen's Kil, extending about twelve German miles [along the Delaware River] under which is included also the said Ferken's Kil, with the intention of drawing to themselves the aforesaid English.*
>
> *This purchase the Governor shall keep entirely intact and inviolate, and thus bring these English families under the jurisdiction, devotion and dominion of [Her] Roy[al] Maj [esty] and the Swedish crown; especially as it is reported that they themselves are not indisposed thereto; and it is rumored that they, as a free people, would submit themselves to that government, which can maintain and protect them, believing that they might shortly increase to some hundred strong.*
>
> *But although there are certain reasons why the Governor should seek to bring these English under the jurisdiction of the Swedish Crown, nevertheless inasmuch as [Her] Roy[al] Maj[esty] herself and the Crown as well as the stockholders find it to be better and more desirable if one could get rid of them out of and away from that place, in a peaceable manner;*

therefore [Her] Most Roy[al] Maj[esty] aforesaid will most graciously leave it to the discretion of Governor Printz to strive for such [a solution] and gradually bring it so far that the English may be removed, in case it can be done with grace and propriety.[1]

In the same instructions, Printz was cautioned to exert effort to retain friendship with the Dutch at Fort Nassau and elsewhere in New Netherland, but if he encountered opposition, he should use his own discretion, and, if necessary, repel force with force. He was reminded that the Swedes had Indian deeds to the land, purchased from the rightful owners, and that Sweden expected to continue to expand her interests and enjoy free commerce along the Delaware River.

Prior to Printz's arrival, a sickness befell both the Swedish population and the Puritans settled on the Varkens Kill. A number died, and some of the English families returned to New Haven, although a few remained behind. An entry in the New Haven court records on October 2, 1644, indicates that one Roger Knapp, afflicted by a sickness, had returned from Delaware Bay where his "armes was burnt" which refers to his guns and ammunition.[2]

In letters written to Sweden shortly after his arrival in America, Printz complained about the English, referring to them as "evil neighbors," and that he continued to resist the pretensions "of the Hollanders, of the Puritans, and of the other English to this place."[3]

Printz wrote of the Puritans from New Haven that they "have lain upon my neck and yet do lay can be seen from the documents which are enclosed here. I believe that I shall hardly get rid of them in a peaceful manner, because they have sneaked into New Netherland also with the Pharisean practices."[4]

The settlers on the Varkens Kill were a constant source of worriment for Printz, because their very presence was a threat that the English might at any time decide to expand the settlement. At the same time the colonists served a useful purpose through their tobacco planting. In the summer of 1644, Printz shipped a consignment of tobacco to Sweden of which 4,991 pounds "were planted here in New Sweden, one part by *our* English at Varkens Kill and one part by our Swedish freemen for which we have paid eight stivers a pound." [5]

His use of the possessive "our" in reference to the English was not accidental, for those on the Varkens Kill had been persuaded to swear allegiance to the Swedish Crown. Governor John Winthrop claimed Printz intimidated the English settlers by threatening to drive them away if they did not shift their allegiance from New Haven to New Sweden. Printz hotly denied this accusation and insisted it was an act of their own free will and they preferred to live under Swedish authority. In fact, he said that the Varkens Kill people had willingly accepted Sir Edmund Plowden as their lord and protector and were in no way loyal to Lamberton or other New Haven officials.[6] Supporting evidence of Printz's statement can be found in the 1648 tract, *A Description of New Albion,* wherein the statement is made by the author, Beauchamp Plantagenet, that one "Master Miles" swore in the "officers there to his Majesties allegiance and to obedience to your Lordship [Plowden] as Governor." [7] I have not been able to identify Master Miles who is not named, incidentally, in the original 1641 edition of the publication. He either preceded Plowden to America or accompanied his lordship in 1642. His mission must have been to acquaint the New Haven settlers that they were not only living on Plowden's grant, but were seated on the specific land the Earl Palatine had selected for his residence at

Watcessit, and to bring them under his lordship's submission. Evidently the people on the Varkens Kill swore allegiance to Plowden when Master Miles told them they had committed a grave offense to the Crown and were to be considered enemies if they did not acknowledge Sir Edmund as their lord and protector. After Plowden failed in his colonization efforts, the English on the Varkens Kill pledged allegiance to Queen Christina in order to maintain good relations with Printz. From then on, he considered them his subjects.

Printz had been a professional soldier in Europe, serving in the imperial forces of Archduke Leopold of Austria, later in one of the regiments of Duke Christian of Braunschweig, and still later as a cavalry captain, major, and lieutenant-colonel in the Swedish forces. He met the problems presented by the Dutch and New Englanders through military maneuvers intended to strengthen the Swedish position on the Delaware. For example, to retain control of the Varkens Kill and prevent further incursions by the English, he constructed a fort on the east side of the river called Fort Elfsborg. The heaviest cannons available in the colony were placed on its bastions, eight 12-pound iron and brass guns and one mortar.

The English settlement on the Varkens Kill was situated very close to Fort Elfsborg, as indicated by the following item included in an inventory of Swedish land holdings in 1653: "Fort Elfsborg with the surrounding 30 morgens [approximately 60 acres] of cleared land *cultivated by the English* a short time ago." [8]

The location of Fort Elfsborg is the key to identifying the site of the little English colony. Lindeström shows the fort on his map of 1654 on the south side of *Asamo Hackingskijl,* one of the Indian names for Salem Creek, near its junction with the Delaware. Amandus Johnson places it a

little south of Mill Creek on an island of upland at "Elsin-
burg Fort Point." Lindeström describes how the mosquitoes
so deviled the garrison that they nicknamed the bastion
Myggenborgh (Mosquito-burg), and were eventually forced
to abandon it because of illness brought on by mosquito
bites.

The garrison at Fort Elfsborg consisted of 13 soldiers, under command of Sven Skutte, second in authority to Printz.
Probably some of them brought their families. No Dutch or
English vessel could thereafter sail up the Delaware without
being challenged by the Swedes at Fort Elfsborg, and none
could enter the Varkens Kill without obtaining permission.

On the site of the former English fort on the Schuylkill,
Printz erected Fort Nya Korsholm, and Mans Kling was
placed in charge of the garrison. Although this post was of
little strategic value in controlling the Delaware River, it
was a key position in the beaver trade with the Minquas and
it rendered Fort Nassau almost useless as a trading post so
far as bartering with the Minquas was concerned. Printz
also erected other fortifications in New Sweden to control
the fur trade, but Fort Christina remained the principal
storehouse. The trade of both the West India Company and
the Delaware Company of New Haven felt the strong in-
roads being made by their Swedish competitors, and one of
the Dutch officials (Hudde) said of Printz's tactics that "no
access to the Minquas is left open, and he, too, controls all
the trade of the Savages on the River . . ."

In June of 1643, George Lamberton and John Thickpenny sailed up the Delaware and into the Christina, and
anchored their pinnace, the *Cock,* about three miles above
Fort Christina. There they intercepted the Minquas en
route to Fort Christina with their furs and began to barter
with them. They had thoroughly prepared for this spring
voyage on behalf of the Delaware Company of New Haven,

and the *Cock* was well supplied with merchandise for the Indian trade, including a large inventory of wampumpeake, which Lamberton had purchased from the Connecticut Indians for use on the Delaware.

Early Sunday morning, June 26, as Governor Printz came from his prayers, Timon Stidden, the barber-surgeon, and Gotfried Harmer, a servant to Hendrick Huygen, brought him reports that Lamberton was not only carrying on a brisk trade with the Minquas, but had bribed them and the Delaware Indians to murder the Swedish settlers and burn their houses and forts. Printz knew that Governor Kieft and his Council at Manhattan Island were strongly antagonistic to Lamberton, having on August 28, 1642, passed a resolution forbidding him to trade on the Delaware unless he paid duty on all the furs he obtained there.[9] He also knew that the Swedish government would support any action he took against the English.

In order to confirm his intelligence, Printz sent Stidden and Harmer (the latter could speak the Indian tongues) with a letter to Lamberton telling him the previous day Indians had stolen a gold chain belonging to his wife, and asking Lamberton's assistance to have it returned. This was a ruse to enable Stidden and Harmer to board the *Cock* and spy on the Englishmen.[10]

Lamberton allowed them to come aboard, and, after some conversation, the Swedish agents requested permission to remain on the pinnace overnight, since many Indians were coming the following day to trade with the Englishmen. They said it would give them a better opportunity to apprehend the culprit who had stolen the gold chain since he could be easily recognized by a mark on his face.

The next day a messenger brought a second letter from Printz to Lamberton, requesting him to come to Fort Christina on a matter of extreme importance. The Englishman acceded to the request, and as they entered the fort, Printz seized Lamberton, Thickpenny, Woollen, and others, and put them under arrest. Printz then interrogated members of the crew concerning the proposed massacre, although nothing incriminating to Lamberton could be discovered. Printz, and his officers, next exposed John Woollen to a continuous grilling, hoping to break him down. Woollen was Lamberton's Indian interpreter, and the Swedes knew that he was present in all of Lamberton's conversation with the Indians. Thickpenny, upon his return to New Haven, deposed that Printz tried to worm a confession out of Woollen by making him drunk and by promising him a house and plantation if he would testify that Lamberton hired the Indians to attack the Swedes. This Woollen flatly refused to do. (See Thickpenny's complete deposition in Appendix.)

Printz then decided to take full advantage of the authority delegated to him in his instructions to administer all controversial matters "according to Swedish law and justice, custom and usage." This meant conducting a court of inquiry, hearing the evidence, rendering a decision, and imposing sentence. He set July 10, 1643, as the date the court would convene at Fort Christina to hear the case of *New Sweden vs George Lamberton et al.,* involving trespass, illicit trading, inciting Indians to commit murder, and the illegal purchase of lands belonging to the Queen of Sweden. In Printz's estimation, the whole subject of Puritan encroachment in New Sweden would then be settled by due process of law, in a test case that would resolve the question for all time.

It was an unusual international tribunal that assembled that hot July day to sit in judgment on Lamberton. The 10 judges selected by Printz acted as both judge and jury. The members were as follows, and I have used the spellings of their names as entered in the court records by the Swedish scribe:

Captain Christiaen Boij, *a young Swedish nobleman who accompanied Printz to America, and was appointed commander of the blockhouse Printz built at Upland, present Chester, Penna. He evidently served as the presiding member of the court.*

Hendrick Huygen, *who was born at Cleef, and was one of Peter Minuit's relatives. He was a member of the first Swedish expedition, and remained for many years in New Sweden as the chief commissary.*

Captain Mons Clingh *was, of course, the well-known Måns Nilsson Kling (Kling was his adopted name as a soldier). He was also a member of the first Swedish expedition who remained in New Sweden as director of Fort Christina. In the summer of 1644 he was placed in charge of Fort Nya Korsholm on the Schuylkil.*

Jan Jansen, *whose participation as a judge was, indeed, strange inasmuch as he was the Dutch commissary or commander at Fort Nassau. His interests lay with the West India Company who strongly opposed the Swedish encroachment in New Netherland, yet he was very friendly with Printz.*

Wessel Evertsen, *a skipper who brought Swedish vessels to New Sweden.*

Sander Lenertsen, *whose name is also recorded as Alexander Lendertsen or Leendertsen, a former Dutch skipper, who was then one of the planters and traders living on the Delaware.*

Oloff Stille, *a millwright, who brought his family to New Sweden in 1641, settling at present Chester.*

Ivert Sievers, *whose name was given elsewhere as Evert Sieversen, one of the early Swedish settlers who came to America in 1641.*

Carl Jansen, *a bookkeeper, also known as Carl Johannsson, a Finn, who was one of the enforced recruits sent to New Sweden because he had run afoul of the law in Sweden.*

David Davidsen, *a Dutch freeman and soldier stationed at Fort Nassau.*

The first witness introduced by the prosecution (according to the minutes of the court) was none other than "the Governor, noble and courageous Johan Printz." Printz was the chief witness, the plaintiff, as well as attorney for the prosecution! He opened his case by asking Lamberton on what basis, and by what commission he had protested against her Royal Majesty Queen Christina of Sweden. This question probably perplexed the judges, who now learned for the first time that in addition to his trading mission, Lamberton had been sent to register protests on behalf of the Delaware Company of New Haven. Printz was thoroughly familiar with these protests, because Lamberton had handed them to him in writing before the trial.

Lamberton obligingly turned over the protests to the court. In them he cited the Indian purchases of the three plots of land he and Turner had made in 1641–1642, and he protested that Måns Kling (one of the judges) was living on New Haven's lands on the Schuylkill, and that Governor Printz had appropriated territory on the Varkens Kill belonging to the English.

Printz then opened a scorching cross-examination of Lamberton, although the language differences complicated the interrogation. By what right did Lamberton pretend to lands on the Schuylkill? Lamberton's answer was that he bought the land from the Delaware Indians two years before with the consent of Jan Jansen, the Dutch commissary at Fort Nassau.

Printz interrupted the Englishman; didn't Lamberton know that the Queen of Sweden owned the whole west side of the Delaware River, having purchased the territory from Cape Henlopen as far north as the Sankikans (present Trenton), which included the entire Schuylkill drainage system? Yes, Lamberton knew that, but Jan Jansen told him to go ahead and buy the Schuylkill lands and settle on them. Lamberton was subtly suggesting that the Dutch encouraged him to occupy lands that the Swedes bought from the Indians. At this point Jan Jansen (a judge) jumped to his feet and exclaimed, "Mr. Lamberton lies like a wanton rascal." That seemed to settle that point.

Printz then interrogated Lamberton about the land on the Varkens Kill and received the reply that the Englishmen had purchased it from the rightful Indian owners. Printz then cited evidence previously given by John Woollen and Robert Cogswell (both members of the original Lamberton-Turner party) that Peter Hollender Ridder on behalf of the Swedes had bought the identical land *three days prior* to Lamberton's purchase. In fact, said Printz, he would call Cogswell and Woollen before the honorable court to testify, but the members of the court said that would not be necessary. They were already convinced that the Swedes bought the land on the Varkens Kill before the English.

Printz next opened up the subject of trading for furs in the territory of New Sweden. Why had Lamberton done so? Lamberton replied he didn't know he was forbidden to do so. To this Hendrick Huygen (one of the judges) said that Peter Hollender Ridder had forbade Lamberton to trade a year before, and Måns Kling said that long before this he had personally warned Lamberton to discontinue trading with the Indians in New Sweden. Evert Sieversen (also a judge) then testified that when Lamberton was warned he paid no attention, and besides, the Governor had written him, in an official letter from Fort Christina, that he should not trade on the Delaware and he ignored that communication, too. By now it was probably very clear to Lamberton, if he understood the full import of the testimony given in both the Dutch and Swedish languages, that impartiality was not a virtue to be found among the judges sitting on his case.

Do you have a commission from the Queen of Sweden to trade in the Delaware? Printz pressed the point. The answer was in the negative, as Printz knew it must be. Didn't Lamberton know that anyone who traded without commission from the recognized authorities in an occupied land was no better than a robber or a rascal and should be hung on a tree? Lamberton replied that although he had no Swedish commission he was willing to pay duty on any furs that he removed from the territory. This reply irritated rather than satisfied Printz, and he promptly answered, "What the Honorable Court allows me that I will have, and no more."

The final charge had to do with Lamberton allegedly inciting the Indians to massacre the Swedes. Stidden and Harmer testified that they had heard such rumors. Four other Scandinavian witnesses, Peter Andriesen, Lasse Anderson, Peer Cock, and Lasse Bonde, also testified to the same effect, the latter revealing that the English settlers on the Varkens Kill had intimated that as soon as Lamberton arrived "the English and the Savages should unite and strike us Swedes dead and chase us out of the River." Indeed, there was testimony that the (White) Minquas and the Black Minquas had already come before Fort Christina with their weapons and acted in a hostile manner as though they intended to scale the walls. But as soon as the Swedish garrison in the fort began to man their guns, the Indians ran away into the woods.

Lamberton admitted he had given the Minquas some cloth and wampumpeake, not to bribe them to kill Swedes and Dutch, but as an incentive to trade with him. Lamberton said that if the court would allow testimony by his interpreter, John Woollen, he would corroborate his statements.

The court asked that Woollen be brought before them for questioning, but Printz hastily said that it wouldn't be necessary. He had already interrogated Woollen, and he would not confess that Lamberton had incited the savages to attack the Swedes. In fact, said Printz charitably, since Lamberton had evidently been honest in his testimony, he wouldn't press the issue of the alleged Indian attack.

The court rendered its decision on the same day as the trial, and in its wisdom, taking a cue from Printz, decided to drop the charges against Lamberton of inciting the Indians to attack the Swedes.

On the other hand, the court found that Lamberton's pretensions to land on the Delaware River were absolutely unfounded. Since the land he bought from the Indians was already in possession of the Swedes through prior purchase, he should by right forfeit it to the Swedish Crown.

Finally, he had admitted he bought 400 beaver skins within "the territory of Her Royal Majesty of Sweden and the Honorable West India Company" without a proper commission. Therefore, the court ordered him to pay double duty on the 400 pelts, and warned him that should the crime of illicit trading be repeated his ship and property would be confiscated.[11]

After paying the double duty of 12 pounds sterling, Lamberton returned to New Haven, where he made a strong protest to the General Court there on August 2, 1643, about the treatment he had received at the hands of Governor Printz. Theophilus Eaton and Thomas Gregson, who had been chosen commissioners from New Haven to represent that jurisdiction at the General Court in Boston (representing the New England Confederation), were instructed to bring Lamberton's complaints before that court in September. The General Court took up the matter, and decided that John Winthrop, as governor of Massachusetts and president of the commissioners for the confederation, should draft letters of protest to be sent to Printz.

Accordingly, the first letter, dated September 18, 1643, written in Latin, was delivered by Captain Nathaniel Turner to Governor Printz, addressed, "To the most worthy lord, lord Johan Printz, governor of the Swedes in Delaware Bay." Winthrop pointed out that Delaware Bay was included in the grants the King of England had given his subjects; that, in addition, the New Haven people had Indian deeds for certain territories along the Delaware which Printz had confiscated; that Printz had interfered with Lamberton's lawful trade; that Printz made false charges that Lamberton had hired the Indians to massacre both Swedes and Dutch; that the English of New Haven demanded satisfaction, with an opportunity for further discussion over the division of boundaries as well as the exercise of trade.[12]

Printz replied on January 12, 1644, also in Latin, a language that he wrote with extreme difficulty because of lack of practice. "I have more often, for the last 27 years," he reported to his superiors, "had the musket and the pistol in my hands than Tacitus and Cicero." His letter was addressed "To the most worthy lord, the lord governor of the English in Massachusetts Bay, *etc.* Greeting," and he strongly defended his position and the action he had taken, denying that he had been unjust to Lamberton. He insisted that the trial had been conducted fairly and in a lawful manner. He emphasized that he was desirous of maintaining friendly relations with the New England colonies.

On March 21, 1644, Winthrop (writing as the chief officer of the confederation) replied to Printz, also in Latin, as was the balance of the correspondence between the two men. His letter was conciliatory in tone, expressing strong hope that the relations between Swedes and New Haven would be "conducted with the utmost peace and accord."

One of the factors that contributed to a better understanding between the two governors was a transcript Printz sent to Winthrop of a second hearing he had conducted. This hearing was held January 16, 1644, and its primary purpose was to give Printz an opportunity to refute John Thickpenny's deposition, which had been very damaging to the Swedes. In the presence of Captain Turner, Isaac Allerton, members of the court, and some of the English from Varkens Kill, Printz asked the English settlers if he had done any injustices to them, driving them from their plantations, or threatening to banish them if they did not swear allegiance to the Crown of Sweden. Their emphatic answer was "No."

Printz then interrogated John Woollen (his name is also given in the New Haven records as Nollin) asking if he had given him beer and wine in an effort to coerce him into testifying against Lamberton, or if he had promised him gold or silver to make false statements. Woollen's answer was also "No."

Printz then turned to Timon Stidden and Gotfried Harmer, asking where they had received information that Lamberton had paid the Indians to attack the Swedes. On their oaths they declared that they had been told by certain Indians that Lamberton had bribed them to kill the Swedes. Moreover, they testified that Lamberton had promised to sell arms and powder to the Indians, a violation of English laws as well as the statutes of the Swedish colony.[13]

When Winthrop read the transcript of this testimony, signed by Nathaniel Turner and Isaac Allerton as witnesses, he had reason to doubt the damaging statement made by Thickpenny, or at least parts of it. Furthermore, as an added gesture of friendship, Printz agreed that if the New Haveners presented a copy of their patent to him, as well as a new commission issued by the confederation, he would allow them to go on with their plantation and trade in Delaware Bay and River.[14]

What would have happened if the Delaware Company of New Haven had immediately taken full advantage of this opportunity and persisted in their efforts to develop their Delaware colony during Printz's administration is difficult to predict. This was expressly against his instructions and contrary to the sentiments he had expressed in his letters and confidential reports to his superiors. Perhaps he knew that New Haven had temporarily deferred its plans for expansion, because the Delaware colony had been a losing proposition to the merchants. For some months thereafter, New Haven's activity on the Delaware resolved itself in periodic trading trips by a few individuals, notably Isaac Allerton. However, the issue was to be revived again in a few years, because New Haven had no intention of giving up its rights to the Delaware.

9

Printz Betrays
the Boston Puritans

On April 22, 1644, Governor Winthrop again wrote Governor Printz, sending his letter by William Aspinwall, a Boston Puritan,

> *whom we have sent with a commission under the public seal*
> *to examine the western bounds of our colony. This is the true*
> *(believe me my lord) and actual cause of this expedition . . .*
> *also to engage in trading with the natives . . . we have*
> *granted him leave of raising in some way or another [money]*
> *for his expenses. For the more fortunate transaction of this*
> *business as much as he and his men shall [not] lack your*
> *counsel and assistance so you will bind the people of our*
> *colony to you and yours with the bonds of greatest gratitude*
> *and duty.*[1]

Aspinwall was one of the Puritans who tried to found a new colony in Rhode Island and who was banished from the church in Boston. In 1642, after acknowledging the error of his ways, he was reconciled with the church, and at the time of his voyage to the Delaware in the spring of 1644, he was not only in good graces with the church, but he had the financial support of a syndicate of influential Puritan merchants.

What had happened was that interest had been re-awakened among these Boston businessmen in finding the great inland lake that had obsessed Thomas Yong, Sir Ferdinando Gorges, Thomas Dermer, Captain John Mason, Captain Neal, and other English explorers. The interest was revived when one Darby Field, an Irishman, accompanied by two Indians, claimed to have seen the lake from a cloudy peak in the White Mountains during an exploring trip. He also looked down upon a sea eastwardly, which he judged to be the "gulf of Canada" as well as a great lake in a westerly direction, from which the river of Canada (St. Lawrence) issued.[2]

The lake, according to a description in *New English Canaan,* was 240 miles in circumference, and within it were many islands, breeding grounds of swan, geese, duck, teal, and other wild fowl. The waters contained an abundance of fish to supply food to the beaver colonies. The Indians reported that three great rivers issued from the lake, and it was originally thought that one was the river of Canada, the second the Potomac, which flowed south to Virginia, and the third, nameless, trended westward and discharged into the South Sea. Laconia was the name given to the district where the great lake and a number of other smaller lakes were situated. On November 17, 1629, Mason and Gorges obtained from the Council for New England a land patent for a piece of territory which they called Laconia.

What inland bodies of water Darby Field saw has never been explained, if, indeed, he saw water at all, and not banks of fog, but it did not take long for the news to reach Boston, where the Puritan merchants were quick to believe his story. They were certain the Irishman had finally located the much sought breeding grounds of the beaver and that a fortune lay waiting for those who first reached the shores of the lake, from which a water route led to the Pacific. Impassable mountains blocked access to the supposed lake from New England, and the French were well established on the St. Lawrence, and the Dutch on the Hudson, so the lake could not be reached via those rivers. Geographical misconceptions of the Delaware River, which seemed to plague the English, made it appear the most logical approach.

On March 7, 1643/44, a petition was submitted to the General Court by Valentine Hill, Captain Robert Sedgewick, William Tinge, Mr. Francis Norton, Mr. Thomas Clarke, Joshua Hewes, and William Aspinwall. Tinge was named in the petition as "treasurer," indicating that funds would be accumulated for the furtherance of the petitioners' interests. The petition requested the court's approval to establish a free company of adventurers, a sort of joint stock company, with authority to take in others. Although the petition said nothing about the lake, which was evidently to be treated as classified information, the adventurers sought authorization that "whatsoever trade they shall discover in those parts within three years next ensuing (if the Lord so bless their endeavors) they may enjoy solely to themselves and the rest of their company for twenty and one years after such discovery is made." [3]

The petition was granted, and for the pursuance of their objective there was also a "commission granted them under the public seal[,] and letters from the governor to the Dutch and Swedish governors." [4] These letters were, of course, for the purpose of guaranteeing them free passage up the Delaware River, and, having a good rapport with Printz, Winthrop no doubt felt that the Swedish governor would cooperate fully. Subsequently, the company

sent out a pinnace well manned and furnished with provi-
sions and trading stuff which was to sail up Delaware River so
high as they could go, and then some of the company under
the conduct of Mr. William Aspenwall, a good artist, and one
who had been in those parts, to pass by small skiffs or canoes
up the river as far as they could.[5]

It was, of course, a secret expedition, so far as its true mission was concerned, because the English had no intention of
revealing Darby Field's discovery to their Swedish and
Dutch competitors. Winthrop deliberately avoided disclos-
ing the aim of the expedition in his letter to Printz by saying the party had been sent only to examine the western
bounds of the colony, which was a falsehood. That alone
must have aroused Printz's suspicions. He knew enough
about Delaware River geography to recognize that its headwaters didn't lead to the bounds of Massachusetts.

Although Governor Kieft allowed Aspinwall's pinnace to
pass Manhattan, en route to the Delaware, he immediately
dispatched runners overland to Jan Jansen at Fort Nassau,
telling him the English were on the way, and instructing
him to prevent their vessel from going up the river above
Fort Nassau. He instructed Jansen to sink the English ship
rather than let it pass the fort. He also kept Printz informed
about what he had done.

Aspinwall's pinnace arrived in Delaware Bay around the
end of May or the beginning of June. As the English came
in front of Fort Elfsborg, on a quiet Sunday morning, a
cannon shot was fired from the fort, a warning that the vessel should proceed no farther. Shortly after, Lieutenant
Sven Skute paddled out from the fort in a small boat, and
went on board the pinnace to confer with Aspinwall, forcing him to fall down lower and weigh anchor. Skute, of
course, was following Printz's orders, and he promptly sent

a messenger up the river to inform the governor that the English had arrived and he was holding them under surveillance, awaiting further orders. In a gesture of magnanimity, Printz sent the messenger back with a passport permitting the English to go up the river, provided they did not engage in trade with the Indians. Furthermore, he sent a Swedish soldier to accompany Aspinwall, as a guide, as far as Fort Nassau, ostensibly giving the Englishman evidence of his good faith that could be reported back to Winthrop. But, unknown to the unsuspecting Aspinwall, Printz had already agreed with Kieft and Jansen that the English must be prevented from ascending the river. This is made clear in a secret note which he sent to Sweden:

> *This journey was prevented for him [Aspinwall] by the Hollanders at Fort Nassau, which I discussed secretly with them, in order that all the blame should not fall on me. As the idea of the Puritans was this: to erect a fort above our post at Zanchikan [now Trenton] and garrison it with people and cannon and then to strengthen their position there, so as to draw to themselves the entire profit of the River here. They brought with them 14 well armed fellows [as well as muskets] bullets and powder enough.*[6]

In a letter to Winthrop dated June 29, 1644, Printz said he was extending the utmost cooperation to Aspinwall and that he wrote "to the officials in our outposts here that they should in no wise hinder him or cause him any annoyance." [7]

It seems quite clear that, despite their suspicions, neither Printz nor Kieft knew that Aspinwall's mission was to find the mysterious lake. The sponsors of the voyage did not intend to build a fort on the Delaware nor to compete with the Dutch and Swedes for the beaver trade on the river proper. Perhaps if they had frankly disclosed the purpose of the mission, both Kieft and Printz would have been less apprehensive. In any event, Jan Jansen displayed an order from Kieft forbidding the English to pass, and Aspinwall, after much argument, was forced to withdraw without going above Fort Nassau, and his mission was a failure.

According to Winthrop, the master of Aspinwall's pinnace

> proved such a drunken sot, and so complied with the Dutch and Swedes, as they feared, when they should have left the vessel to have gone up to the lake in a small boat, he would in his drunkenness have betrayed their goods, etc., to the Dutch, whereupon they gave over and returned home [reaching Boston July 20, 1644]; bringing their action against the master both for his drunkenness and denial to proceed as they required, and as by charter party he was bound, they recovered 200 pounds of him, which was too much, though he did deal badly with them, for it was very probably he could not have proceeded.[8]

To add insult to injury, Sven Skute, according to the same entry in Winthrop's journal, made Aspinwall pay 40 shillings for the shot he had been forced to waste when he fired across the Englishman's bow at Fort Elsborg.

Some years later the New England Confederation took note of the Aspinwall incident as one of their numerous grievances against the Dutch. The passages quoted below give the English view of what happened, and it is of interest that Printz's name is not even mentioned, so successful had been his strategy to put the blame on the Dutch:

> Richard Callicott, sometime agent for the company of adventurers for the Lake Lyconnia, allowed for the general court, for the Massachusetts, complaineth, that about the year 1644, he did present to the said Dutch governor, letters from the court of Massachusetts, wherein liberty for the English vessel to pass up Delaware Bay and River, by the Dutch fort,

for discovery and in further prosecution of the said company's occasions, was desired, and by a verbal promise, freely and fully granted by the Dutch governor.

Notwithstanding which, in an underhand and injurious way, he presently sent a vessel, well manned to the Dutch fort at Delaware, with command to John Johnson [Jan Jansen], his agent there, rather to sink said vessel than to suffer her to pass; by means whereof Richard Callicott and his company were forced to return, and whereby their whole stock, which at least was £700 was wasted, and their design overthrown, beside the hope of future trade and benefit.[9]

Although the records do not reveal any further attempt by the English to seek the lost lake via the Delaware River, individual English traders continued to visit New Sweden. Many of these traders came to do business with the Swedes, and there is record, for example, of an English boat arriving in the fall of 1643 with oak planks.[10] In 1644, Captain Nathaniel Turner sold duffels to the Swedes for use in the Indian trade; Richard Malbon of New Haven brought corn and sewant; William Whiting, an English trader, in 1644 sold the Swedes 7,333 pounds of tobacco, as well as beer and sewant.[11] Many, many other examples could be cited to illustrate the commerce of individual English traders with the people and government of New Sweden. Supply ships from Sweden were arriving less frequently, and interest in the colony was waning. Tobacco raising had not proved profitable, and Indian wars in which the Minquas were engaged interfered with the supply of beaver pelts. The backers of the Swedish company were dissatisfied with the return on their investments. Printz needed the merchandise sold by the English traders to maintain trade with the Indians and also to supply the settlers. As long as the English traders did not deal directly with the Indians, the relationship was a happy one.

In the winter of 1643–1644 an incident occurred that is not found in the Dutch or Swedish contemporary accounts, but is worthy of note. A bark was sent from Boston, under command of one Captain Luter, with six or seven men, for the purpose of conducting trade with the Indians along the Delaware. This voyage, too, was financed by Boston merchants. The English party remained during the winter with their countrymen seated on the Varkens Kill, and in the spring sailed off to trade.

The beaver trade usually began in April and continued throughout the summer months. Before the arrival of Europeans, the natives, who understood conservation, waited until the beaver bore their young before trapping the adults. This practice was ignored as more and more traders sought pelts and was a principal factor in contributing to the extinction of the beaver along eastern waterways.

As the number of beavers decreased, the trade became more highly competitive. The Indians also grew more sophisticated. They were no longer satisfied to exchange pelts for sewant and cheap European merchandise; they demanded guns and powder. Realizing the danger of placing firearms in the hands of primitive peoples whose only weapons had been the bow and arrow and stone knives and axes, the Europeans agreed during the days of the early contacts with the Indians that they would withhold firearms. The agreement was soon broken, in what almost amounted to a mania for furs. Printz claimed the Dutch were the first to give the Indians guns in order to corner the fur market, and the Dutch said the Swedes were the first. Both accused the English of giving cheap firearms for as little as 10 beaver pelts and as much as seven or eight pounds of powder for one skin. All three nations were later to regret teaching the Indians to use firearms.

The Luter party had a large assortment of trade goods in

their bark, including arms and powder, and after three weeks of barter they had accumulated 500 pelts, mostly beaver and otter. The news spread through the local tribes that a party of English traders had a wondrous assortment of goods to barter, and one day a party of 15 Indians came aboard the bark bringing bundles of pelts. As Luter and his men started to examine the skins, the Indians drew hatchets they had hidden under their clothing, and attacked the whites. They killed Luter and three others, looted the vessel, and carried away as prisoners an English boy, and the party's "linkister," or interpreter to the Indians, an Englishman named Redman. Shortly after they had gone ashore another party of Indians came along, slew the sachem of the raiding party and took all the stolen goods.

Redman and the boy lived among the Indians for five or six weeks and were well treated. In fact, Redman was given 40 skins and 20 fathoms of wampum by his captors, but since it was known that he bore a grudge against Captain Luter, the accusation was later made that he had betrayed his commander to the Indians, for which the chief paid him in skins and wampum.

News that the Indians were holding an Englishman and boy in captivity reached Governor Printz, and he saw an opportunity for ingratiating himself further with Winthrop. He enlisted the assistance of friendly Indians to effect the release of the prisoners. Redman and the boy were given haven at the Swedish fort until another bark from New England made an appearance, and they were sent to New Haven, and thence to Boston.

Redman was eventually tried for his life, and found guilty by a grand jury, but his trial was deferred in expectation of the arrival of additional evidence from the Delaware. Later he was acquitted.[12]

In 1646, Luter's bereaved widow, Elizabeth Luter, petitioned the Massachusetts authorities for financial relief for herself and children. This interesting and touching document, not previously published, appears in the Appendix of this volume.[13]

10
Further English Attempts to Settle the Delaware

≈≈≈≈≈≈≈≈≈≈≈≈≈≈≈≈≈≈≈≈≈≈≈≈≈≈≈≈≈

Following the Luter tragedy, Governor Printz apparently was not bothered for some time by intruders either from Boston or New Haven, and, on February 20, 1647, he was able to report:

> *As to the English Puritans, with whom I had most to do at first, I have at last been able, with the authority of Her Majesty, to drive them from hence; and they have not been heard from for a long time, except that one Captain Clerk was sent here last year, from North England [New England] to try to settle a few hundred families under Her Majesty's flag, which I, in a civil way, refused, referring the matter to Her Majesty's further resolution.*[1]

The above translation, made in 1912 by Amandus Johnson, was slightly modified in his second translation in 1930, and the words "to drive them from hence" were replaced with "to get them out of here." Clerk's name is spelled Clerck in the second translation, and he is identified as "one of their commissaries from North England."

The pages of history are strangely silent about this alleged settlement effort by Captain Clerk, but in any event, it did not materialize nor has Captain Clerk yet been identified.

Final settlement attempts brought the irascible Sir Edmund Plowden back on the stage for his last personal role in the drama of the Delaware settlements. Early in 1649, he assembled 450 settlers in England and chartered a vessel to bring them to America to populate his beloved New Albion. Once again, lawsuits brought against him (this time for back rents which he allegedly owed) while he was preparing the expedition interfered with his plans.[2] The project was ultimately cancelled, and the money he had spent on preparation no doubt added further to the Earl Palatine's financial burdens.

Sir Edmund was not one to readily abandon hope, and in 1650 he reprinted Beauchamp Plantagenet's *Description of New Albion,* hoping that the glowing description of his American province would arouse interest among potential settlers. Then, on March 21, 1650, he petitioned the Committee for Plantations, requesting permission to transport guns and ammunition to New Albion. His request was granted with the understanding that he would not use this ordnance against the Puritan government. Among those who obtained leases from the Earl for tracts in New Albion was Sir Thomas Danby, who intended to establish "Danby Fort," a town and manor near *Watcessit* on a section of the 10,000 acres he leased. But these plans never materialized either. The proposed expedition was cancelled. There the matter rested, while Plowden continued his many and sundry battles in the English courts, and there is no further record of Sir Edmund ever again attempting to settle his province between then and his death in 1659.

Governor Printz in far-off New Sweden knew nothing about Sir Edmund's activities in England, or he, too, might have been thrown into a fit of anger to learn that his sovereignty was in danger of being challenged again by the Catholic nobleman, for whom he had no affection. In fact, things were relatively quiet in New Sweden, and the excitement had subsided between Printz and the New Englanders. This prompted him to write in 1650 (referring especially to the Dutch)

> *a few times and in several places begun to build within our poles and limits, but I have immediately let it be torn down again, so that if the new Governor [his long-awaited successor from Sweden] brings enough people with him, the Hollanders will quickly get tired and give up this in no less manner than the Puritans have done, who in the beginning were the most violent, but now they leave us entirely.*[3]

Printz underestimated the persistence of the New Haveners, who never forgot that they had in their possession Indian deeds giving them ownership rights to lands along the Delaware. Nor did they forget that their countrymen had settled on the Varkens Kill. Of the various groups or individuals among the English who attempted trade or settlement in the Delaware River valley—Thomas Yong, Sir Edmund Plowden, the Virginians, the Marylanders, the Boston Puritans, and the Delaware Company of New Haven —none held more stubbornly to what they considered their rights than the New Haveners. At the very moment Governor Printz was writing about having gotten rid of the English, a major movement was afoot in New Haven to establish another colony on the Delaware.[4]

Moreover, Printz didn't count on the trouble that the Dutch were planning for him. In 1647, Governor Kieft was succeeded by Peter Stuyvesant, a sturdy Dutchman, then about 55 years of age, a virile and picturesque soldier with a violent temper and a silver-bound peg leg, that replaced a limb he had lost in battle. As an experienced military man, Stuyvesant quickly sized up the situation on the Delaware, where Printz held mastery with less than 80 or 90 men. Stuyvesant understood the weakness of Printz's position, essentially one of too few men and too little matériel, and he knew that the Swedish forces could not match the ships and men the West India Company had placed under his command. Stuyvesant decided there had been enough threats and protests, and the time was ripe for action to bring the territory under Dutch control again. In June of 1651, he marched overland from Manhattan to Fort Nassau with an armed force of 120 men. There he had a prearranged rendezvous with 11 Dutch vessels that had sailed down the Atlantic Coast, into Delaware Bay, and up the river to meet him. The Dutch forces outnumbered the Swedes three or four to one, and Printz immediately realized that he could not repel this pincer movement applied to New Sweden by land and sea. He offered no resistance as the Dutch vessels sailed up and down the river drumming and cannonading.

The local Indians were naturally awed by this display of Dutch military strength, which was unlike anything they had ever seen before. When Stuyvesant summoned them to confer with him at Fort Nassau they were pleased and flattered. Wise old Mattahorn was the spokesman, and he said that all nations were welcome on the Delaware, and that everyone knew the Dutch were the earliest comers and discoverers long before the Swedes settled on the river. Actually, said Mattahorn, in answer to Stuyvesant's queries, the Indians had sold the Swedes only a few small plots of land, and the Swedes were occupying other places against the will and consent of the Indians, who had received no compensation for their property.

When the series of conferences ended, Stuyvesant had paid the chiefs well, and had in his possession Indian deeds for all the land he wanted. It made no difference to him that (despite what the Indians had told him) the Swedes and the English of New Haven also had Indian deeds for the identical land.

Stuyvesant dismantled Fort Nassau, and built a stronger fortification at the Sand Hook (present New Castle, Delaware), which he called Fort Casimir, and in one fell swoop made himself in effect master of the Delaware. Printz sent vigorous written protests to Stuyvesant, and urgent appeals to the Swedish Crown for the protection of the colony, but nothing happened. The directors of the West India Company were not sure whether to be pleased when they heard from Stuyvesant that he had bested the Swedes and proclaimed ownership over the Delaware by a show of military force. They didn't know whether the Swedish chancellor would send a fleet to wipe out the Dutch settlements in New Netherland or demand damages of Holland at home. Printz, in the meantime, discouraged at the lack of support from the homeland, angered that his many letters were unanswered, frustrated at his lack of soldiers and supplies, decided to return home, and he sailed for Sweden in the fall of 1653 without waiting for a successor to replace him.

As the balance of power changed on the Delaware, leading citizens of the town of New Haven were protesting to Governor Eaton because of

> *a sense of difficulty in carrying on their family occasions with comfort in this place, there being more in the town than can well subsist together, and therefore they think there is a necessity that some should remove; also that Delaware Bay hath been propounded as a fit place to receive plantations which may be for the good of posterity.*[5]

A special "Towne meeting" was held December 17, 1650, and since the issue was deemed too weighty to be put to a hand vote, everyone was allowed to speak his mind. The majority of the citizens agreed, after free discussion, that some part of the town should remove for the good of posterity, and that Delaware River was the "fittest place" to remove to.

During the months that followed there were many discussions about the Delaware project, but for one reason or another action did not materialize. But the issue was not laid aside nor forgotten, and in 1654 it loomed as a matter of paramount importance. This time, not only New Haven, but people from other Connecticut towns, as well as Massachusetts, were discussing movement in a body to the Delaware. As the New Englanders planned to remove their families, major political changes were again taking place in their "promised land." Governor Johann Rising, who succeeded Printz as the ranking official in New Sweden, captured the Dutch Fort Casimir on May 21, 1654, renaming it Fort Trinity. The fort, in a bad state of disrepair, was garrisoned by only a handful of Dutch soldiers, and its recapture was easily accomplished. Once more the Swedes were in control of the Delaware.

Scarcely had Rising become acquainted with his subjects and his Indian allies (with whom he had several pow-wows to win their affections) when he was visited, June 18, 1654, by Edward Lloyd of Maryland, who pointed out to him that the English owned the Delaware River on the following counts:

> *1. That they had discovered it; 2. That they had it through a donation from King James and all that which was situated between such and such a degree along the coast; 3. That Sir Edward Ployde [Sir Edmund Plowden] and Earl of Great Albion had a donation of this river from King James.*[6]
>
> *Rising refuted these claims by saying that the Spaniards*

had been in Delaware Bay long before the English (purely a surmise on his part), and that the Swedes had title deeds from the Indians for the territory from Cape May and Cape Henlopen as far north as the river extended. In a letter written back to Sweden, he commented, "The Virginians who were here requested to be allowed to buy land and plant colonies. I said I would not allow it since I had no orders." [7]

Had Rising known upon his arrival in New Sweden of the growing movement afoot in New Haven by his English rivals, whose Indian deeds to Delaware lands were as valid as those in the royal chancery at Stockholm, he probably would have been gravely concerned about the destiny of New Sweden. It didn't take long for the news to reach him, following an item of business recorded by the New Haven Court on July 5, 1654:

A letter was now by order of this court sent to the Sweeds at Delaware Bay, informing them of the propriety which some in this colony have to large tracts of land on both sides of Delaware Bay and River, and describing a neighborly correspondence with them, both in trading and planting there, and an answer hereof &c. [8]

Rising received the letter mentioned in this citation, signed by Governor Eaton, and dated July 6, 1654. This letter, portions of which are torn and undecipherable, was preserved in the Royal Archives in Stockholm. It is printed for the first time in the Appendix of this volume. Although Eaton stood firm in his position that New Haven owned lands along the Delaware, he expressed a sincere willingness to maintain ties of friendship with the Swedes.

On August 1, Rising replied, in Latin, to Eaton's letter, the delay occasioned by the time required for the communications to be carried by vessel. (The records indicate that some of the traders also served as couriers to carry correspondence between New Haven and New Sweden during their regular voyages. Among them were Isaac Allerton, Henry Rutherford, and Jacob Svensson.)

Eaton referred Rising's letter to the commissioners of the confederation then meeting in Hartford. The commissioners replied officially in English on September 23, and from the passages quoted below from their letter it is clear that the New England officials took exception to its contents:

> *Mr. Eaton, one of the present commissioners has showed us the copy of the letter he wrote you by order of New Haven court, dated July 6, 1654, and your answer thereto in Latin, dated Agust 1, 1654, the contents whereof seem strange to us all. We were many years since informed of their just title, and of the unjust disturbance their agents found in their planting and trading there, both by Monsieur William Kieft, the former Dutch governor, and from Monsieur John Printz, your predecessor; and thereof Mr. John Winthrop, governor of Massachusetts colony, and president of the commissioners, wrote to them both in September, 1643, and thereunto, a few months after, received their several answers but without any satisfaction.*
>
> *What you wrote concerning a treaty or conference before Mr. Endicott, wherein New Haven's right was silenced or suppressed, and what you affirm concerning the right the Swedes have to lands on both sides of Delaware Bay and River from the capes, &c, is either your own mistake, or at least the error of them that so inform you.*
>
> *We have perused and considered the several purchases our confederates of New Haven have there made, the considerations given acknowledged by the Indian proprietors under their hands, and confirmed by many Christian witnesses, whereby their right appeareth so clear to us, that we cannot but assent their just title to the said lands, and desire they*

may peaceably enjoy the same with all the liberties thereunto
belonging, and in their name and behalf do assure you they
will by no means disturb you in any of your just rights, . . .[9]

The letter put Rising on the horns of a dilemma. It was
his sworn duty to preserve Swedish sovereignty on the Delaware, but he did not want to do anything to affront New
England. He had bought much-needed tobacco on credit
from Isaac Allerton, to whom a large sum of money was
already owed. To obtain food to sustain the Swedish settlers
he had purchased provisions from Richard Lord, a Hartford
merchant, in the amount of 2,196½ rix-dollars which he
agreed to pay by draft through the Swedish commercial
college.[10] He needed New England's support and couldn't
afford to antagonize the confederation. Furthermore, a
treaty had been signed by Sweden and England whereby
both nations agreed that their countrymen in the New
World should "cultivate true friendship and refrain on both
sides from all injuries and annoyances." Rising was obligated to uphold this treaty, which did, in fact, improve the
situation between New England and New Sweden.

As Rising deliberated on a course of action, a special
committee was named in New Haven to supervise preparations to colonize the Delaware, consisting of Robert Seely,
William Davis, Thomas Munson, and Thomas Jeffery. The
elders of the colony declared they were willing to further the
project by lending their full support.[11]

One of the things the committee did was to treat

with the proprietors about the purchase of the lands [on the
Delaware] and understand that they are out about six hun-
dred pounds, but are willing to take three hundred pounds
to be paid in four years, that is one hundred pounds at two
years end, another at three years end, and the last at four

years end, which they accepted of, if a suitable company appeared this Spring to plant it, . . .[12]

Evidently the proprietors were the stockholders in the former Delaware Company of New Haven, although several of the principals were now dead. Lamberton, Turner, and Thomas Gregson, for example, were lost at sea in 1646 on their return voyage to England on the "Great Ship" built in New Haven.

Governor Stuyvesant also exchanged letters with New England leaders at this time about New Haven's pretensions to the Delaware. He held to the position that such expansion was against the best interests of the West India Company "whose indubitable right is to all that land betwixt the river called Conneticut & that by the English named Delaware." [13] As a military man, Stuyvesant was apprehensive of an English maneuver to the Delaware which would leave New Netherland caught in an English vise from the north and south.

As New Haven persisted with plans to send families to the southern colony, Stuyvesant again protested the intent of "Your Countriemens there to settle a considerable Company in the Southriver called De la ware baye, a place we not only pretend unto, but have lawful right unto by lawfull Commission from our States-General and lawfull purchase from the natives." [14]

To this, Governor Eaton replied that his people didn't want a foot of land that belonged to anyone else—only that which they had paid for.[15] Stuyvesant answered that he had already made clear to the governors of Massachusetts and Plymouth his position concerning Dutch rights. He said he had been as tolerant as he dared to stretch his authority in allowing New Haven vessels to pass freely for trade in Virginia and Delaware, but the directors of the West India

Company simply would not allow an unauthorized settlement on their Delaware property.

In an effort to arrive at peaceful means to settle their differences (which also involved issues other than the Delaware which are not now relevant), Stuyvesant met with the commissioners of the confederation in Hartford in September of 1650. It was agreed, after discussion of the problems affecting New England and New Netherland, that each party should name two representatives to arbitrate the issues in disagreement.

To resolve the controversy about the Delaware, the arbitrators decided that most of the offenses or grievances occurred during the administration of Stuyvesant's predecessor, Kieft, for which the present governor was not responsible. It was agreed, however, that Stuyvesant would acquaint the directors of the West India Company of New Haven's injuries so that reparations could be considered. Meantime, both sides stood firm in their claims to the Delaware, and the arbitrators were not authorized to make concessions. Therefore, the situation was to remain *in statu quo* leaving both parties

> *to plead and improve their just interests at Delaware, for planting or trading, as they shall see cause, only we desire that all proceedings there, as in other places, may be carried on in love and peace, till the right may be further considered and justly issued, either in Europe or here, by the two states of England and Holland.*[16]

The confederation took a neutral stand toward New Haven on the Delaware question, refusing to give unqualified support in the plans to send colonists to found a new settlement. The commissioners felt they had made good progress with Stuyvesant on other matters. Accordingly, they did not want to antagonize him and disturb the good trade relations that then existed between them and New Amsterdam.[17]

Stuyvesant assumed that no further colonization attempts would be made until the Dutch and English governments resolved the question confronting their respective New World colonies. He was advised by the directors that the Dutch ambassador had been authorized to initiate discussions in London. Early in 1651, a rumor reached Stuyvesant that the New Haveners were busy outfitting five or six vessels with the objective of bringing the entire Delaware River under English rule. This was, of course, a gross exaggeration, but in the fall of the year a single vessel carrying 50 men, under command of Robert Crane and Lieutenant Seely, sailed from New Haven for the Delaware. So far as Stuyvesant was concerned, New Haven was acting unilaterally and contrary to the terms of the agreement he had signed with the confederation. The particulars of this expedition and what happened when the vessel reached Manhattan Island is revealed in the following passages from a petition submitted later to the confederation by Jasper Graine and William Tuttill:

> *And whereas your petitioners, straightened in the respective plantations, and finding this part of the country full, or affording little encouragement to begin any considerable new plantations for their own comfort and conviency of posterity . . . resolved upon a more difficult remove to Delaware . . . a vessel was hired, and at least fifty of us set forward in the spring, and expecting the fruit of that wholesome advice given at Hartford the last year, in the case by the arbitrators jointly; we went to the Manhattoes, which we might have avoided, and from our honoured governor presented a letter to the Dutch governor, upon perusal whereof, (without further provocation) he arrested the two messengers and com-*

mitted them to a private house, close prisoners under guard;
that done, he sent for the master of the vessel to come on
shore, as to speak with him, and committed him also; after
which, two more of the company coming on shore, and de-
siring to speak with their neighbors under restraint, he com-
mitted them as the rest, then desiring to see our commissions
and copy them out, promising to return them the next day;
though the copies were taken, and the commissions de-
manded, he refused to deliver them up, and kept them, and
the men imprisoned till they were forced to engage, under
their hands, not then to proceed on their voyage towards
Delaware, but with loss of time and charge, to return to New
Haven, threatening that if he should after find any of them
in Delaware, we would seize their goods, and send their per-
sons prisoners into Holland, and accordingly they returned,
though their damage thereby, as they conceive, doth amount
to about £300 . . .[18]

Their mission thwarted, New Haven complained bitterly
to the confederation when the advance party of settlers were
forced to return to the home port. New Haven officials insisted that the Delaware "in the judgment of those that have
often and seriously viewed the land, and considered the
climate, is a place fit for the enlargement of the English colonies at present, and hopeful for posterity, that we and they
may enjoy the ordinances of Christ, both in spiritual and
civil respects."

An argument they felt very convincing was the following:

They fear that if the English right be not seasonably vindi-
cated, and a way opened for the speedy planting of Delaware,
the Dutch, who have laid already an injurious hand both
upon our persons and rights, they having (as is reported)
lately begun a new fortification and plantation upon our duly
purchased lands, will daily strengthen themselves, and by large

offers, draw many of the English to settle and plant under them, in so hopeful a place, which will not only be dishonourable to the English nation, but inconvenient to the colonies, and of mischievous consequences to the persons who shall so settle, in reference to that licentious liberty there suffered and practised . . .[19]

I have emphasized the reference to the Dutch fort, because this could only be Fort Casimir at the Sand Hook, present New Castle, Delaware. At this time it was the only new Dutch fort under construction; in fact, it was the only Dutch stronghold on the Delaware after Fort Nassau was abandoned. Previously, I have pointed out that Lamberton purchased three tracts from the Indians, two of which have been accounted for, and the above reference seems to indicate clearly that the third tract encompassed present New Castle.

The commissioners took under serious consideration New Haven's complaint, in view of what had been agreed at the Hartford conference, and they voted to write Stuyvesant a strong letter "to assert the English right, and to require satisfaction for the damage done to our friends and confederates of New Haven." They also told New Haven that they did not feel it was advisable to

enter into a present engagement against the Dutch, choosing rather to suffer injuries and affronts (at least for a time) than in any respects to be too quick, yet if they shall see cause again to endeavour the planting of their fore-mentioned purchased lands in Delaware, at any time within these twelve months, and for that end shall at their own charge transport together 150, or at least 100 able men, armed, with a meet vessel or vessels, and ammunition fit for such an enterprise, all to be allowed and approved by the magistrates of New Haven jurisdiction, or the greatest part of them, that then, in case they meet with any hostile opposition from the Dutch or Swedes, while they carry themselves peaceably and inoffensively, that may call for further aid and assistance, the commissioners do agree and conclude that they shall be supplied by the several jurisdictions, with such a number of soldiers as the aforesaid commissioners shall judge meet, they the said plaintiffs bearing the charges thereof, for the true payment whereof, the purchased lands and trade there with the natives shall be engaged till it be satisfied, provided also, and it is agreed, that such persons as shall transport themselves to the aforesaid lands in Delaware, either out of New Haven colonies or any of the other three, shall be and remain under the government and jurisdiction of New Haven till the commissioners of the United Colonies shall otherwise order the same.[20]

A letter was dispatched to Stuyvesant, although it was probably milder in tone than New Haven would have preferred, and, at the same time, Governor Eaton wrote Edward Winslow in London telling him how New Haven had been injured by the Dutch and Swedes in their attempts to colonize the Delaware. The commissioners of the confederation also addressed a letter to Winslow recounting that 50 New Haven people had been turned back by Governor Stuyvesant; that the English nation had been dishonored by this affront; and asking for an opinion about the validity of the Indian deeds in possession of the New Haveners, since there had been no recent improvement of the lands. Also, the commissioners wanted to know

whether the parliament hath granted any late patents, or whether, in granting they reserve not liberty and encouragement for such as have or shall plant upon their formerly duly purchased lands, as also how any engagement by the colonies against the Dutch, upon the afore-mentioned occasion, will be resented by the parliament, of which we desire information by the first.[21]

Between the lines of the latter inquiry, one senses that the commissioners had knowledge both of Sir Edmund Plowden's patent and Lord Baltimore's, but, without specific reference to either, they were attempting to ascertain where New Haven stood in this complex of Indian deeds and royal charters for the same lands.

I have been unable to find Winslow's reply to this inquiry, but, if one was written, it did not deter the New Haven people, although things remained quiet for some time. On the 30th of the 11th month 1654, Thomas Munson and John Cooper, representing the committee making plans for the Delaware settlement, petitioned the court again

> *on behalf of a company of persons intending to remove to Delaware Bay wherein they propounded that for the enlargement of the kingdom of Christ, the spreading of the gospel, and the good of posterity therein, that they may live under the wings of Christ, they would afford some encouragement to help forward so public a work.*[22]

The petitioners stated that there were 50 or 60 persons who had already expressed a desire to settle on the Delaware, and they requested that two magistrates, Samuel Eaton and Francis Newman, be given the court's permission to go in person to the Delaware under New Haven's protection. They also requested cannon and powder and financial assistance to purchase a vessel.

The court gave permission for the magistrates to accompany the settlers, but withheld its decision on the other requests pending further study. The court records also contain the following highly significant passage which illustrates that the proposed settlement was being planned on a large scale.

> *And for their encouragement they purpose when God shall so enlarge the English plantations in Delaware as that they*

*shall grow the greater part of the jurisdiction, that then due
consideration shall be taken for the case and conveniency of
both parts,* as that the governor may be one year in one part,
and the next year in another, and the dept. governor to be in
that part where the governor is not, *and that the general
courts for making laws be ordinarily but once a year, and
where the governor resides, and* if God much increase plantations in Delaware and diminish them in these parts, then possibly he may see cause that the governor may be constantly
there and the deputy governor here.[23]

The significance of the latter words should not be overlooked. What they mean is that the New Haven Puritans
seriously considered making the Delaware River the principal seat of their government, a fact that is not generally
known.

Discussions were still in progress in 1655, and on April
19 of that year, the court agreed to lend the company two
small cannon, along with shot, musket balls, and a barrel of
powder to transport to the proposed settlement.[24]

John Cooper went to the Massachusetts Bay colony to enlist settlers, but he did not receive much encouragement,
according to the report he made to the New Haven court on
March 16, 1655. The records do not clarify the reasons, but
the people in Boston may have heard of the impending
clash between the Dutch and Swedes as a result of Rising's
capture of the Dutch fort. Not long before, a seaman,
Thomas Doxey, in the employ of Isaac Allerton, had written
a letter from the Delaware to John Winthrop, Jr., in which
he said that "heare is a grete difference beetwixte the Swede
and the Dutch bouthe of them strivinge for to bee Masters
of the River and Soe by that means the trad is mutch hin-
dred and Detes hard for to gette . . ." [25]

After listening to Cooper's report, Stephen Goodyear was
quoted as saying

notwithstanding the discouragements from the [Massa-
chusetts] Bay, if a considerable company appear that will go,
he will adventure his person and estate to go with them in
that design; but a report of three ships being come to the
Swedes seems to make the business more difficult. After much
debate about it, it was voted by the town in this case that
Goodyear, Sergeant Jeffery, and others may go to Delaware
carrying the commissioners' letter and treat with the Swedes
about a peaceful settlement of the English upon their own
right, and then after harvest if things be cleared, the company
may resort thither for the planting of it.[26]

Evidently, the letter was carried to Rising, either by
Goodyear and Jeffery, or others, for in his report written
June 14, 1655 and sent to Sweden, Rising had this to say:

Those of New Haven (indeed the whole republic of New
England as may be seen by the enclosed copy of their letter)
lay claim stoutly to a large part of this country (concerning
which I wrote and reported last fall); and last spring they had
about a hundred men ready to come here and take possession
of it. But they gave up their design in the hope that the Eng-
lish would capture Cuba, Hispaniola, etc., whither then a
good many of them intended to transport themselves.[27]

I have found no indication in the New Haven records of
any intention of settling on the Caribbean islands, and
Rising may have been reporting one of many rumors that
reached him.

In the summer of 1655, nine adventurers from New England suddenly appeared in New Sweden. They said that they
had heard the Swedes were all dead and came to take possession of the river. They had no commission or passport,
other than a document they had signed themselves. On
July 17, Governor Rising, mindful of the treaty between

Sweden and England, assembled a court to examine the Englishmen and to ascertain whence they came and the true purpose of their mission. When the hearing ended, they were allowed to leave, provided they returned the same way they had come.[28] I have found no other reference to this English party, although it is entirely possible they may have been reconnoiterers from New Haven who did not want to disclose their true identities.

Before the beginning of a settlement could be made by the New Haveners, the Dutch moved to take decisive military action against the Swedes. Following Rising's capture of Fort Casimir, Stuyvesant immediately began to lay plans for its recapture. He sent to Holland for more ships and soldiers, and when they arrived he collected several small vessels, and on August 26, 1655, set sail for the Delaware, trimmed for battle. His fleet, carrying 317 soldiers and sailors, consisted of two battleships, two armed merchant ships, two *bojerts,* and a sloop. Fort Trinity (formerly Casimir) capitulated on September 1, and two weeks later Rising surrendered Fort Christina, after the Dutch "killed our cattle, goats, swine and poultry, broke open houses, pillaged the people, . . ."

With the fall of the two strongholds, New Sweden was finally at an end, although the Swedish colonists who submitted to Dutch rule were allowed to keep their lands. If there were any English families still living on the Varkens Kill, which is uncertain, they, too, were compelled to change their loyalties again.[29] Governor Rising and 37 of his followers and officers were returned to Europe in a Dutch vessel.

The West India Company, which had gone deeply into debt through its colonizing efforts in South America and on the Guinea coast of Africa, was further burdened by the costs of Stuyvesant's conquest on the Delaware and the other expenses attendant upon maintaining installations in New Netherland. The company took the opportunity to relieve a part of this indebtedness by transferring Fort Casimir and the little town that grew up around it to the rich commercial city of Amsterdam. The land conveyed to the city extended from the west side of the Christina River to Bombay Hook, and as far west as the Minquas county. Consequently, in 1656, Fort Casimir became the property of the burgomasters of Amsterdam, who gave the little town a new name, New Amstel, after a suburb of the Dutch city. Thereafter, the Dutch officials in the Delaware colony were appointed by the city of Amsterdam, with the New Netherland officials of the West India Company serving in both advisory and protective capacities. The city's interest in the colony was solely "to promote commerce." For a while the company retained ownership of the land at Fort Christina and above, but in the autumn of 1663 this, too, was transferred to the city.

The change in administration evidently did not halt the discussions at New Haven about the proposed Delaware settlement until the outbreak of the first Anglo-Dutch war. New Haven seized this as a chance to eliminate her Dutch rival from the Delaware by pressing the New England Confederation to declare war against New Netherland. Massachusetts, however, which stood to lose profitable trade, refused. New Haven then turned to the mother country for support. Cromwell, always friendly to the colony, responded by commissioning Robert Sedgewick and John Leverett to organize an expedition against New Netherland. The war ended before the attack could be launched, and Sedgewick used his forces against French Acadia, to the benefit of Massachusetts and the complete frustration of New Haven.

Thereafter, New Haven gradually became reduced to a series of small agricultural communities, and the merchants found their chief business in marketing the produce of the colony at New Amsterdam in exchange for furs used to purchase goods at Boston. Thus, New Haven became economically dependent upon the colony she had originally broken away from. Interest in the Delaware faded away for a number of reasons, not the least being that Charles II and his brother James, Duke of York, had other ideas for anglicizing the much-disputed buffer zone that had so long been everyman's land.

11
Maryland "Discovers" the Delaware

After the Dutch regained control of New Amstel, the Swedish, Dutch, and Finnish families along the Delaware became subjects of the city of Amsterdam. Back home in Sweden, efforts were made by Charles X, Queen Christina's successor, to regain the colony and obtain indemnities for Swedish losses, but it was wasted energy. The Delaware was forever lost to Sweden. Individual Swedes and Finns (as well as a few Dutch settlers) were unhappy under the new administration. A number of colonists, unable to pay their debts, fled to Maryland to live in Lord Baltimore's province. The appearance of these aliens made the Maryland authorities more aware than ever before of the foreign community within the limits of their eastern boarder.

Dutch ownership of the Delaware continued to be contested by several English factions. Sir Edmund Plowden still retained his royal charter, which he felt gave him incontestable rights to settle New Albion, and there can be no question that the Crown intended him to have full ownership under his patent. When he made his will July 29,

1655, New Albion was still uppermost in the earl's thoughts, and he spoke of his "family kindred and posterity" taking possession of the territory, building schools and churches, and converting the Indians to Christianity.[1]

The New Haveners had Indian deeds which they insisted gave them outright ownership of three tracts on the river, and New Amstel was built on one of these tracts. The Calverts, according to the Maryland charter, claimed all the territory along the entire western bank of the river below the 40th parallel. This may have overlapped Plowden's grant, and it certainly encompassed part of the New Haveners' tracts. It would have overtaxed the wisdom of a Solomon to sit in judgment on the validity of these English claims against those made by the Dutch, who had been there the longest, and were the first to cultivate the lands not previously occupied by a Christian nation. In the background of the controversy, silenced by the Dutch conquest and not inclined to appropriate money for further colonization, was the Swedish government still claiming proprietorship on the basis of Indian deeds, as well as rights of ownership resulting from occupation.

Whether the Dutch officials at New Amstel, employed by the city of Amsterdam, or the West India Company (who continued to maintain a garrison at Fort Christina, now called Fort Altena), were fully aware of the conflicting English claims is doubtful. But there can be no question about their apprehensiveness of the English. The fear of an English invasion—from New England, Virginia, or Maryland—became almost a phobia with Jacob Alricks, the city of Amsterdam's chief official at New Amstel, who bore the title of Director and Commissary-General. William Beekman, the West India Company's ranking officer at Fort Altena, shared Alricks' fears. Alricks went so far as to write Stuyvesant that "The Governor of Maryland, also, requested of the English in New England last year [1658] assistance to take this river, which was denied and refused, according to your Honor's declaration, because the said Governor is a Papist." [2]

When a party of 14 Englishmen was shipwrecked off Cape Henlopen in 1657, and subsequently rescued by the Indians, the rumor spread up and down the river that the English of Virginia were planning to assault the Dutch forts and seize control of the Delaware.[3] The members of the English party, ransomed by Alricks, declared themselves fugitives from Virginia—runaway bondsmen seeking their freedom. Both Alricks and Beekman, however, were suspicious, believing them to be an advance party sent by either Virginia or Maryland, to pave the way by infiltering the population preliminary to a full-scale English attack.

Dutch fears of English incursions on the Delaware are well illustrated in the following excerpt from a Dutch account written in 1650,

> *The English have sought at different times and places to incorporate this river which they say is annexed to their territory, but this has as yet been prevented by different protests. We have also expelled them by force [on the Schuylkill] well knowing that if they once settled there, we should lose the river or hold it with much difficulty, as they would swarm there in great numbers.*
>
> *There are rumors daily, and it is reported to us that the English will soon repair there with many families. It is certain that if they do come and nestle down there they will soon possess it so completely, that neither Hollanders nor Swedes, in a short time, will have much to say . . . The report now is that the English intend to build a village and trading house there, . . .*[4]

Meanwhile, in the Province of Maryland a new governor, appointed by Cecil Calvert, Josias Fendall, took office, and

Alricks received intelligence that Fendall intended to enforce Lord Baltimore's rights and privileges to the letter under the terms of the Maryland charter. After conferring with Beekman, Alricks promptly wrote Governor Stuyvesant on Manhattan Island that he learned that Fendall had "strict orders to make a close inquiry and investigation concerning the limits and jurisdiction in his district in these latitudes, and in case they are in somebody's possession to notify the same of it, summon to surrender it, and do his further duties according to his power and the circumstances of the case." [5]

At long last—27 years after the Maryland charter was granted—Lord Baltimore's government began to look seriously toward the eastern bounds of the province where intruders were challenging their lordship's sovereignty. Although this is purely a surmise, it is possible that the failure of Sir Edmund Plowden had something to do with the Calverts' sudden interest in the Delaware. The Earl Palatine had not succeeded in colonizing New Albion and was nearing his death in England. It was certainly clear to Cecil Calvert that there was little chance of his having a friendly Catholic neighbor on his eastern flank.

At a session of the Maryland Council on August 3, 1659, there was considerable discussion about the aliens seated on the western bank of the Delaware River and what should be done about them. After deliberation, Colonel Nathaniel Utie was ordered to "repair to the pretended Governor of a People seated in Delaware bay within his lordship's Province & that he doe give them to Understand that they are seated within this his Lordship's Province without Notice given to his Lordship's Lieutenant heere & to require him to depart the Province." [6]

Utie, a member of the Assembly, was also a councilor, as well as a colonel in the militia. He lived on Spesutia Island (which means "Uties Hope") at the head of Chesapeake Bay, and had been licensed to trade with the Indians. Fendall selected him as a courier, knowing that Utie had a bold and arrogant manner that would impress the Dutch, and that he could be stubborn, in fact, overbearing, if the situation demanded. Utie was, in fact, the ideal messenger to carry Fendall's letter to the "Commander of the People in Delaware Bay," in which he stated that he (Fendall) was the rightful governor of that territory, and that he does "require & command you presently to depart forth of his lordship's Province or otherwise desire you to hould me excused if I use my Utmost endeavor to reduce that part of his Lordship's Province unto its due obedience to him." [7]

In retrospect, it is now clear that the Maryland authorities had no intention of invading New Amstel and provoking hostilities with the Dutch, with whom England had recently negotiated a treaty. Fendall carefully avoided making any reference to the Dutch nation in his communications, speaking of them with deliberate vagueness as "a people." The inference he apparently intended to be drawn from his correspondence was that there were unwelcome strangers settled on Lord Baltimore's grant, but he was uncertain who these "people" were. There can be no doubt that he was fully informed as to the identity of the "people," and his aim was to frighten them away by intimidation, threat, and all other means short of provoking trouble between England and the United Netherlands.

On September 6, Colonel Utie arrived at New Amstel accompanied by his brother, his cousin, a Major Jacob de Vrint, and a servant.[8] New Amstel then had about 110 houses (compared to 350 on Manhattan Island), and its population numbered approximately 600. Although there is no record of the dress of Utie and his party, it is reasonable to assume that he and de Vrint were resplendent in their military uniforms. Since their mission was to impress and intimidate, they probably wore their shining back and breast plates with the overlapping tassets to protect the thighs, and plumed helmets. They probably rode into New Amstel on the sleekest horses that Maryland could provide, the sun sparkling on their swords, and one can imagine Utie striding into Fop Outhout's hostelry to demand the best accommodations the innkeeper could offer a ranking officer in the service of his majesty, the King of England, and a personal emissary of Lord Baltimore.

For three days Utie and his men surveyed the town, strutting imperiously along the streets, examining the waterfront, counting the houses, noting the condition of the fort and the inadequacy of the defenses. Utie accosted townsfolk on the streets, addressing them through de Vrint, who acted as his interpreter. He told them they had no rights on land that belonged to Lord Baltimore, but if they deserted New Amstel, they would be permitted to live in Maryland under his lordship's government. Otherwise, Utie warned, he would be forced to drive them away and plunder their homes. All this time Alricks did nothing, offering no objection to the subversion of his subjects. Finally, Utie demanded an official hearing, and Alricks by now was so frightened that he was willing to agree to almost anything. He hurriedly sent a messenger to Fort Altena, asking Beekman to come at once.

In the transfer of New Amstel to the city of Amsterdam, the West India Company had guaranteed the city against loss. Alricks knew that Beekman had a responsibility to protect the company against any claims brought by the city. Also, he needed moral support. He didn't know what Utie might do next. Even at that moment a troop of English soldiers might be marching from Maryland to invade New Amstel.

Utie informed Alricks, Beekman, and the members of the

council assembled to hear him that the Dutch were occupying the limits of Lord Baltimore's territory and their presence could no longer be tolerated. He said that Lord Baltimore owned the land by virtue of a royal charter granted
him by no less a personage than his Royal Majesty, King
Charles I, to which the Great Seal of England was affixed.
He emphasized that neither the West India Company nor
the city of Amsterdam had any rights to the land and they
were trespassing on English territory. He gave Alricks and
Beekman two alternatives, first to leave immediately, or,
second, to declare New Amstel subject to Lord Baltimore's
government. If they refused, Utie hastily added, he would
not hold himself responsible for any blood spilled, because
Lord Baltimore, according to his charter, had the power to
make war without consulting anybody.

Alricks' defenses at the time consisted of about eight soldiers, two cadets, and one sergeant, a number of members of
the garrison having fled during the past several months to
settle in Maryland.[9] Beekman's garrison at Fort Altena consisted of no more than 21 soldiers in the employ of the West
India Company. They knew that their combined forces
could not protect the town against an English invasion.
Alricks asked Utie to allow him three weeks to consult with
his superiors. He and Beekman decided they must seek assistance from Stuyvesant. To this request, the colonel replied,
"I have no order to grant a delay, for we must take advantage of our opportunity," but he reluctantly agreed to the
three-week extension. Colonel Utie and his party then returned to Maryland after warning Alricks for the last time
that the settlement would be invaded if his acquiesence were
not forthcoming in three weeks.

Alricks hastily wrote a letter to Governor Stuyvesant at
Manhattan, telling him what had happened: that the situation was critical; that Utie meant business; and that the

Maryland government had 500 men under arms awaiting orders to march against New Amstel.

When Stuyvesant received Alricks' letter he was furious, and he addressed a scathing reply jointly to Alricks and Beekman, telling them they had given a "stupid answer" to the "frivolous demands of Nathaniel Utie," and had erred in allowing the English party free access to the town to spy on the Dutch forces and to sow "seditious and mutinous seeds" among the citizens. He said that they should have arrested Utie as a spy and sent him to Manhattan in chains to be tried. He added that he was sending Captain Martin Crieger, burgomaster at Manhattan, and Cornelis van Ruyven, secretary, with 60 Dutch soldiers, to reinforce the garrisons at New Amstel and Fort Altena. When and if the English came, the Dutch would be prepared to repel the invaders. Stuyvesant, wise in the ways of diplomacy, had reason to believe that Utie was bluffing, and no bragging colonel in the Maryland militia could intimidate him.

Three vessels sailed from Manhattan on the 23rd of September, carrying the defending forces, and they dropped anchor at New Amstel three days later.[10] After their arrival, Crieger and van Ruyven surveyed the situation and they found the defenses in a deplorable state. They urged Alricks to enlist 50 townsmen and arm them to join their forces in defense of the town. But the men of New Amstel were not interested in taking up arms to fight to protect a colony in which they were persecuted by the administration. Crieger informed Alricks that he must take drastic steps to keep up the city's forces to protect the settlement. He said that the soldiers he brought must shortly return to Manhattan, where they were needed to keep the garrison there up to its full strength in the event of an emergency, and an Indian attack might come at any moment. Alricks took the position that it was the West India Company's duty to protect the city's colony against the English, because the company had guaranteed clear title to the land it conveyed to the city. Arguments ensued and ugly memoranda passed back and forth. The result was a miserable wrangle among the headstrong Dutchmen, each holding to his own fixed views.

Stuyvesant had given van Ruyven and Crieger instructions to arrest Utie if he returned at the end of the three-week moratorium. But Colonel Utie did not show up on the appointed day, nor thereafter. No English troops marched against New Amstel. In due time, van Ruyven, Crieger, and their men returned to Manhattan, and Governor Stuyvesant took complete charge of the situation.

On the same day that Stuyvesant ordered Crieger and van Ruyven to go to New Amstel he commissioned two others as envoys to Governor Fendall—Augustine Herrman and Resolved Waldron. They were instructed to deliver a letter from Stuyvesant demanding the return of all servants and freemen who had fled from New Amstel to Maryland; secondly, to register an official complaint about the reprehensible conduct of Colonel Utie who had made threats and demands without exhibiting

> any legal document, order or qualification from any state, prince, parliament or government, only a manufactured paper in the form of instruction, without time or place, where or when written nor signed by order of any state, prince, parliament or government, demanding and threatening in case of refusal to bleed the aforesaid Fort and Colony of New Amstel, adding thereto that he should take and invade the fort by force of troops hostiley within three weeks' time, if the same was not surrendered willingly, which directly contradicts the 2d, 3d, 16th and the last article of the Confederation and Articles of Peace made between the Republics of England and of the Netherlands in the year 1654.[11]

I have emphasized the last clause to accentuate the fact that the diplomatic relations between the European nations had a pronounced influence on their American colonies. When there was war between the mother countries, or when a state of peace existed, it had an important bearing on the attitudes of their respective colonial officers. To understand fully the relations between the Dutch and English in America, one must be aware of the European background, and that the relations between nations changed as certain events transpired.

The two envoys were also authorized to assert the Dutch right to occupy the Delaware River under patents granted the West India Company by the States-General, as well as by right of land purchases from the Indians. Finally, they were to insist that any dispute between Dutch and English over land ownership, under terms of the late peace treaty between the two nations, should be settled in Europe on higher diplomatic levels. Officially, Herrman and Waldron were not instructed to discuss the validity of the respective claims of the Dutch and English, although they did so and with notable skill as debaters.

Augustine Herrman, a Bohemian by birth, was a merchant, and a highly respected member of the New Netherland colony. He was well educated, a surveyor by profession, a merchant by choice, and he possessed skills in the graphic arts. Little is known about Waldron, and Stuyvesant doubtless selected him because of his ability to interpret the English language for Herrman, although the latter could read and write English. Herrman kept a journal of the mission, making the first entry on September 30, 1659, when he and Waldron left New Amstel with an attachment of soldiers and guides and pressed through the wilderness toward Patuxent in Maryland, where they would meet the Maryland Council.[12] Herrman was so impressed with what he saw that he subsequently returned to Maryland and was given permission January 14, 1660, to inhabit the province, where he became a large landholder, lord of a manor called Bohemia.

The envoys traveled for six days before reaching Patuxent for their conferences with Fendall, Philip Calvert, then a member of the council as well as secretary of the province, and the six councilors, one of whom was the pompous Colonel Utie. A series of meetings was held—individual sessions with Fendall or Calvert, or both, and formal sessions with all the members of the council present.

The inadequacy of the English maps in depicting the Delaware came as a surprise to Herrman, who was well acquainted with Dutch maps and charts which, at this late date, represented both the Delaware and Hudson systems in full detail. Philip Calvert showed the envoys three maps, "One was printed at Amsterdam, by direction of Captain Smith, the first discoverer of the great bay of Chesapeack or Virginia; the second appeared also to be printed at Amsterdam, at the time of Lord Balthamoer's patent; we knew not by whom or where the manuscript one was drawn." [13]

Calvert attempted to use the three maps to show the extent of Lord Baltimore's grant, but Herrman wrote that "All differed one from the other." The Smith map, as we know, did not even show Delaware Bay, and any Dutch maps printed in Amsterdam as early as 1632, when Lord Baltimore's charter was granted, did not contain entries appearing on manuscript maps.

Herrman himself was responsible for rectifying many of the English cartographical deficiencies, when, in 1670, he completed a map of "Virginia and Maryland," engraved by W. Faithorne in London in 1673. Herrman's map was partially completed as early as 1660, when he was permitted to inhabit Maryland, and was doubtless inspired by the inadequacies of the English maps he saw during his trip as an envoy. It portrays the entire tidewater area of Virginia and Maryland with accuracy, and also delineates Delaware Bay and River, showing the major tributaries by name, the names of white settlements, as well as the names and locations of Indian towns then in existence.

The discussions with the Maryland authorities opened with Herrman and Waldron reading a declaration in which they reviewed the historical background on which the Dutch based their claims to New World lands. "The English," the declaration stated, "established and seated their Colony of Virginia by Distinct pattents from the Degree 34 to about 38. The Dutch the Manhattans from 38 to 42 and New England from the degree 42 to 45." [14]

Then the two envoys presented an interesting, if somewhat exaggerated, interpretation of the reason for the existence of the buffer zone:

> *King James of England Did Will[,] Comannd and require that the Colony or province of Virginia and the province of New England should remaine asunder and not meete together within the Distance and space of a hundred leagues which was allotted for the Dutch plantations then called by the Generall name of Manhattans, after the name of the Indians they were first seated by . . .*[15]

Since the charter to the London and Plymouth Companies was issued twenty years *before* the Dutch settled Manhattan Island, the reader can readily recognize the error of the argument. Moreover, as discussed in Chapter 3, the Crown had no intention of reserving the buffer zone for anyone other than the English.

Neither Fendall nor Philip Calvert attempted to refute Herrman's claim because the facts were apparently not known to them. When they did present their arguments on other issues Herrman was never at a loss in refuting them. For example, when they insisted that Lord Baltimore's patent included Delaware Bay and River, Herrman replied that "Sir Edm. Ployten had, in former times, set up a claim to Delowar Bay, and that, therefore, one claim was as good as the other." [16] The English retaliated by saying that Plowden had no commission (which was untrue) and that his patent was of no value (which was also untrue); furthermore he "lay in jail in England on account of his debts" (which was true).

Herrman promptly answered that if Plowden's grant was invalid "it was not certain whether my Lord Balthamoer's claim to Delowar Bay, should he have any, was not [also] obtained by falsehood and misrepresentation."

When Philip Calvert stated that the English claims to land in North America dated as far back as Sir Walter Raleigh, Herrman replied by saying the Dutch derived their rights from the King of Spain since the Dutch were subjects of Spain at the time Columbus discovered America, and that when they achieved their liberty, Spain turned over to the United Netherlands all the colonies in regions formerly claimed by Spain. His statement was correct, because under the treaty of Münster, in 1648, Spain confirmed to the Dutch possession of her colonies, although Herrman's attempt to trace Dutch ownership of New World lands to the discoveries of Columbus was a tenuous argument.

Calvert then said that the specific area under discussion, namely the Delaware, had been first discovered by the English, and that it was, in fact, named for Lord Delaware. Herrman, mindful of Henry Hudson's voyage as an employee of the East India Company, replied that the Dutch had been in Delaware Bay long before Lord Delaware ever came to Virginia. This, too, is factual.

So the discussions went, each party making claims re-
futed by the other, but conducted in a friendly fashion, with
frequent recesses for wine and meals. As a final gesture,
Governor Fendall laid before Herrman and Waldron an impressive copy of the patent Charles I issued to Cecil Calvert.
While the English officials went to hold court at the next
plantation, Herrman and Waldron asked permission to bor-
row the document, written in Latin, which they pored over
like two classical scholars.

"*Rex &c Omnibus ad quos &c salutem. Cum predilectus
et perquam fidelis Subditus noster Cecill Calvert Baro de
Baltimore in Regno nostro,*" and so on they patiently read,
and translated into both English and Dutch. They labored
on through the stilted royal phraseology and learned that
the loyal and well-beloved Baron of Baltimore had been
excited with a laudable and pious zeal to propagate the
Christian faith and enlarge the empire and dominion of his
Royal Majesty in the New World. They noted that he had
supplicated the Crown to grant him a certain thereinafter
described territory of America "*certam quandam Regio-
nemn inferius describendam in terra quadam in partibus
Americe, . . .*" Then they saw the phrase inserted routinely
in the preamble of the charter that would eventually ex-
clude the Calverts forever from any rights to the Delaware
"*hactenus inculta et barbaris nullam divini Numinis no-
ticiam habentibus in partis occupatis,*" "hitherto uncultivated," except by "barbarians having no notice of the divine
Deity."

Herrman recognized that according to the terms of the
preamble of the charter it was the English king's intention
to grant to the Calverts only land that was still occupied by
savages and had not previously been planted or colonized
by any Christian nation.

He and Waldron immediately set to work to compose a

new argument, the final and most logical refutation of the Calverts' claims. In their opening declaration at the start of the conference, Herrman and Waldron had already pointed out that

> *the said River was in the primitive tyme likewise possessed and a Collony planted in the Western Shore within the mouth of the Sowth Cape called the Hoore Kill to this day, The Dutch Nations erecting there and all over the Countrey their States Armes and a little fforte, but after some tyme they were all slained and murthered by the Indians Soe that the possessions and propriety of this River at the first in his Infancy is Sealed up with the bloud of a great many Sowles. After this, in the year 1623 the fforte Nassaw was built about 15 leagues up the River on the Eastern Shore [it was actually built in 1626], beside many other places of the Dutch, and the Dutch Swedes to and againe settled, . . .* [17]

Their arguments, now reinforced with a highly important technicality, Herrman and Waldron requested another audience with the governor and council. They then informed these gentlemen, according to Herrman's journal, that

> *we found it was set forth in the preamble that Lord Balthamoer had applied to and petitioned his Majesty for a tract of country in America, which was neither cultivated nor planted, but only inhabited as yet by barbarous Indians. In answer, whereunto, we maintain that our South River, called of old Nassaw River, had been long before occupied, appropriated and purchased by us in virtue of a commission and grant of Their High Mightinesses the Lords States General of the United Netherlands, and therefore that it was His Royal Majesty's intention and justice not to have given away and granted that part of a country which had been previously taken possession of and settled by the subjects of Their High Mightinesses the Lords States General, as already declared*

and demonstrated, and that Lord Balthamor's patent was invalid where it makes mention of Delowar Bay, or any part thereof, as well as in various other respects and particulars.[18]

Governor Fendall answered the argument by saying that Charles I knew what he was doing and intended to include the western shore of Delaware Bay in the grant, regardless of the phraseology of the charter, but it was a feeble defense. There were further discussions and arguments to conclude the series of conferences, and the Maryland authorities finally handed the envoys a written reply to be carried to Stuyvesant which purported to answer the original declaration. They stated that they declined to yield up any indebted fugitives from New Amstel on the grounds that New Amstel was actually on Maryland soil, and the courts of Maryland were open to the creditors of the fugitives. They defended Utie's action, and finally re-emphasized their original position that the Dutch had no title to the Delaware of any kind.

There was no meeting of minds as a result of the conference, no pact was signed, and no agreements made looking toward future discussion to arbitrate the opposing views. Nevertheless, it was a moral victory for Stuyvesant. His envoys had shown themselves capable of standing firm against the threats of the governor and council on even terms. The envoys' firmness and determination not to yield to Maryland's demands must have impressed Governor Fendall and Philip Calvert, who now recognized they could not take over New Amstel merely by demanding its surrender through threat and intimidation.

The logic of Herrman's reasoning, and the acuteness of his legal argument relative to the *hactenus inculta* provision must have given the Maryland authorities doubts about the real extent of Lord Baltimore's territory, even though

Fendall pretended to reject it as insignificant and irrelevant. Had they been able to anticipate the events to follow they might have chosen a different course of action.

In 1660, Cecil Calvert, not gifted with prophecy to see into the future, had no intention of allowing one foot of land in his province to be usurped either by the city of Amsterdam or the West India Company. Upon receipt of dispatches from Fendall and his brother Philip, telling him about the visit of the Dutch envoys, and the persistence of the "people" to retain New Amstel, he appointed Captain James Neale as his attorney to visit Holland and formally register a protest at Amsterdam with the Assembly of XIX (the executive committee of the Dutch West India Company). In August of 1660, certain deputies of the Assembly of XIX granted an audience to Captain Neale and listened to his protests on behalf of Lord Baltimore.

Neale engaged an Amsterdam notary to translate the protest from English to the Dutch language, and he delivered a copy to the deputies for their further consideration.

The protest did not mince words. It called upon the West India Company to immediately surrender New Amstel and *demanded* its submission and obedience to Lord Baltimore. If the company refused to comply, Captain Neale said in the protest that he reserved the right to "seek and reduce the said Colonie to and under his Lordship's obedience, at such time and place, where and whenever he shall find fitting." [19] This was strong language, reminiscent of the threats Colonel Utie had used to intimidate Alricks, although Captain Neale had been vested with the full authority of his lordship, whereas Utie had acted under Fendall's direction, not as a direct representative of Lord Baltimore. Neale submitted to the Dutch deputies a copy of a letter given him by Lord Baltimore when he left England, authorizing him to go to Maryland from Amsterdam, communicate with the

Maryland governor, and "to employ or make use of all possible and proper means to reduce those people, who are settled on my land, under the obedience of the government of Maryland." [20]

The deputies did not take Neale's protest lightly. They knew that the West India Company's interests in New Netherland were being menaced in Connecticut, as well as along the Hudson and the Delaware, by the English. They knew that the English population in America outnumbered the Dutch. They were also concerned about the substantial investments the company had made to put New Netherland on a profitable basis, "which amount to far beyond ten tons of gold." [21] New Netherland was reaching the point where it could subsist alone and begin to produce revenue for the company. The deputies did not want to antagonize Lord Baltimore and risk seizure of New Amstel, and at the same time it was out of the question to accede to Neale's request.

The deputies prepared an answer for Neale, telling him they had read his protest with great surprise in view of the fact that the West India Company

> *with good right for a long series of years, the aforesaid demanded place possessed and still occupy under the government of the High and Mighty Lords States General of the United Netherland, without the said Baron of Baltimore, or anyone else, having put forth the least claim thereto, and that they accordingly, do intend the same to hold, their settlers in their good right, to maintain and defend against whomsoever it may be.*[22]

Having made a bold reply to Neale, the deputies then secretly agreed to draw up a petition to be submitted to the States-General "requesting them to be pleased to instruct and commission their Ambassador going to England, not only to complain to the King of such usurpations, but also to request redress and then to negotiate a settlement of the boundary between us and them in that country." [23]

The lengthy remonstrance prepared by the deputies on November 5, 1660, and submitted to the States-General, urged that diplomatic channels be used to try to resolve the several differences between the company and the English. The company urged that the King of England be asked:

> *First—That Baron Baltimore, who resides in England, may desist from his unfounded pretensions and consequently leave our people yonder unmolested.*
>
> *And at least allow this matter to remain* in statu *until Commissioners on both sides should there make and agree upon a boundary between Merrilant and New Netherland.*[24]

Neither Captain Neale nor Lord Baltimore was aware that Neale's mission had provoked this action, since the only reply they had received had been a flat denial of Baltimore's rights with the warning that the West India Company would defend New Amstel against all attempts of Maryland to invade the Delaware.

Meanwhile, at Lord Baltimore's instigation, Charles II had written the governor of Virginia telling him that the Crown fully supported Baltimore "to the end that we him in his just rights would protect and defend, do charge and command you and every one of you to be aiding and assisting unto his officers in the establishment of his jurisdiction there . . ." [25]

After departing Holland, Captain Neale sailed to Maryland, but before his arrival, a letter dated December 14, 1660, was received by Philip Calvert (who had succeeded Fendall as governor) from his brother, Lord Baltimore. The letter instructed Philip to

*think upon some speedy and effectuall waye for Reduceing
the Dutch in Delaware Baye[,] The New England men will
be assisting in itt and Secretary Ludwell of Virginia assured
me before he went from hence that the Virgineans will be soe
too But it were well to be done with all Celerity convenient
because perhaps the New England men falling upon them at
Manhatas may take in the head to fall upon them at Delaware
too and by that means prtend some title to the place &c.*[26]

It goes without saying that the military movement
planned by Lord Baltimore was of major proportions, involving a united effort on the part of Maryland, Virginia,
and the New England Confederation to invade the whole
of the Dutch New Netherland. Yet he had his own personal
apprehensions of the assistance he could expect from his
countrymen—doubtless by now aware that the New Haveners had made an attempt at settlement on the Delaware—
lest those English in New England should seize Manhattan
Island and then move on to occupy the lands on the Delaware they had purchased from the Indians.

Captain Neale met with Governor Philip Calvert, the
secretary, Henry Coursey (who had succeeded Philip Calvert), and the members of the Maryland council on July 1,
1661. He presented the commission issued to him by Lord
Baltimore granting him authority to muster and train soldiers to move against

*certaine Ennemie Pyratts & Robbers who have invaded and
usurped a parte of our said Province of Maryland lying upon
the South Side of Delaware Baye within the degree of forty
Northerly Latitude, . . . And to seize to our use all or any
howses and Goods of the said Ennemies Pyratts and Robbers
or their Abettors which shall be upon the Shoare within the
lymitts of our said Province . . .*[27]

In weighing the decision as to whether or not to launch an attack against the Dutch, Governor Calvert and his council were mindful of a number of considerations. First of all, since the Utie mission two years earlier they had substantially increased their trade with the Dutch both at New Amstel and at Manhattan Island. In fact, English tobacco merchants had learned how to defraud the Crown of customs due on tobacco by ''delivering the same at sea, by carring the same to New England and other Plantacons and thence shipping the same in Dutch bottoms, and also by rolling the same to the plantacons of the Dutch lyeing contiguous to Delewar Bay and the Manhatoes . . .'' [28]

Customs amounting, it was claimed in London at a meeting of the Council for Foreign Plantations, "of tenne thousand pounds per annum or upwards" were being lost through this evasion of the Navigation Act.[29] Although it cannot be said that the Maryland governor and his council were conspirators in this fraudulent trade, the fact remains that Dutch merchants and ship captains were necessary to the success of commerce, especially in tobacco, which was rapidly taking the place of beaver pelts as the American commodity most in demand in Europe.

Secondly, the council was in doubt whether or not the town of New Amstel actually lay within the bounds of the Province of Maryland, and since his lordship had authorized war only against those who had usurped some part of his province they were hesitant to take action that might prove precipitous.

Thirdly, the council was not as optimistic as his lordship about the Virginians and New Englanders joining Maryland in a campaign against the Dutch. This, they concluded "doth not at all seeme likely the Dutch Trade being the Darling of the People of Virginea as well as this Province and indeed all other Plantacons of the English and this

Province alone not being able to beare the Charge of the Warre that will thence insue with the West Indian Company . . ." [30]

In short, the council was averse to taking any military action against New Amstel, and to delay the decision it was decided to write Lord Baltimore concerning the affair

> *and that Observacon may be taken at the head of the Baye of Chesepeack thereby to finde certainely whether the said Towne of New Amstell Doe lye within the fortyth degree of Northerly Latitude or not and further that tryall be made whether Assistance from Virga may be had and from New England for Reduceing and maytenance of that place against the Dutch.*[31]

All this, due to slow communications, differences of opinions, and the unavailability of ready funds to support the cost of a united attack, would take months, perhaps years, to bring to a head. Thus, the situation remained *in statu quo,* with the Dutch still in control of the Delaware. Captain James Neale was given a seat on the Maryland council where internal controversies and troubles with the Indians utilized his talents as a military advisor, and the proposed attack on New Amstel was deferred. In England, other developments were taking place which would bring another English faction into the controversy over the Delaware, which eventually forced Maryland's hand.

12

The Duke of York
Seizes the Delaware

On March 12, 1664, Charles II granted his brother, James Stuart, Duke of York (destined to become James II), a patent in free and common socage, conveying proprietary rights to lands in America from the St. Croix River in Maine to and including the *east* side of Delaware Bay and River. The territory, with all the "lands, islands, soils, rivers, harbors, mines, minerals, quarries, woods, marshes, waters, lakes, fishing, hawking, hunting, and fowling," comprised practically all of New Netherland, including the Dutch capital on Manhattan Island, the *east* side of the Delaware River (now the state of New Jersey) encompassing a large portion of the buffer zone James I had originally created between Virginia and New England.

Not included in the Duke's grant was the territory along the *western* shore of the Delaware still under Dutch control, where New Amstel and Fort Altena were situated, and further south the settlement recently begun by the Dutch on the site of Swanendael, then called the Hoerenkill (Harlots Creek). All this territory Lord Baltimore considered part of his province, although his Maryland government had done nothing since the Herrman-Waldron mission to remove the Dutch.

The Duke's patent completely ignored all previous English grants and commissions in the same area, including Sir Edmund Plowden's charter for New Albion and New Haven's land purchases from the Indians along the eastern shore of the Delaware, which never had royal sanction anyway. Maryland, however, was not included. There seems no question that Charles II intended to respect his father's grant to Lord Baltimore when he patented the territory to his brother.

This patent to the Duke of York was the first move in an imperious plan, an inevitable step in England's course to secure her economic position in the New World. The grant was a direct result of the economic nationalism intended to create a self-sufficient British empire from which foreign trade and commerce were to be excluded.

The Laws of Trade and Navigation, the so-called Navigation Acts, were designed to enable England to triumph over France, Spain, and Holland in the struggle for world power. The Act of 1651—the first of the Navigation Acts—was directed mainly against the Dutch, who, through their business acumen, the quality of their merchandise, and financial resources, enabling them to give more liberal credit than the English, had been able to dominate the world trade. In an attempt to cripple this Dutch competition, Parliament declared in 1651, among other things, that no products of Asia, Africa, or America could be carried to England, Ireland, or the English colonies except in English, Irish, or colonial ships, manned by sailors who, for the most part, were British subjects.

The Navigation Act of 1660—a re-enactment of the Act of 1651—prescribed that no foreign ships could import any of the products of the English colonies into England. There were other provisions in the statute to guard further against the intrusion of foreign, especially Dutch, competition. Thus, British colonial policy came to be dominated by the mercantilistic principle that the interests of the mother country took precedence over that of any of the colonies singly or in combination. This intended monopolization of colonial trade provided by the Navigation Acts was one of the seeds of the American Revolution, later nourished by George III. But as early as the 1650's the acts proved entirely unenforceable in the American colonies, principally because of the existence of the Dutch in New Netherland and the unwillingness of colonial merchants to conform to the law.

The Dutch shipped to New Netherland in Dutch vessels, and English merchants in Virginia, Maryland, and New England traded freely with the Dutch in American ports. As a result, tobacco, furs, and other goods originating in those areas in America under English control were shipped to Holland in Dutch vessels. English revenues from tolls and tariffs suffered as a result of this stratagem, and it became obvious that the restrictive trade laws could not be effective as long as the Dutch remained in control of New Netherland.

Furthermore, economic, social, or political unification of the English colonies was an impossibility as long as a dominant European power held an expanse of territory between New England on the north and Maryland and Virginia on the south, especially since that power controlled the two major eastern rivers leading to the sea—the Hudson and the Delaware. The Hudson, and its affluents, as well as the Mohawk, was a gateway to the north and west, to the Great Lakes and to the St. Lawrence. It controlled the fur trade with the Iroquois Confederacy of the Five Nations, and was the key to the exploitation of a vast, inland territory. Similarly, Dutch control of the Delaware, a no less important river than the Hudson, also blocked English expansion, and deep penetration of the territory west of the Susquehanna River. There could be no lasting English settlement on the Schuylkill nor expansion west of the Alleghenies as long as a rival nation held the Delaware.

Parliament urged Charles II to bring the matter to a head and redress the grievances of the kingdom by taking action against the Dutch, who were ruining the colonial trade, reducing the national income, and menacing economic expansion in the New World. At the same time, in Holland, the States-General, through its diplomatic representatives in London, was demanding a delineation of the boundaries between New England and New Netherland, as well as the boundaries between Maryland and New Netherland, as discussed in the previous chapter. It was a moment of decision for Charles II. Should he recognize the rights of the Dutch in New Netherland by a suitable compromise or deny them altogether and risk war with Holland by enforcing England's claim to the whole region?

Charles II, restored to the throne following the Civil War and the beheading of Charles I, had a capacity for intrigue and duplicity. Although he stood more than six feet tall and had a good figure and vigorous health, his swarthy complexion and large, ugly mouth gave him a homely appearance. Once, viewing his portrait, he said, "Odds fish! I am an ugly fellow."

Influential Englishmen then living in London, who had personal scores to settle either with the Dutch or with English colonial officials, agitated for Charles to take action against the Dutch. Prominent among these were George Baxter, who had been Stuyvesant's English secretary; John Scott, who had been a troublemaker on Long Island; and

Samuel Maverick, who had found dissatisfaction with the theocratic administration in Massachusetts. These three men appeared as witnesses before the Privy Council to explain why the Navigation Act was ineffective, and why England must possess New Netherland to assure its future economic security. Lord Chancellor Clarendon lent the weight of his office to support their position.

The King's brother James, Duke of York, a narrow, obstinate, covetous, and revengeful man, had no more love for the Dutch than his brother Charles or the Stuarts who had preceded them. He had been a refugee in Holland during the period of political upset in England, and his experiences there were distasteful to him. Moreover, as governor of the Royal African Company (in which both he and the King were principal stockholders), he had seen the depressing effect of Dutch competition in the English trade for gold and slaves.

James held the position of Lord High Admiral of the English navy, and being of a restless and energetic disposition, he chafed at the temporary idleness of his fighting ships. From his point of view, war with the Dutch seemed most desirable, even though a state of nervous peace had existed between the two countries for ten years following the signing of a treaty in 1654. As head of the navy, James could order English vessels away for an attack on the Dutch colonies without the formality of a declaration of war. He knew that the Dutch lacked both military and civil strength in the New World despite the trading activity of the West India Company and the city of Amsterdam. The entire population of New Netherland was probably not more than 10,000, compared to approximately 50,000 people in New England, 35,000 in Virginia, and 15,000 in Maryland.

If James seized New Netherland and succeeded to the crown as Charles' heir presumptive, the territory on his accession would become a royal possession. This was an important consideration to Charles II, who was ambitious to increase the influence of the empire, and who looked with more favor on his brother's ambitions than he would have greeted the same plans proposed for personal gain by a grantee unrelated to him.

It was agreed in the Privy Council that a proper plan was for the King to grant the territory occupied by the Dutch to the Duke of York, who would immediately move for its sudden and unheralded seizure with a minimum of bloodshed. There was nothing to be gained by openly declaring war and alerting the potential enemy. If England moved first and secretly, and with a certain amount of deceit, the Duke would have New Netherland in his possession before the Dutch were aware of what was going on. The Dutch government could then retaliate by declaring war against England if the States-General were so inclined, but their task would be all the more difficult with their New World bases in English hands.

Evidently Charles II gave no thought to arbitration or an effort for peaceful settlement with the Dutch. The rationale for the coup was that James I had taken possession of the entire seaboard between the 34th and 45th parallels when he granted territory to the London and Plymouth Companies in 1606. The fact that settlements were made only at Jamestown, and later at Plymouth in 1620 after the failure at Sagadahoc, with no permanent English occupation in the intervening buffer zone, was a technicality that both Charles and James Stuart chose to ignore.

The Dutch claim, based on positive occupancy begun in 1624 on both the Delaware and the Hudson, and continuing for more than 40 years, would seem to qualify their rights under the canon of international law as laid down by Queen Elizabeth in 1580, and reaffirmed by the House of Commons in 1621. But this was of little concern to the King, Lord Clarendon, or the Duke of York and his coadjutors. International justice had nothing to do with the Crown's final decision. It was to England's economic interests to possess the New Netherland, and have it she must, despite the treaty then existing between England and Holland. The King not only granted the land to his brother and endorsed the master strategy, but he gave James £4,000 to help pay for the conquest.

To carry out the tactical details of the plan, Charles appointed a royal commission consisting of Colonel Richard Nicolls, Colonel George Cartwright, Sir Robert Carr, and Samuel Maverick. Its mission was actually twofold. The first was to look into American affairs generally on behalf of the Crown, especially to try to resolve the civil and ecclesiastical differences between Connecticut and Massachusetts, and to settle the disputes between New Plymouth, Rhode Island, and the Providence plantation about the limits and bounds of their respective charters and jurisdictions. The commissioners were authorized to visit all the English colonies, to hold hearings on criminal and civil matters, and resolve all controversies according to their own discretion.

Secondly, its mission, in the phraseology of private instructions issued to the four commissioners on April 23, 1664, was

> the possessing Long Island, and reduceing that people to an entyre submission and obedience to us & our government, now vested by our grant and Commission in our Brother the Duke of York, and by raising forts or any other way you shall judge most convenient or necessary soe to secure that whole trade to our subjects, that the Dutch maye noe longer ingrosse and excercise that trade which they have wrongfully possessed themselves of . . .[1]

Lest the Dutch get wind of the impending attack and move their fleet to defend New Netherland, the announced purpose of the mission was the investigation of internal affairs in New England. The reduction of the Dutch was the secret phase of the mission, carefully concealed as the expedition was planned. The subterfuge proved effective, and Dutch agents, aware of preparations being made in England for the voyage, reported to Amsterdam that a commission was being sent to New England to solve the strictly local problems there. Some of the directors of the West India Company were not satisfied with this explanation, suspecting an English attack, but the States-General did not take any defensive action.

Although the private instructions were clearly pointed at the conquest of the principal Dutch settlements on the Hudson, nothing was said about the Delaware River. Both the King and the Duke of York were aware of Lord Baltimore's protest to the Assembly of XIX of the Dutch West India Company through Captain Neale, and that Neale had since been sent to Maryland to plan an attack against New Amstel. The King and the Duke of York also knew that Article XII of Lord Baltimore's charter invested his lordship and his heirs with full authority to wage war and to pursue, vanquish, captivate, and even put to death, enemies and ravagers. There was no point in utilizing the Crown's finances for an attack on the Delaware which would benefit Lord Baltimore and not the Duke. Moreover, that territory lay well beyond the limits of the land granted to the Duke.

On May 15, 1664, the four commissioners set sail from Portsmouth, their squadron consisting of the frigate *Guinea* and three other armed vessels, having aboard three companies of seasoned troops, consisting of 400 or 450 soldiers, in addition to the ships' crews. Colonel Nicolls, a devoted royalist, in command of the expedition, was appointed by the Duke as Deputy Governor, chief administrator over his new duchy in America. Nicolls, a well-educated man of 40, son of a barrister, had served on the continent with the Duke and was rewarded with the post of Groom of the Bedchamber to the Duke. He served the Duke both in Europe and America with loyalty, discretion, and untiring energy. The commissioners were ordered to proceed against New Netherland, as they should see fit, using force only if it could not be avoided. They were to assure the Dutch residents that if they submitted to English rule they would be taken into protection and could continue to enjoy all their possessions and have the same freedom of trade as other English subjects.

After a sojourn in Boston, where volunteers were recruited to join the expedition, the English vessels sailed down the coast. On August 26, 1665, the *Guinea,* Nicolls' flagship, anchored in a little bay called Nayack, now Gravesend Bay, between Coney Island and New Utrecht. By August 29, the other vessels arrived, piloted by New Englanders familiar with the waters of Manhattan. Nicolls moved to blockade the Narrows, seize the blockhouse on Staten Island, and prepare to besiege Manhattan Island. By now, Governor Stuyvesant, aware of the English ships in Dutch waters, sent a message inquiring as to their purpose, which was answered by Nicolls, who stated that it affronted the English Crown

> to *Suffer any Forraigners how near soever they be Allyed to usurp a Dominion and without his Maties Royal Consent to inhabit in those or any other his Maties Territoryes, hath Comanded me in his name to require a surrender of all such Forts, Towns or Places of Strength which are now possessed by the Dutch under your Comands And in his Maties Name I do Demand the Town scituate upon the Island commonly known by the name of Manhatoes with all the Forts there-*

*unto belonging to be render'd unto his Maties Obedience and
protection into my hands.*[2]

Fort Amsterdam, guarding the town at the southern extremity of Manhattan Island, was garrisoned with less than
150 soldiers, and in the town there were not more than 250
civilians able to bear arms. Resistance was useless and
merely postponed the inevitable, although Governor Stuyvesant bravely stood firm. The details of the correspondence
between Stuyvesant and Nicolls, and the military action
against the fort, have been adequately treated in a number
of reliable sources and need not now detain us. On September 8 (August 29 on the English calendar), the city and fort
surrendered to the English. The name of the fort was
changed to James and the town to New York, both in honor
of the Duke.

The conquest occurred exactly 55 years after Hudson's
"discovery" of the Hudson River, and 38 years after Manhattan Island was purchased from the Indians and first
settled by the Dutch. One author termed the English conquest a "lawless capture or seizure . . . a buccaneering enterprise, planned and carried out under conditions that
made it a flagrant example of bad faith." [3] This appraisal
was made because Charles II encouraged the conquest in
defiance of the law of nations as then understood, and
against a friendly power with whom he had signed an agreement not to right by force wrongs such as those he alleged
to excuse his own use of force.

If the attack on Manhattan Island was a violation of the
law between nations, what subsequently happened on the
Delaware was a more flagrant example of immorality in international politics. The Duke of York, it will be remembered, had received no title to land on the western shore of
the Delaware. Moreover, on June 24, 1664, after Nicolls'

expedition left England, the Duke presented to Sir John Berkeley and Sir George Carteret that part of his patent east of the Delaware lying within certain designated degrees of latitude. Sir George, Vice-Chamberlain and Treasurer of the Navy, and Sir John, a member of the Privy Council, were both loyal supporters of the Duke, and they called their grant *Nova Caesarea*, i.e., New Jersey.

Thus, in view of this grant, the four commissioners had no jurisdiction of either side of the Delaware River, but this did not prevent their making a decision to invade New Amstel. They evidently had no written instructions from the Duke or Charles II to do so, but if their action was not approved by the Crown before the fact, it was certainly endorsed afterwards. The Duke of York had two secret ambitions, to rule England as an absolute monarch and to re-establish the Catholic Church, and any military maneuver that extended the power of the English empire had his approbation.

Nicolls, Carr, and Cartwright—former officers in the royal army—were all capable of commanding a force to move against the Dutch at New Amstel, but, after discussion, the task was assigned to Sir Robert Carr. It was agreed that Nicolls would remain in New York to handle administrative matters there and set up the new government. During the next several months he would establish courts, English modifications of those already existing under the Dutch; form a law-making body consisting of justices sitting with himself and a newly-formed council; and draw up the "Duke of Yorks Laws" for the province.

Maverick and Cartwright planned to return to Boston at the earliest possible moment to carry out the commission's instructions with regard to New England. The instructions to Sir Robert Carr, dated September 3, 1664, were signed by Nicolls, Maverick, and Cartwright, and open with the following sentence. I have supplied the emphasis:

> *Whereas we are informed that the Dutch have Seated them-*
> *selves at Delaware bay on his Maty of Great Brittaines' Terri-*
> *tories without his knowledge and consent and that they have*
> *Fortifyed themselves there and drawn a great Trade thither,*
> *and being assured that* if they be permitted to go on, the
> gaining of this place [Manhattan Island] will be of small
> advantage to his Maty . . .[4]

What this obviously means is that the commissioners now
recognized, from the intelligence they had received, that
the capitulation of Manhattan Island, although necessary
and much to be desired, would not eliminate the Dutch
threat to the English colonies as long as Delaware remained
under enemy control. It was also clear to them that, although
Lord Baltimore pretended to the western shore of the Delaware, his officials in Maryland were unwilling to interrupt
their profitable trade with the Dutch by moving against
New Amstel.

Knowing that Charles Calvert had succeeded his brother
Philip as governor of Maryland, Nicolls instructed Carr how
to counter any objections that the new governor might
make:

> *To My Lord Baltimore's Soun you shall declare to all the*
> *English concerned in Maryland that his Matie hath at his*
> *great Expense Sent his Ships and Souldiers to reduce all*
> *Foraigners in those parts to his Maties Obedience, and to that*
> *purpose only you are Employed, but the Reduction of the*
> *Place being at his Maties expence, you have Comands to keep*
> *possession thereof for his Maties own behoof and right, and*
> *that you are ready to join with the Governr of Maryland*
> *upon his Maties Interest in all occasions, And that if My Lord*
> *Baltimore doth pretend right thereunto by his Patent (which*
> *is a doubtful Case) you are to say that you only keep posses-*
> *sion till his Maties is informed and satisfied otherwise. In*
> *other things I must leave to your discreccon, and the best*
> *Advice you can get upon the place.*[5]

The phrase, "which is a doubtful Case," suggests that Nicolls was aware of the dispute over the bounds of Maryland. Article 3 of the private instructions Charles II issued to the Nicolls' commission told them that before leaving England they should study all the pertinent charters that had been issued by "our Royall Father for the undertaking and settling those plantations and any other Charters which have been granted to any perticular Colonies by our father and ourselfe, or the late usurping powers . . ." [6]

Should the commission encounter difficulty in interpreting the provisions of the respective charters, Charles II made available to them his council at law and the office of the Secretary of State. He also suggested that the commission make authentic copies of the relevant charters and take them to America for later reference.

Assuming that Nicolls was familiar with Baltimore's charter, he perhaps reasoned that his lordship would not be able to retain the territory along Delaware Bay below the 40th parallel. This, then, would give the Dutch stronger reasons to enforce their claims, and his objective was to reduce the enemy, not strengthen his position. Later, Nicolls wrote Lord Arlington, then Secretary of State, that his principal motive in ordering Carr to attack New Amstel was that the Marylanders were illicitly engaged in the tobacco trade with the Dutch, and would soon be "overawed with so powerful a neighbour as the town of Amsterdam would have proved in short time." He emphasized a fact already known to the Crown, perhaps, that due to the trade at New Amstel, circumventing the Navigation Act, Lord Baltimore was not very "solicitous to take it from the Dutch." [7]

Nicolls was very exacting in his written instructions to Sir Robert Carr. He instructed the commander first to make peace with the Swedes and Finns living under the authority of the city of Amsterdam; next, he should assure the Dutch farmers and burghers that if they submitted to English rule they would not be harmed, and their lands, homes, and possessions would not be molested. Nicolls knew that if Carr could win the support of the citizenry, Governor Alexander d'Hinoyossa, the thirty-five-year-old ranking officer of the city's colony, who had succeeded Jacob Alricks, would be deprived of their assistance. The garrison at Fort Amstel, including officers, numbered only 30 men (although Nicolls did not know the exact size of the defending force prior to the attack), and Nicolls reasoned that d'Hinoyossa would need assistance from the citizens to repulse an attacking force.

Sir Robert Carr sailed to the Delaware in the *Guinea*, under command of Captain Hugh Hyde, her 40 guns ready for action. Accompanying him was an armed merchant ship, the *William Nicholas*, under command of Captain Thomas Morley. Lieutenant John Carr (promoted to the rank of captain before the campaign ended) and Ensign Arthur Stocke were two of the English officers in charge of more than 100 foot soldiers transported by the vessels, eager for their first American battle. (Manhattan had surrendered without military action, which was probably a disappointment to the English soldiers who had crossed an ocean to fight for their monarch.)

The expedition arrived off New Amstel on October 1, 1664, after some difficulty in navigating the shoals of the river and bay. Carr remained on board the *Guinea* during the early phases of the attack, but went ashore in time to commandeer the supplies and material. The fort fell on the first day of the attack, which was preceded by three days of discussions wherein Carr won the support of the burghers. Governor d'Hinoyossa, however, refused to surrender immediately and put up a feeble defense, but withheld orders to fire on the English vessels, which might have delayed the attack. The *Guinea* first directed cannon shot at the structure, after which the English troops, who had landed prior to the bombardment, under command of Lieutenant John Carr and Ensign Stocke, scaled the rear wall. The Dutch officers and men fled as the attackers overran the stronghold, suffering most of their casualties in their retreat. Before sundown, the English standard was flying over Fort Amstel.

The fort, its equipment, weapons, and provisions, as well as the houses, arms, slaves, livestock, and personal possessions of the city's officers and soldiers were all legitimate spoils of battle. Strictly speaking, all the pillage was the property of either the Crown or the Duke of York, but Sir Robert was nobody's fool. He knew that the Duke's patent did not include the west shore of the Delaware, and as the commanding officer, who had risked his life and the lives of his men in the engagement, he had his own ideas about the disposition of the spoils.[8] His instructions provided that "all the Canon Armes and Amunicon wch belongs to the Governmt shall remain to his Maties," but nothing was said about lands, houses, and personal property.

Sir Robert's account of the engagement is contained in a letter he wrote Colonel Nicolls on October 13 from Fort Amstel, which he now called "Dellawarr Fort." Here are pertinent excerpts:

> *Whereuppon I landed my soldiers on Sonday morning following & commanded ye shipps to fall down before ye Fort with muskett shott, wth directions to fire two broadesides apeace uppon yt Fort, then my soldiers to fall on.*
>
> *Which done, the soldiers neaver stopped untill they stormed ye fort, and soe consequently to plundering: the seamen, noe less given to that sporte, were quickly wthin & have gotten good store of booty; so that in such a noise and confusion noe worde of comand could be heard for some tyme; but for as many goods as I could preserve, I still keepe intire. The loss*

on our part was none; the Dutch had tenn wounded and
3 killed.

The fort is not tenable although 14 gunns, and wthout a
greate charge wch inevitably must be expended here wilbee
noe staying, we not being able to keepe itt. Therefore what I
have or can gett shalbe layed out upon ye strengthening of
the Fort, . . .[9]

Sir Robert deliberately minimized the extent of the spoils
for reasons known best to himself, conveying the impression
to Nicolls that the goods he had taken were needed for the
maintenance of the fort. Actually, he confiscated all the possessions of the city of Amsterdam, including 100 sheep, 30
or 40 horses, 50 or 60 cows and oxen, 60 or 70 Negro slaves,
the corn and hay recently harvested, cloth, linen, shoes,
brandy, wine, tools, a sawmill, a brewhouse, nine sea buoys
wtih their chains, and unsold cargo stores in the fort
amounting to £400 sterling. There was no accounting of the
plunder taken by individual soldiers and sailors. Carr also
sent a boat to the little Dutch settlement at the Hoerenkil
where his soldiers also pillaged the homes.

Sir Robert generously divided among his staff officers the
booty that had belonged to the administrative officers in the
employ of the city of Amsterdam. He gave Lieutenant John
Carr the house, servants, lands, and personal possessions
owned by Gerritt Van Sweeringen, the schout or sheriff.[10]
He also gave the younger officer a tract of meadowland that
had belonged to Governor d'Hinoyossa, and a transcript of
the patent covering the latter property (later confirmed by
Nicolls) is given in the Appendix of this volume. He rewarded Ensign Stocke, who was promoted to serve as the
commissary, with certain houses and other possessions of
Peter Alricks (nephew of the former director, Jacob Alricks),
including 11 Negro slaves.[11] He granted Captain Hugh
Hyde and Captain Thomas Morley a large tract of land

near the head of the Delaware River to be known as the Manor of Grimstead.[12]

The richest prize Carr kept for himself—the estate of Governor d'Hinoyossa on Burlington Island, with its gardens, dykes, houses, cultivated fields, livestock, and servants, where d'Hinoyossa and his family lived in comparative luxury. D'Hinoyossa owned a number of Negro slaves that Carr sold to English planters in Maryland for beef, pork, corn, salt, and other commodities.

Carr also gave lands to certain of his soldiers for their services in the campaign. Among these were Mr. William Tom,[13] John Ogle,[14] Thomas Wollaston, James Crawford, John Askue, Robert Scott, John Marshall, John Cousins, John Boyers, and others. A transcript of the patent conveying land to William Tom, typical of those issued, is given in the Appendix. To these common soldiers, some from poor working families in England, the possession of large tracts of land was something they could never have attained in their homeland. Several of them remained on the Delaware as residents after leaving military service.

Sir Robert did not bother to obtain from the other three commissioners consent for his program of sharing the Dutch wealth. He referred to himself as having been appointed as "sole and chiefe commander & disposor of the affayres in the behalf of his Majesty of Great Britaine, of Delaware Bay and Delaware River," and he alone felt authorized to dispose of the spoils to suit his fancies.

Sir Robert was by no means as harsh to the Dutch citizens in his surrender terms as he was to the officers and garrison; in fact, he was more generous than the residents had reason to expect from an invading force. The burghers, farmers, and private citizens were allowed to retain their homes and personal property. Any resident who did not want to live under English rule was free to depart unmolested within six months. Everyone was guaranteed freedom of conscience in church disciplines; the Dutch magistrates were allowed to continue in office, subject to the authority of Governor Nicolls. All the magistrates and inhabitants, Swedes, Finns, and Dutch alike, were told they must take an oath of allegiance and submit to the king of England, after which they were as free as Englishmen to enjoy the privileges of the colony. The surrender terms seemed to impose no undue hardships, because there had been no strong loyalties to the city of Amsterdam, and many of the residents were glad to be free of d'Hinoyossa, a tyrannical, unprincipled administrator, primarily interested in his own personal gain.

When Nicolls eventually learned of the booty Carr had acquired he promptly reported to London that Sir Robert claimed that what he had, " 'Tis his owne, being wonn by the sword." Nicolls said he did not approve of Sir Robert assuming the role of a "private Captain" appropriating property to himself, and disposing of houses, farms, and livestock to others that he deemed fit to have them.[15]

Nicolls was so incensed over the reports that he received at New York about Carr's actions that he intended to go to the Delaware and personally take charge, but the records do not clearly state that he did so. If he went to the Delaware, he did not stay, for Sir Robert Carr remained the governing officer there until February of 1665, enjoying for a short period of about five months his newly-acquired lands and estate. The commissioners tried earlier to persuade him to return to New York, but he claimed to be ill. In the commission issued by the King, the four commissioners were instructed to cooperate and decide courses of action by majority vote. In Carr's absence, the others could not efficiently conduct his majesty's affairs.

But Carr did not immediately return, and Maverick and Cartwright went to Boston without him, while Nicolls remained at Fort James to govern the Duke's new subjects. On January 16, 1665, Cartwright, then in Boston, wrote that Sir Robert "cannot be perswaded to leave Delaware as yet." [16] Colonel Nicolls finally prevailed upon Sir Robert to leave Delaware and come to New York, and from thence he went to Boston. He arrived in Boston on February 4, complaining of a leg injury he had received on the Delaware which prevented his wearing a boot and which was the reason he had not been able to join the other commissioners earlier. Later in the year he returned to New York, where he lay ill for ten weeks from an ailment he got "in his travills to Delaware & Maryland."

Sir Robert was not the only commissioner with a complaint. Cartwright and Maverick both protested that they had not received a farthing from the booty taken at Delaware, which they understood was worth £10,000.[17] In reply to this, Sir Robert lamented that he had nothing to show for the battle in which he hazarded his life, and of d'Hinoyossa's former estate on Burlington Island he wrote, "I heare is given away, and one is come over to take possession of it." [18] He then petitioned the Earl of Arlington to ask the King that he be granted a tract of land on the Sagatucket River, where he aspired to become governor of the English subjects in the province of Maine.

Like Sir Robert Carr, the other commissioners also claimed that they had gained nothing in their service on behalf of the Duke and the Crown, and that they had neither money nor credit. Nicolls wrote that he had expended his own money in the Duke's interests, for which he had not been compensated. Perhaps it was his knowledge that the commissioners, and some of the officers, had been inadequately compensated that caused him to write the Earl of Arlington in April 1666 recommending that the Crown confirm to Sir Robert Carr, Captain John Carr, and

Ensign Stocke, in recognition of their meritorious services, the lands "of which they have been in possession ever since the taking of the place." [19] There is nothing in the records as to what action, if any, was taken in London upon receipt of Nicolls' request. The former Governor d'Hinoyossa also wrote Governor Nicolls from St. Marys, where he had sought refuge after the English attack, asking that his Delaware estate be returned to him. D'Hinoyossa said that if Nicolls was not agreeable to his request he would personally appeal to the Duke of York. [20]

It is known that Sir Robert Carr left Boston for England sometime in 1667, but he was still in poor health. Upon his arrival in England he died in Bristol without ever returning to London.

Captain John Carr succeeded Sir Robert on the Delaware and was placed in command of the English army of occupation (about 20 soldiers), and became head of the governing council of Dutch and Swedish magistrates. Various writers have assigned such relationships to John Carr as a son, cousin, or brother of Sir Robert. It is known that Sir Robert had at least one son, but that this son was Captain John Carr has not yet been established with certainty. On December 15, 1668, Captain Carr was ordered to deliver Burlington Island and "whatsoever else was delivered to you there by Sr Robt Carr to Peter Alricks." [21] Alricks was a brilliant and resourceful Dutchman who had come to America from Groningen prior to the English attack. The burgomasters of Amsterdam employed him as an official in the colony, where he acquired large land holdings. He lost these lands, as well as other possessions, to Carr's forces after the attack. After the smoke of battle lifted, Alricks became friendly with the English, who soon realized that his influence and ability could be utilized to their best interests. Within a few years his position as a landowner had been restored, and the

English not only conveyed d'Hinoyossa's Island to him, but other tracts were patented in his name, and he acquired considerable real and personal property.

* * * *

When news of the victory of the Duke of York's forces at Manhattan Island and New Amstel reached the New Haven Colony it again reawakened interest in the Delaware. The English merchants still smarted over their high-handed treatment by the Dutch, and as one final gesture it was decided to write Governor Nicolls in the hope of enlisting his sympathies. The following letter was composed and dispatched to him:

> *Right Honble, Att a genll meeting of Deputies from ye severall Plantacons of this Colony, it was agreed yt a letter should be prpared and sent to informe Yor Honor of ye great wrong and injury this Colony have suffered from ye Dutch at Delaware Bay, about 14 yeares agoe, being violently repulsed wth great damage out of theire just purchase and possession there; for we had purchased a great tract of land on ye one and ye other side of ye Bay or River, and a plantacon begun by sundry psons, & a trading house set up; wch ye Dutch pillaged and burnt, and soe wholly destroid ye designe at yt tyme. Two or 3 yeares afterwards, a new attempt was made and a vessel sent, wch was then alsoe stopt at the Manhatoes, and sundry of ye principall psons imprisoned by the Dutch Governor, soe yt nothing yt way hath ever bin attempted since, although ye Indians of whom we purchased ye land doe still owne our right & much desire ye coming of the English. But thus much only to acquaint Yor Honor wt is further intended upon a further search of or records to be improved by Yor Honor as yor wisdom shall think fit; humbly desiring alsoe that or just claime to ye pmises, wn more fully psecuted, may be admitted. Thus craving Yor Honors pdon for this*

boldness, with humble service presented, rests, Yor Honrs humble Servt.[22]
    20 Decr, 1664   *Wm Jones*

Needless to say, Colonel Nicolls had no intention of further complicating the situation by assisting New Haven to place colonists on the Delaware River. If he answered the letter, the reply has been lost, but it is certain that he took no action favorable to the New Haveners.

An entry in the New Haven court records in 1666 indicates that Matthew Gilbert, a prominent civil officer, had gone to the Delaware, presumably to make further inquiries about the long-awaited settlement.[23] But nothing further was done, and as pointed out in an earlier chapter, the New Haveners lost interest in expanding their colony, having received no encouragement from the Duke of York's government.

The Treaty of Breda, proclaimed August 14/24, 1667, ended the war between the Dutch and English. By the terms of the treaty Surinam (Dutch Guiana in South America), which the Dutch had taken from the English, was allowed to remain in Dutch hands, and the New Netherland remained in England's possession. The Duke of York's government continued in power at New York and on the Delaware, although Nicolls, who had repeatedly asked to be relieved of his assignment, was now permitted to return to England. He was succeeded as governor by Francis Lovelace. Under Lovelace's administration, New Castle was incorporated as a "bailiwick" and the government on the Delaware was strengthened by a centralized authority over the entire river. This was vested in a high sheriff, Edmund Cantwell, and the bailiff or chief magistrate, Peter Alricks, with six assistant magistrates.

*   *   *   *

In July of 1663, before the English attack and during the era when the city of Amsterdam ruled the Delaware, Peter Cornelis Plockhoy, a Dutch Mennonite, settled 41 people at the Hoerenkil, with the permission and encouragement of the burgomasters. Plockhoy, a zealot, envisioned an ideal, semi-socialistic community in the New World, based upon the equality of man and held together by Christian principles. The Hoerenkil, at the site of the ill-fated patroons' colony of Swanendael, overlooking Delaware Bay, seemed to Plockhoy an ideal location. The area was also called *Sikonesse* or *Sickoneysincks* from the Indian name of the nearby creek.

Following the attack by Sir Robert Carr's soldiers in the fall of 1664, Plockhoy remained at the Hoerenkil for several years, and then moved to Germantown, where he died. Some of his followers—and others, both of Dutch and English origins—continued to occupy the Hoerenkil and the surrounding area. Politically the community fell under the jurisdiction of the Duke of York's government, although, like New Castle, it was part of the territory the Calverts continued to claim under their Maryland patent. Although some doubt still existed in Maryland as to whether New Castle lay below the 40th parallel, there was no question that the Hoerenkil, almost 100 miles south of New Castle, was definitely within Maryland's bounds.

For about five years following the establishment of the Duke of York's government on the Delaware, Lord Baltimore did practically nothing to exercise his authority over the territory. Then he suddenly decided to settle colonists on what he called the "seaboard side" of his province, which included the territory along Delaware Bay south of New Castle. He took several steps to accomplish his purpose. First, he established Worcester County (still in existence), which comprised part of the seaboard side, including the

Hoerenkil. Then he created a second county (no longer in existence), which he called Durham, comprising the area from the Hoerenkil as far north as the 40th degree of latitude, although at the time he was still uncertain where this degree crossed the Delaware.[24] Special incentives in the form of low rents were established, particularly to attract English and Irish settlers to the two new counties.

He also ordered the surveyor-general of the province, Jerome White, to find exactly where the 40th parallel crossed the territory. In compliance with instructions, White made his surveys, and on November 26, 1669, wrote a highly important letter which he addressed to Governor Lovelace in New York. He stated that he found New Castle to lie 39 degrees, 30 minutes in northerly latitude (definitely south of the 40th parallel), and, according to the terms of the Maryland patent, clearly on Lord Baltimore's territory. He said that Lord Baltimore appreciated that his majesty had graciously sent troops to reduce this town from the usurped power of the Dutch, and he was grateful that it had since been so ably protected by the Duke's government. But since the town was definitely within the Maryland patent, his lordship now intended to assert his ownership.[25]

Meanwhile, Lord Baltimore had again written from England urging his son, Governor Charles Calvert, to seat persons on the "seaboard side," particularly in the Hoerenkil area. His lordship said he was willing to lease lands at the low rent of one shilling per 50 acres, and he instructed his son that if he met any opposition in the expansion program he should counter force by force, if necessary. His lordship also instructed that the surveyor-general lay out at the Hoerenkil and on the "seaboard side" two proprietary manors for himself in every county, each to contain at least 6,000 acres.

Although Lord Baltimore made no overt effort to challenge the Duke of York's authorities at New Castle, he seems to have been deliberately creating a test case at the Hoerenkil. He was fully aware that his actions would be considered a confrontation by the Duke, and perhaps he selected the smaller of the two settlements because it was poorly defended and could put up little resistance. In retrospect, it is now clear that he not only intended to seat Marylanders at the Hoerenkil, but he had decided to overthrow the Duke of York's government there.

At a council meeting held at Fort James in New York on May 17, 1672, a report sent by Captain John Carr from New Castle was read informing the authorities that Lord Baltimore had sent a surveyor to lay out land at the Hoerenkil, without the knowledge or approbation of the English officials.[26] Governor Lovelace was disturbed by this information, but in August he received another report from Carr which had far more serious consequences.

He learned that a certain Captain Thomas Jones rode to the Hoerenkil with a party of horsemen, and there plundered several of the inhabitants and carried away their goods. Jones held a cocked pistol to the breast of one of the magistrates, threatening his life if he did not follow orders.[27] Lovelace interpreted the incident as having been provoked by a brigand, unaware that on June 20, 1672, Governor Charles Calvert commissioned Thomas Jones of Worcester County to be captain of all military forces of that county with authority to muster and train soldiers to be used to overcome all enemies.[28] In fact, he also issued orders to Captain Paul Marsh of Somerset County to assist Jones and obey his orders in any military action against an enemy of the province.[29] In the protesting letter he dispatched to Philip Calvert, who succeeded Charles Calvert as governor, Governor Lovelace said that the Duke of York would not tolerate such "horrid Outrages," and he hoped that Maryland would promptly bring Jones to justice.[30]

The letter brought no results, and it appears that Captain Jones returned to the Hoerenkil for the second time, bringing a larger force of horsemen to sack the settlement. Whereupon, according to a deposition by Helmanus Wiltbanck, Jones formed a court of his own men and demanded that all of the settlers take an oath of allegiance to Lord Baltimore. Since they were unwilling to do so (having previously sworn allegiance to the Duke of York), Jones committed them to prison overnight without food or water, threatening to carry them all to Maryland as prisoners and confiscate their properties. They were thus coerced into taking the oath of allegiance to Lord Baltimore.[31]

Captain John Carr, upon learning of the incident, wrote Governor Lovelace to advise him that not only had the Maryland government seized the Hoerenkil, but the Marylanders were now making plans to bring the whole Delaware River south of the 40th parallel under Maryland's jurisdiction, and New Castle was in a vulnerable position. With his small contingent of soldiers, Carr was in no position to repulse an attack, and, as Jacob Alricks had done when threatened from the same direction a decade before, he turned to his superiors on Manhattan Island for assistance.

Lovelace was uncertain about how far he should go in defense of territory which his predecessors had invaded in the Duke's behalf, but which lay beyond the bounds of the Duke's patent. To make matters worse, the attackers at the Hoerenkil, who now threatened New Castle and the entire river, did not represent any enemy nation. They were his own countrymen, acting under the instructions of a nobleman in possession of a charter bearing the Great Seal of England. There was only one person with sufficient authority to make the final decision: that was the Duke of York himself. Lovelace dispatched a courier on a vessel bound for London with full details for his royal highness, asking what course of action he should follow.

While awaiting a reply, he ordered Captain Carr to strengthen his defenses at New Castle and ready his garrison so that it would be able to move into action within an hour's notice. He further instructed him that if an attack came he should try to persuade the attackers that the Duke of York had been in control of the territory for eight years without his authority being questioned. If words did not repel the invaders, he instructed Carr to stand his guard, and if the attackers broke the peace, he was to use all possible means to defend the fort and the town.[32]

While these two English factions prepared for the inevitable clash, developments were ensuing in Europe which again brought the Dutch into the controversy. The ink on the Treaty of Breda was scarcely dry when, in 1672, as the culmination of power politics in which France was now involved, England declared war on the Netherlands. That meant that Lord Baltimore and the Duke of York had to lay aside their personal differences, and their respective provinces in the New World began to prepare for possible attack by the common enemy.

13
The Dutch Recapture the Delaware

~~~~~~

The war between the Dutch and English brought major naval action at Solebay where the Dutch won an advantage over the allied fleets of England and France, then in league. In this engagement, Colonel Nicolls, late governor of the Duke of York's province, was killed by a cannon ball at the foot of the Duke, who commanded the British fleet. Although the Dutch maintained their dominant position on the seas, destroying the enemy in almost every encounter, their land forces in Europe were not as fortunate, suffering serious defeats.

With the enemy in control of the Atlantic trade routes, the effects of the war were felt in the English colonies. Not only was commerce interrupted, but the colonists lived in fear of Dutch raids.

In the summer of 1673, a rumor reached the English at New York that a Dutch squadron had been dispatched against the West Indies and was on its way to the Atlantic coast. Governor Lovelace had doubts about the authenticity of the report, although he assembled English troops at New

York from several points, numbering about 350 men, to defend the town. The contribution to this force from the colony on the Delaware was nine men and a corporal, and Captain John Carr also came to lend assistance.[1] After a while, when no Dutch ships appeared, Lovelace dismissed the reinforcements, leaving about 80 soldiers in the garrison at Fort James under the direct command of Captain John Manning. Captain John Carr remained for a time at Fort James. Governor Lovelace went on an official trip to Connecticut to confer with Governor John Winthrop, leaving the garrison in charge of Captain Manning.

On July 28, an alarm was received that Dutch ships were in the Atlantic, and the next day at 3:00 P.M. the enemy was sighted off New York. But this was no small complement of raiding vessels; it consisted of a fleet of some 27 ships under the joint command of Cornelis Evertsen, Jr. and Jacob Binckes. Fifteen of the vessels were warships, heavily armed, reinforced with other men-of-war, and accompanied by English prizes now manned with Dutch crews. With about 1,600 aboard, and confident of victory, the Dutch commanders dispatched the following message to the English:

> *This force of Warr now lying in yor Sight are sent out by the High and Mighty States and his serene Highness the Prince of Orange for to destroy their Enemies: Wee have sent you therefore this our Letter together with our Trumpeteer to ye and that you upon sight hereof Doe Surrender unto us ye ffort called James promiseing good Quarter—or by refusall wee shall be obliged immediately to proceed both by water and Land in such manner as we shall finde to be most advantageous for the High and Mighty States, Dated in ye ship* Swanenburgh *Anckored betwixt Staten and Long Iland New Yorke ye 09 of August 1673.*[2]

Captain Manning, who had sent a courier to Lovelace in Connecticut when the Dutch were sighted, replied that he wanted to discuss the matter with the mayor and alderman, and asked the enemy to forbear hostilities until 10 o'clock the next morning. The Dutch commanders returned the messenger with a note to the effect that they would give Manning half an hour to make up his mind, after which they would begin an attack. When no reply was received, the Dutch vessels fired 2,000 rounds from ten of their ships' cannons, killing and wounding some of the Dutch soldiers. Then they landed about 600 men to storm Fort James. Many of the Dutch burghers were, of course, overjoyed to see their countrymen moving against the English and joined the landing party. Manning could offer no effective resistance against such an overwhelming attacking force, and he was compelled to surrender.

The English soldiers were put under guard and imprisoned in a church, and the Dutch plundered their belongings and other English goods in the fort. According to the English account, the soldiers were taken aboard the Dutch ships the next morning "and soe carried us some to Newfoundland and ye Portinguall Ilands where they Inhumanly left us and some to Cales wch we have not heard from as yett." [3]

The majority of the magistrates and constables willingly swore allegiance to the States-General and the Prince of Orange. Fort James was renamed Fort Willem Hendrick and New York became New Orange.

The river settlements of Esopus (present Kingston) and Albany also surrendered to the Dutch without opposition. Evertsen and Binckes, who jointly acted as a council of war, confiscated the property of the Duke of York and his agents, and on August 12 commissioned Captain Anthony Colve, an infantry captain, who had commanded the land party, as governor-general of the Duke's former province. One of

Colve's official acts was to appoint Peter Alricks schout or sheriff and commander of the settlements on both sides of the Delaware River. In the commission he issued to Alricks, Colve referred to the fact that he had received a good report of Alricks' previous service under the Dutch government on the Delaware as ensign and commissary.[4] Colve doubtless knew that Alricks was also respected by the English, and he realized that the transition from one government to another could be made with least friction by appointing an administrator friendly to both.

Alricks took an oath testifying that he would be true and faithful to the States-General and the Prince of Orange, and that he would help to maintain the Dutch Reformed Church. Evertsen and Binckes had previously agreed that the inhabitants on the Delaware, regardless of their national origins, would be allowed to retain possession of their homes, lands, and personal property. Three courts of justice were established at New Castle, Upland (present Chester, Penna.), and the Hoerenkil, with magistrates as the presiding officers. The citizens accepted the new government without complaint or resentment, having had so many administrative changes that they probably felt another one would have little effect on their pattern of living. There was no resistance, no military action, and no bloodshed on the Delaware.

Immediately following the capture of New York, Binckes dispatched a vessel to the Board of Admiralty at Amsterdam with letters reporting the good tidings, and documents giving full details of their successes, culminating in the recapture of New Netherland. The vessel was attacked in the Atlantic by the English, and the pilot, in obedience to his orders, destroyed all the documents by throwing them overboard to keep them from falling into the enemy's hands. Thus, the States-General was completely in the dark as to the outcome of the expedition, and what was needed to preserve the captured colony. The pilot "was a man so little observant that he could not impart any information" when he reached Holland except that New York had been taken.[5] Some time later, Cornelis Van Ruyven, who left New York January 10, 1674, with additional dispatches from Binckes and Evertsen, arrived in the Netherlands with news of the capture of the English colony.[6]

The late Victor H. Paltsits, historian of the State of New York, and an eminently qualified scholar, was in process of translating into English several unpublished Dutch manuscripts pertaining to the action of the Dutch fleet at the time of his death in 1951. Some of these documents were evidently among those retained by Binckes and Evertsen and taken back to Holland with them, and others are copies kept in Holland. They are extremely important because their contents provide data not previously known. Among these documents are two sets of secret instructions adopted October 12, 1672, intended to govern the movement of the Dutch squadron under Evertsen's command. They reveal that after leaving Zeeland, Evertsen was instructed to sail to the English island of St. Helena, displaying the English and French flags for the purpose of deceiving the defenders, and then to capture the island and the fort. Using St. Helena as a temporary base, the squadron was to operate in the surrounding waters until June 1673, for the purpose of sacking English ships returning with rich cargoes from the East Indies.

If the attack on St. Helena failed—or should the spoils prove insufficient—the commander was instructed to cross the Atlantic and to cruise along the coasts of Virginia, New Netherland, and Newfoundland "ruining there whatever shall be possible, so that should the design against the Island of St. Helena have miscarried, which is not surmised, to acquire through this [cruise] so much booty that the ex-

penses of this equipment shall be generously defrayed."
Apparently there was nothing explicit in the original instructions about seizing Fort James, New York, and recapturing the former Dutch colony on the Delaware. It is entirely possible that the decision may have been made on the
spot by Binckes and Evertsen, after receiving intelligence
from Dutch burghers who came aboard their vessel when
the fleet lay off Staten Island. When they learned that the
English defenses were less than adequate, and that the governor was absent, they knew that victory was assured.

Cornelis Evertsen was a popular young commander, son
of a valiant Dutch vice-admiral who had died in battle.
The admiralty of Zeeland linked his name with Abraham
Krynzoon, another naval hero, who, under the auspices of
Zeeland, captured the British colony of Surinam in April
1667. Binckes, a bold seaman, who was to lose his life in
battle a few years later, had been dispatched by the admiralty of Amsterdam.[7] His original mission was entirely
separate from Evertsen's, and with his small squadron of
four men-of-war he had meet Evertsen's forces in Mar-
tinique. There they combined the two squadrons into a
formidable fleet and steered a course for New York. The
capitulation of the fort and city came so quickly and easily
that the two commanders suddenly found themselves masters of the Duke's province with the responsibility of organizing a new government.

They then set up a military administration with the only
officer under their command capable of handling the situation having previously had no more authority than that of
an infantry captain. Historians who have concluded that the
Dutch fleet was sent from Holland for the express purpose
of recapturing New Netherland can now read the instructions to Evertsen and learn that he and Binckes were on
separate raiding missions with the objective of gathering
booty.

With the cooperation of the New York Public Library, in whose manuscript room are preserved the Dutch texts of the secret instructions, as well as Paltsits' translations written in his own hand, I have reprinted both translations in the Appendix.

In the same collection of documents is an inventory of the papers which were handed to Captain Evertsen in a sealed tin box when he sailed from Zeeland to St. Helena. The inventory lists the two sets of instructions referred to above, information about the winds, two signal charts used by ships of the East India Company, and a cipher to be used in all official communications. The cipher itself is an interesting and unusual document giving numerals to be used in representing nautical and military terms. Each number had a specific meaning, and it would have been virtually impossible for an enemy to decode an intercepted message without having the ciphered references. The reader has seen in an earlier chapter that the Spanish ambassadors in England used coded messages to communicate with their king, and it was doubtless common practice among other nations. To the best of my knowledge, the Dutch naval code of 1672–1673 is the only one that has been preserved. It is a lengthy document, and I have cited only a few of the entries to illustrate the general pattern:

		[CODE NUMBER]
Verovert	[conquered]	134
Een	[one]	130
Twee	[two]	137
Acht	[eight]	143
Schepen verlooren	⌈ships⌉ ⌊lost ⌋	212

Another document translated by Paltsits is a "Memorandum of the commissioned mariners who have promised to join the squadron of Captain Binckes and Evertsen." It appears in his longhand (the brackets are also his) as follows:

> *Captain Adrian Centsz Vos, the Ship* d'Offerhande *Abraham's* [*Sacrifice*] *carrying 36 pieces and 160 Crew Captain Constant, the* Salamander, *32 pieces, 150 Crew Captain Pieter Marousz,* Ram, *36 pieces 160 Crew Capt. Thomas Nett, the* Eelena [Helen] *24 pieces, 100 Crew Captain Cornelis Marinusz,* Nassow, *28 pieces, 115 crew, Captain Thobias Thobias,* Wulpenburgh, *28 pieces, 120 crew Capt. Mels Cornelissen*[?] *14 pieces, 80 crew, Capt. Warwyck, the* Jager [Hunter] *26 pieces from Zeeland Capt. Jan. Spaignaert, de* Brack [Beagle] *10 pieces Capt Clement, the* Eenhorn [Unicorn] *14 pieces.*

Perhaps the most interesting document in the collection from the viewpoint of American history is "The list of ships taken and burnt by the Dutch under commander Cornelis Evertsen in James River in Virginia in July 1673." The list includes the names of 12 English vessels, along with the names of the captains of eight of the vessels, whose aggregate cargoes of 9,200 hogsheads of tobacco was, indeed, a rich prize. What evidently occurred was that before meeting Binckes, Evertsen's forces had captured seven of the English vessels, and destroyed five by setting them afire. No doubt the tobacco from the five destroyed ships was salvaged and transferred to the other vessels. The seven prizes were presumably in the custody of the Dutch squadron when New York was taken. A transcript of the document follows:

			HOGS-HEADS
The Pearl of Bristol	Jan Reed	taken	700
The Pearl of London	Tho:ffox	taken	1000
The John & Matthew of London		taken	1000
The Posthorn of London	Mr. Moore	taken	800
The Elias of London	Benj. Caper	taken	700

The Friendship of Briston	Rich. Speed	burnt	700
The Robt of Briston	Morgan Taylor	burnt	650
The Madaras of London		taken	1050
The Plymo. of Plymouth		burnt	700
The Mary of Liverpool		burnt	350
The Panas of London	Robt Cocdas	taken	500
The Maryland Merchant	Jo Stobrok	burnt	650

Yet a sloop of New York, taken with victuals

24 ships destroyed	at Plymouth
7 ditto	at Briston
2 ditto	at Tapsham

By the time Governor Lovelace returned to New York, in answer to Manning's summons, the fort and town were already in the enemy's hands. Lovelace was arrested and detained, and when Binckes and Evertsen departed from New York he was carried back to Europe on Binckes' vessel. The commanders left two armed vessels at New York under Colve's direction, but the other vessels in the squadron all sailed away. Evertsen took the ships under his command to Cadiz, where he arrived in December, after conquering the island of St. Eustatius.

Captain Manning was later held for court martial, accused of not having the garrison in a proper state of defense; of going aboard enemy vessels to treat with them; of allowing enemy vessels to approach the fort without firing on them; of allowing the enemy to send small boats ashore without opposition; of striking the English flag and running up a flag of truce before the landing party was in sight of the fort; and of causing the fort gate to be opened to the enemy.[8]

Most of these accusations he denied, and as one looks back at the incident it seems clear that if Lovelace had been present he could not have handled the situation differently. The handful of English soldiers, under Manning's com-

mand, could not have withstood battle with the Dutch landing party that outnumbered them more than ten to one. If
Manning had not surrendered, the Dutch fleet would have
bombarded both the fort and town, destroying private and
public property and wounding or killing civilians.

*　　*　　*　　*

With an enemy nation again in control of New Castle and
the Hoerenkil, and the Duke of York's government deposed,
Govenor Charles Calvert seized the opportunity to strike on
the Delaware, and the Hoerenkil was again selected as the
point of attack.

Calvert learned from one of the commissioners he had
appointed to govern the Hoerenkil that the inhabitants
there had taken an oath to be true to the new Dutch regime,
violating the pledges they had made to Captain Jones to submit to Lord Baltimore's authority. On October 1, 1673, he
commissioned Captain Thomas Howell to raise 40 men and
take the settlement from the Dutch by force and surprise,
and to defend it by force, if necessary.[9]

In early December of 1673, Captain Howell thundered
into the Hoerenkil town, leading his band of horsemen,
armed to the teeth, brandishing their swords. The inhabitants were so terrified that they readily submitted without offering resistance. Although Howell's men did not
harm the people, they killed many of the cattle. After the
soldiers were billeted in the town for several weeks, and all
ties with the Dutch authorities severed, Captain Howell returned to Maryland to advise Governor Calvert that the
inhabitants were poor and were unable to maintain the
troop of soldiers.

What orders Howell received from Calvert are not known,

but when he returned he assembled the townsfolk, as well as those living in the surrounding area, and ordered all the men to bring their guns and ammunition the day before Christmas on the pretense of having a military drill. When the men had all gathered in the town, Howell and his soldiers took their guns and ammunition. Then, Howell said, it caused him much grief to tell them he had been instructed to burn all their houses to the ground and not leave a stick standing. He would give them 15 minutes before he set fire to their dwellings. Several expectant mothers entreated Howell to spare one house for their relief because of the bitter cold weather. He replied that he must obey his orders and could spare none of the buildings, but if God would save one they could have it.

His men then fired all of the buildings. Some of the residents were held prisoners while their homes were burned to prevent their saving food and personal property. A thatched barn was set afire three times by flying sparks, and, as Providence would have it, each time the winds extinguished the flames. Howell said that since God intended the barn to be saved he would not meddle further with the deity, but would allow it to stand as shelter for the pregnant women. The barn was the only building spared.

Howell's men also gathered the boats from the creek and took them with them when they departed, as well as the guns and ammunition they had collected. They left the inhabitants with no means of transportation, no weapons to defend themselves against possible Indian attack, and their homes reduced to ashes. The nearest settlement from which relief could be had was more than 60 miles away.

From five depositions relating to the incident, which were made a number of years later,[10] some details are available relating to the hardships suffered by specific individuals. For example, Howell's men tortured Harmon Cornelison, a merchant and Indian trader, by holding a flame to his fingers, to force him to confess where he had hidden a store of beaver pelts. When he disclosed the hiding place, they stole all the pelts from him. They also broke into his chest and took all of his savings.

A party of Howell's horsemen rode to the plantation of John Roads (Rhodes), Jr., about eight miles beyond the town. There they set fire to his tobacco house, which was full of tobacco, next his milk houses, and finally his dwelling. They carried wheat sheaves and piled them alongside the house to feed the flames. The owner's father, John Roads, Sr., and a neighbor, Thomas Tilley, later tried to reach New Castle by going overland, but unable to defend themselves without weapons, they were attacked by Indians and killed.

Richard Platte's house was destroyed by fire, as well as his storehouse full of tobacco and corn. When he asked Howell's permission to build a thatch shed to shelter his wife and young children, Howell's reply was that it was death to build anything. Fearful that his family would suffer lingering deaths through exposure to the severe winter weather, Platte pleaded with Howell to shoot him along with his wife and children. To this Howell replied that his commission didn't reach as far as murder.

Howell's reward from the Maryland government for his acts of cruelty and pillage amounted to "2000 lbs. of tobacco for 35 men @ 400 lbs of tobacco p. man 14,000 pounds of tobacco—to the same Howell for his lieutenant 700 lbs of tobacco, for his ensign 600 lbs, for his sergeant 500 lbs— In all 1800 pounds to Howell for pvisions and necessaries 776 pounds for his attendance upon a prisoner of warr [June 1674]." [11]

Some of the dispossessed occupants of Hoerenkil town went to New Castle or New York, causing Colve to issue a proclamation which he sent to Commander Peter Alricks at New Castle. He stated that

> *as some English of Maryland have driven some of the subjects of this government out of their dwelling-houses in a very strange and cruel manner and have ruined the same by burning their houses, whereby several have doubtlessly been deprived of all their means of subsistence, therefore I consider it necessary to proclaim hereby, that all such exiles, English as well as Dutch, who may come here with certificates from Commander Alrigs, that they are among the sufferers, shall be provided with means of support.*[12]

In order to prevent a recurrence of similar incidents, Colve ordered that all inhabitants of the Delaware were commanded to place themselves immediately under Alricks' orders if an enemy appeared, and it would then be decided how to counter the enemy and inflict the most harm on him.

A few families, principally because of the expectant mothers, remained at the Hoerenkil after Howell's party rode away. They probably crowded together for a miserable existence in the barn that Howell had spared until they were able to build new homes in the spring, assisted by men from New Castle who came to their relief. Among those who remained were Hermanus Wiltbanck, John Kiphaven, Alexander Moulston, Harmon Cornelisen, Anthony Inlose, and Elizabeth Roads, widow of John Roads, Sr.[13]

No other Delaware River settlement was exposed to so many tragic episodes in the 17th century as the Hoerenkil. From the time the Indians massacred the patroons' colonists in 1632, the attack by Sir Robert Carr's troops in 1664, the raid by Captain Jones in 1672, and finally the cruel assault by Captain Howell in 1673, the little community along Delaware Bay was, indeed, "sealed in blood" and anguish.

*   *   *   *

The Treaty of Westminster ended the war between the English and Dutch. William, Prince of Orange, and his States-General fully realized that they could not hold the reconquered American province, surrounded as it was by a growing and aggressive English population. The Prince made an offer of the restitution of New Netherland to Charles II as evidence of a desire for peace and understanding. Charles referred the offer to Parliament, who immediately recommended acceptance. The treaty, signed in February of 1674, but not proclaimed in America until July, contained this provision: "That whatsoever countries, islands, towns, ports, castles, or forts have or shall be taken on both sides, since the time the late unhappy war broke out, either in Europe or elsewhere, shall be restored to the former lord or proprietor, in the same condition they shall be in when the peace itself shall be proclaimed." This meant that New York and the Delaware settlements were returned to England.

Edmund Andros, a major in a dragoon regiment, was appointed to receive the Dutch surrender in New York from Colve. The Westminster treaty ceded the New Netherland territory to the English crown, but on June 29, 1674, the Duke of York obtained a new patent from his royal brother with enlarged authority. The Duke then conferred his commission on Andros to govern the province in his name.

On October 15, 1674, Colve, having received a message from the States-General, assembled the burgomasters and schepens at New York to announce that he had received orders to return the province to the English and to return home with his garrison.[14]

Andros arrived on the *Diamond* on October 22, anchoring off Staten Island. He sent a message to Colve telling him he had orders to receive the province from him pursuant to the peace treaty signed by their respective governments.[15]

On November 10, Colve surrendered the city and fort to Andros, asking that certain privileges be granted. Among those was his request that the personal debts of the English officers still standing from the time of the Dutch capture be paid; that sentence and judgments passed during his administration should stand; that the Dutch citizens be allowed to retain their church privileges; that the West India Company's creditors be paid; that the tax which he had levied on exported beavers and other peltries to pay for building fortifications be allowed to stand. Andros, who had orders to receive the settlement in a friendly manner, with kindness to the Dutch, agreed in principle with the requests. Colve absolved the burgomasters and schepens of their oaths of allegiance to the Dutch, and Andros reinstated the former laws and courts that had existed under Lovelace's administration.

On the Delaware, the magistrates in office at the time of the Dutch attack were also reinstated to their former positions. There was an important exception: Peter Alricks was removed from office "he having proferr'd himself to ye Dutch at their first coming, of his own Motion and acted very violently (as their cheife Officer) ever since." [16] In his stead, Captain Edmund Cantwell and Mr. William Tom were commissioned to take possession of the fort at New Castle and the military stores, and Cantwell was authorized to administer the oath of allegiance to the newly-appointed commissaries. William Tom had been a collector of quit rents under the Lovelace administration and Cantwell high sheriff at New Castle.

When the mixed population of Dutch, Swedish, Finnish, and English colonists on the Delaware learned that the government of His Highness, the Duke of York, had again regained control, it caused them little concern. Among the justices newly appointed by Governor Andros, Hans Block, John Moll, Peter Cock, Israel Holm and others of both Dutch and Swedish origins were also well known to the common people, having, like Cantwell and Tom, served in previous regimes. The people were already familiar with the Duke of York's Laws published March 1, 1664, under which they had lived for nine years prior to the Dutch recapture.[17]

There was, however, an area of contention on the Delaware that caused the residents concern, and that was the Hoerenkil, which was still claimed by Lord Baltimore. Andros, new on the scene, was unaware of all the incidents that had occurred before his arrival, and he was not familiar with all the details in the dispute with Maryland about the extent of the Duke's province. Immediately upon taking office, he wrote the governors of Maryland and Virginia to advise them that the territory was again under the government of the Duke of York. He said he had issued orders to his subjects that nothing be done by the residents to injure the neighboring colonies, and he hoped the two governors would do likewise.[18] The Maryland government at the time was again having serious Indian troubles, this time with the Susquehanna-Minquas, and this took precedence over land matters. Meanwhile, Andros had appointed magistrates for the Hoerenkil, and the older residents there, now recovered from Captain Howell's assault, had been joined by new colonists, and a number of additional homes were built.

Captain Cantwell wrote Andros in May of 1676 that the people living at the Hoerenkil were anxious to receive patents for their lands because there is dispute over "where they live and under whoos governmt." [19] Hermanus Wiltbanck also sent several communications from the Hoerenkil, where he still resided, notifying Andros that it was reported that Lord Baltimore intended to have the Hoerenkil again, and that Maryland surveyors were again surveying the lands.[20]

Meanwhile, in Maryland, Governor Thomas Notley on June 24, 1677, took notice that there were several persons seated at the Hoerenkil on the seaboard side of the province who pretended to be under the government of New York. A special warrant was granted to William Stevens for 8,000 acres on the seaboard to be proportioned among those who would seat the area, with seven years liberty to land paying his lordship two shillings rental yearly for every 100 acres. Those that seated nearest the Hoerenkil shall have "one thousand acres of land for a family haveing in itt three working hands at the least." [21]

It was also decided that a letter should be sent to Governor Andros in New York asking whether those encroached on the land "do own him for their governor," that there might be a satisfactory understanding between the two governments.

By 1680, the Hoerenkil had grown to such a point that the residents urged the government to build a prison, courthouse, stocks, and a whipping post. The occupants were also agitating to give the settlement a new name, because of the unfavorable connotations of the English equivalent, Whorekill, which was now widely used to designate the area.[22] Despite the fact that the Duke of York's administrative officers were now well established, and the people looked to Andros as their governor, they were still apprehensive about Lord Baltimore. On August 10, 1681, two residents wrote that they expected Lord Baltimore to come any day and subdue them by force. They emphasized that a few years before they had seen houses burned and provisions destroyed, which might happen to them if they opposed Lord Baltimore. They reported that Lord Baltimore had proclaimed that he would support and protect those who received title to their lands from him; otherwise he would take away all the privileges of those living under the Duke of York's government.[23]

Thus the controversy over the Delaware between the Duke of York's government and Lord Baltimore, which had begun many years ago with Colonel Utie's mission, continued unresolved. It was still unsettled on October 27, 1682, when William Penn arrived at New Castle as the new proprietor of the disputed lands.

14
Conclusion

≈≈≈≈≈≈≈≈≈≈≈≈≈≈≈≈≈≈≈≈≈≈≈≈≈≈≈≈≈≈≈≈≈≈≈

When William Penn petitioned for his charter for Pennsylvania, the differences between the Duke of York and Charles Calvert, the then Lord Baltimore, over ownership of the lands along Delaware Bay and River were still unsettled, although on two occasions hearings had been set before the Privy Council, but no action taken.

In obliging Penn (and conveniently settling the £15,000 debt that Charles II owed Penn's late father, Vice-Admiral Penn), the Crown's problem was how to dovetail the patent for Pennsylvania with the borders of the neighboring colonies without affronting other grantees. From the beginning, Penn wanted to secure for his province a clear and certain water route to the sea—and that meant access to Delaware River and Bay. His petition was referred to the Committee for Trade and Foreign Plantations, and at the very outset he ran into conflict with the bounds of Maryland, as well as the pretensions of the Duke of York. Penn's petition encountered much and various opposition, particularly from agents of the Duke (who was in Edinburgh, temporarily banished from his brother's court) and Lord Baltimore (who was then in America).

In the negotiations, Penn played a skillful part, finally winning the Duke's support and the cooperation of Sir John Werden, the Duke's secretary. It was Werden who, acting under the Duke's instructions, altered the bounds described in the first petition so that they were acceptable to Penn and the Duke of York, as well as Lord Baltimore's agent.[1]

In the charter, as finally approved by Charles II, the southern bound of Pennsylvania was given as "a circle drawne at 12 miles distance from Newcastle Northwards and Westwards unto the beginning of the fortyeth degree of Northern Latitude." This eliminated any conflict between Penn's patent and the Duke's pretension to the lands at and near New Castle and with his claim to lands running southward to Cape Henlopen including the Whorekill settlement. But the description, as time would prove, could not be reconciled with the geography. A circle drawn on a 12-mile radius from New Castle did not touch the 40th parallel for the simple reason that the line lay north of the circle.

On none of the contemporary maps was the 40th parallel accurately located. For example, John Smith's map, and a map published by Lord Baltimore in 1635 to accompany *A Relation of Maryland*[2] show the 40th parallel well to the south of its actual location. Penn was to be plagued with the same anomaly as Lord Baltimore, whose charter, as the reader saw in an earlier chapter, assumed that the 40th parallel crossed Delaware Bay, which it does not. Incomplete and inaccurate information in England about Delaware Bay and river was at the root of the controversy that ultimately developed between Penn and Lord Baltimore about certain of their bounds.

Penn's eastern bound was given in his charter as the Delaware River "from 12 miles distance northwards of New

Castle Towne." What this meant was that the western bank of the Delaware River *south* of the 12-mile circle continued to be owned by the Duke of York, but Penn owned the same bank *north* of the 12-mile circle. This, too, was an unusual situation and one that Penn found intolerable. To reach Philadelphia from the ocean Penn had to sail up a river whose western bank, as far north as the southern boundary of Pennsylvania was claimed by the Duke of York. The Duke's town of New Castle, which then dominated the river, stood as a formidable barrier between his province and the sea. Penn knew that several years before burdensome duties had been levied at New Castle and the Whorekill, in the name and authority of the Duke, amounting to 10% on all goods imported from Europe and on all furs and peltries exported. These duties were also applicable to the Quaker settlers along the opposite side of the Delaware in West Jersey, and although Penn was instrumental in having them lifted, there was no assurance they would not be reinstated at some future date.

To complicate the situation even further, Lord Baltimore continued to assert his rights to the west bank of the Delaware River south of the 40th parallel. Penn was apprehensive lest the future find the Duke of York and Lord Baltimore in open controversy, and no matter who emerged victorious, free navigation rights to the Delaware might be denied his settlers. Even though Penn was on friendly terms with the Duke, he knew enough about this conniving man not to trust his future actions. Penn's only practical recourse to protect his province was to find some way of controlling the western shore of the Delaware River. He was not worried about the eastern shore of the river because that area was in the possession of friendly Quakers.

In the spring following application for his charter, Penn opened negotiations with the Duke to acquire the Duke's lands along the river and bay. He was fully aware that possession of the territory would inevitably bring him into conflict with Lord Baltimore, but that was the risk he was willing to take as the lesser of two evils. Initially, the Duke was not disposed to divest himself of any of the lands under his jurisdiction and he declined Penn's offer.[3]

The details of the further negotiations between Penn and the Duke are not known, and their bargaining was of a personal nature not formally recorded. Penn was persistent, and in due time won over the Duke to his argument. On August 24, 1682, the Duke executed four legal documents conveying his lands along the Delaware to Penn. Much has been written about this transaction, which I will only briefly summarize.

The first document was a valid and effective lease for 10,000 years for all the land below the southern border of Pennsylvania and within the 12-mile circle, including the town of New Castle. The second document was an absolute deed, or in legal language, a Deed of Feoffment, for the same area. The third was a legally valid lease for 10,000 years for all the land south of the 12-mile circle, extending down the River to Cape Henlopen, including the Whorekill. The fourth was a Deed of Feoffment for the latter territory.

As a consideration for the land at New Castle and within the 12-mile circle, Penn agreed to pay the Duke, or his heirs, a token rental of five shillings annually at the Feast of St. Michael the Archangel, when demanded. For the land below the circle extending to Cape Henlopen Penn agreed to pay the Duke, or his heirs, one rose at the Feast of St. Michael annually when demanded, as well as one-half of all the rents or profits he collected from tenants on the land, to be paid also on the same day.[4]

The most interesting facet of this transaction is the fact that the Duke of York did not have legal title to the lands

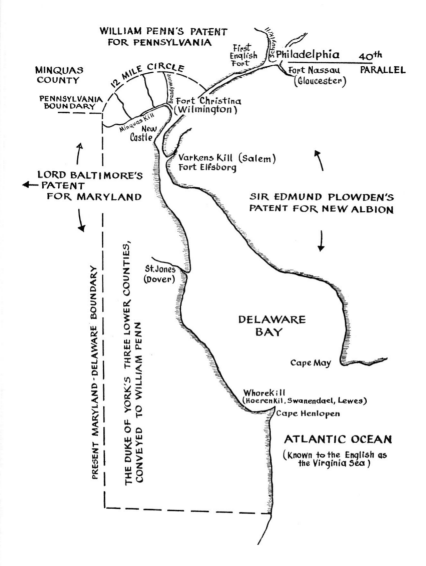

Lord Baltimore's Maryland patent overlapped the Duke of York's three lower counties lying below Penn's Patent of Pennsylvania. Penn's acquisition of the lower counties led to conflict with Lord Baltimore, ultimately decided in Penn's favor.

he conveyed to Penn. He possessed the territory along the western shore of the river, with the knowledge and consent of his royal brother, as part of the spoils of the 1664 campaign against the New Netherland, but the King had not patented it to him. This omission was remedied on March 22, 1683 (seven months after he executed the four documents to Penn) when the Duke received a royal grant for the lands he had already conveyed. The Duke had sold what he did not legally possess, and retroactively (through what lawyers usually term "covenants for future assurance") he made the transaction a legal one. Yet, while the instrument was being drawn up to legalize the conveyance to Penn, both the King and his brother were fully aware that Lord Baltimore's charter encompassed the identical territory!

Arriving at New Castle, October 27, 1682, on his first visit to America, Penn took possession of the town and the lands along the river extending south to Cape Henlopen. Through the ancient ceremony of livery and seisin he became the new proprietor of the Duke's province by accepting from the town's commissioners "one Turf with a Twigg upon it," and "a porringer with River water and Soyle."

Penn's legacy from the Duke of York was an uncertain land title and the problems and controversies that had plagued three nations in the long struggle for control of the Delaware valley. He inherited the remnants of the wasted Lenni Lenape tribe who had been mistreated by both traders and settlers; he inherited land intrigue; he inherited the aftermath of wars and changing administrations resulting from European power politics; and he inherited a suspicious population with its Swedish, Finnish, Dutch, and English factions, some of whom were even hostile to him. Above all, he inherited the mistrust of the Calverts, the resentment of the heirs of Sir Edmund Plowden, and the jealousy of New Haven merchants, all of whom had claims to the lands along the Delaware that Charles II and his scheming brother James, Duke of York, chose to ignore in favor of their own selfish interests.

Without laboring the details of the conflict that developed between William Penn and Lord Baltimore, and their early confrontations, suffice it to say that the case was ultimately referred to the Committee for Trade and Foreign Plantations. At the very beginning the matter of *hactenus inculta* loomed as a basic issue. In a session held June 12, 1683, the Committee phrased the question as follows:

"Whether, in the Year 1632, the Dutch were possessed of the Lands claimed by Mr. Penn; which Mr. Penn's Agent undertakes to prove, in a short time, and their Lordships will then take this Matter into further Consideration." [5]

The argument before the Committee was advanced at first by agents representing Penn and Baltimore who were both in America, but no decision could be made until they returned to England to present their claims in person. On September 2, 1685, following a session of the Committee when the two principals were present, it was recorded that, "Mr. Penn having produced divers Proof to make out that the Country of Delaware was inhabited by the Swedes and Dutch before the Date of my Lord Baltimore's Patent," the said "Evidences and Proofs" were loaned to Baltimore for study to enable him to make further argument. [6]

This evidence consisted of depositions taken from early Dutch and Swedish settlers, which Penn had obtained in America and which clearly showed that the Dutch had settled the Whorekill and elsewhere on the Delaware prior to 1632, when Lord Baltimore's charter passed the Great Seal. [7]

When the hearings were resumed on October 8, Baltimore presented an account indicating "in the year 1642, one Ployden [Plowden] sailed up the Delaware River, and did

not see any House there at the time," and he also introduced a deposition by Garrett Van Sweeringen which he
thought would help his case.[8]

The hearings continued, and on November 7 their lordships resolved to report their opinion to His Majesty the
King along the following lines:

> That for avoiding further Differences, the Tract of Land
> lying between the River and Bay of Delaware, and the East-
> ern Sea, on the West side, and Cheasepeak Bay on the other,
> be divided into two equal Parts, by a Line from the Latitude
> of Cape Hinlopen, to the 40th Degree of Northern Latitude;
> and that one half thereof, lying toward the Bay of Delaware
> and the Eastern Sea, be adjudged to belong to his Majesty;
> and that the other half remain to the Lord Baltimore, as com-
> prised within his Charter.[9]

The reference to "his Majesty" was none other than the
former Duke of York, now James II, who had acceded to
the throne following the death of Charles II. Undoubtedly
the part James played in deeding the land to Penn in the
first place had a strong influence on the decision rendered
by their lordships. Had they decided in favor of Lord Baltimore it would have placed the reigning monarch in the
embarrassing position of having conveyed land to one subject which was legally owned by another. Little wonder they
seized on the technicality of *hactenus inculta* as the legal
loophole to validate Penn's claim. Then to soothe Baltimore's ire they generously returned to him half the territory
that he already owned!

The official decision was rendered on November 13, 1685,
at the court at Whitehall in the presence of the King and
the honorable Lords of the Committee for Trade and Foreign Plantations. Having examined the matter in dispute

concerning a Tract of Land, in America, called De La Ware, Their Lordships find that the Land intended to be granted to the Lord Baltimore's Patent, was only Land uncultivated and inhabited by Savages. And that this Tract of Land, now in Dispute, was inhabited and planted by Christians, at and before the Date of the Lord Baltimore's Patent . . .[10]

They recommended dividing the territory, as they had agreed on November 7, "His Majesty, well approving of the said Report."

On two later occasions, during the reign of Queen Anne, Lord Baltimore attempted to have the order of 1685 laid aside, but he was not successful.[11] The decision had resolved for all time the principle at issue; namely, on the basis of *hactenus inculta,* Penn became the owner of the seaboard side of the peninsula, giving him access by water to his colony. It is true, however, that the dispute was not settled, because the question of Baltimore's northern bound, and how to project lines on the peninsula to divide the territory in compliance with the order of 1685, continued to be a point of contention. After Penn's death in 1718, the boundary dispute was continued by his heirs in conflict with the heirs of Charles Calvert, whose death preceded Penn's. At one stage in the long litigation, the Calvert heirs attempted to reopen the *hactenus inculta* question by claiming "not withstanding these words were in the Preamble, yet, they were not inserted by way of Restriction in the body or granting Part of the Defendants said Charter." [12] Their argument, however, did not shake the 1685 decision, which stood as a finding of fact.

In 1732, an agreement was reached with articles drawn and signed, but a fresh controversy arose over the location of the true Cape Henlopen, a benchmark in the dividing line, as opposed to what was termed the "false cape" at present Fenwicks Island. A decree in favor of the Penns in 1750, assessing the costs against the Calverts, did not settle the dispute and the surveyors John Watson, in 1750–1751, and Charles Mason and Jeremiah Dixon, in 1763–1767, were engaged to run survey lines acceptable to both parties. After almost a century of argument and controversy, the division of the territory was approved in 1769 by George III.

The territory legalized to Penn in the 1685 decision became known as "the three lower counties" of Pennsylvania. These three counties formed their own assembly in 1704 and became a colony of the Crown. In September of 1776 a convention of delegates from the lower counties met at New Castle and framed a constitution for "the Delaware State," and today these selfsame counties—New Castle, Kent, and Sussex—constitute the state of Delaware. If the decision of 1685 had been favorable to Lord Baltimore this territory would have become part of Maryland. The identity of Delaware as a separate state was rooted in the Dutch settlement at the Whorekill (present Lewes and originally Swanendael) which permitted Penn to invoke the *hactenus inculta* question, the legal basis on which his ownership was adjudged.

*　　*　　*　　*

West Jersey was the name given by the English to that part of the present state of New Jersey that bordered on the Delaware River. European possession of the area dated from Fort Nassau, built by the Dutch in 1626, and the Indian purchase made by Peter Hollander Ridder on behalf of the Swedes in 1641. As a further step in Swedish territorial expansion—and to block the English from New Haven—Ridder bought the land from present Raccoon Creek to Cape May from the Lenni Lenape chiefs. Whether or not any Swedes settled there following the purchase of the land is unknown, although it is unlikely, for the main settlements were then in the process of being established along the western shore. There was little reason for Swedish or Finnish farmers to cross the river at this early date and separate themselves from their countrymen on the west shore, where land was freely available.

When Printz built Fort Elfsborg in 1643, it is possible that some members of the Swedish garrison may have erected log cabins and cultivated the land in the vicinity of the fort. It is a certainty that the first documented occupancy by Swedes and Finns in West Jersey occurred in the area between Salem Creek and Raccoon Creek, although this was merely an offshoot of the main area of occupation on the west bank of the river which was the nucleus of Swedish, later Dutch and English activities. The political center in the 17th century never moved from the western side of the river, the area now encompassed by the State of Delaware.

English occupancy began with the New Haven settlements on the Varkens Kill in 1641 or 1642, as discussed in earlier chapters. When Sir John Berkeley and Sir George Carteret received their grant from the Duke of York in 1664 the area was wide open for English expansion, although their colonization efforts were far less aggressive than the Duke might have expected. The new proprietors commissioned Philip Carteret, a relative of Sir George's, as their first governor. He arrived in 1665 with a small party of settlers, but he gave little attention to the land area bordering the Delaware River, still occupied by a few scattered Swedes and Finns, but concentrated his attention on East Jersey. The whole area, however, remained under the joint proprietorship of Berkeley and Carteret for about 10 years.

As late as 1672 there were still only sparse settlements in West Jersey, and the Quaker, George Fox, described his visit that year as follows: "Then we had that wilderness country to pass through, since called West Jersey, not then inhabited by English; so that we have travelled a whole day together without seeing man or woman, house or dwelling place. Sometimes we lay in the woods by a fire, and sometimes in the Indian wigwams or houses." [13]

In 1674, Berkeley turned over his proprietary rights in New Jersey to two Quakers, John Fenwick and Edward Byllynge, for £1,000. As time went on, the two co-owners quarreled about their respective shares, and the Friends in London, who opposed their members taking their differences to court for settlement, prevailed on the two proprietors to submit their dispute to William Penn for arbitration in 1676.

A basis for dividing the territory was agreed upon, but Byllynge's insolvency resulted in Penn and two other Quakers being named as trustees to accommodate Byllynge's creditors. Meanwhile, Fenwick settled at Salem in 1675 with his family and a few friends and disposed of 148,000 acres to about 50 purchasers, many of whom settled on the lands. Soon he, too, was in financial difficulties, and Penn and the other two trustees acquired control of part of his land.

The upshot of these tangled land matters was a division of the territory into East Jersey and West Jersey, with the latter passing into the hands of the Quakers.

When Edmund Andros arrived at New York in 1674 as governor, his authority from the Duke of York included jurisdiction over New York, as well as New Jersey, despite the fact that the Duke had transferred the New Jersey territory to Berkeley and Carteret a decade before. The Duke completely ignored his former grant, and he treated the east bank of the river (as well as the west bank) as part of his domain. As a result of a strongly-worded Quaker remonstrance, perhaps inspired by Penn, the Duke was finally persuaded to accept New Jersey as independent of New York, which brought an end to Andros' control.

I can add nothing to Pomfret's thorough and detailed study of the English settlements in New Jersey, and a repetition of his account seems unwarranted.[14] After Penn's followers settled in Pennsylvania, the pages of a new chapter opened on both sides of the Delaware River, and this story has been fully told in the histories of New Jersey, Delaware, and Pennsylvania.

*   *   *   *

An epilogue to the story of the English activities along the Delaware is the final effort made by an heir of Sir Edmund Plowden to assert what he believed were his undisputed legal rights to the territory granted his ancestor.

Thomas Plowden, the second son of Sir Edmund, who received the New Albion charter as part of his father's estate, did nothing about it. He made no further effort to continue his father's colonizing attempts, nor did he protest the King's grant to the Duke of York in 1664, which included much, if not all, of the territory embraced in the charter. Today, when one considers that the state of New Jersey, the heart of New Albion, with its cities, towns, universities, and industrial establishments, has a worth of billions of dollars, it seems incredible that a man possessing legal ownership would allow ancestral property to be confiscated by a scratch of the pen without a word of protest.

In 1698, Thomas Plowden devised the New Albion charter to his son Francis. As the reader has seen in an earlier chapter, the document was in the custody of his son-in-law when Francis drew his last will and testament. After his death the charter somehow vanished and has not been seen since.

The years passed, and in 1773, one of Sir Edmund's great-great-grandsons, Francis Plowden of Plowis Arms, Welshpool, revived the New Albion claim, which had then lain

dormant for more than a century. It seems that Francis
Plowden discovered the official enrollment copy of the charter in Dublin and recognized its significance. On good legal
advice, he petitioned the King, requesting that he be restored to the enjoyment of the family tract and collect compensation from those illicitly living on it.

His petition was referred to the Lords of the Committee
of Council for Plantation Affairs, and thence to the Lords
Commissioners for Trades and Plantations, neither of whom
took any action. The petition was evidently circulated from
desk to desk until it was pigeon-holed by one of the King's
ministers who may have considered it as coming from some
crackpot. The clouds of the American Revolution were
gathering, and there were graver problems at court than a
document purported to have originated with an alleged fifth
Earl Palatine of New Albion claiming restitution of a family
estate in far-away America. There the matter rested for a
number of years.

Following the close of the Revolution, Francis Plowden
renewed his efforts to gather profits from New Albion, now
part of a former British colony that had become an independent state. In 1784, he printed a pamphlet bearing the
unwieldy title of *The Finest Part of America to Be Sold or
Lett, From Eight Hundred to Four Thousand Acres, in a
form, All that Entire Estate, called Long Island, In New
Albion, lying near New York.* In the pamphlet he asserted
his inherited rights to New Albion and offered to sell or
lease acreage to potential lessees. The pamphlet, now a collector's item, because only six copies are known to exist,
included what was purported to be an accurate English
translation of the Latin text of the original charter (although
it was not a faithful translation), as well as other relevant
documentation.

About the same time, Francis Plowden sold part interest

in New Albion to Charles Varlo, an English attorney, and then appointed him governor of a hypothetical colony and sent him to America as his agent. Varlo's mission was not to recover New Albion, but to sue the residents for back rents, and, for a consideration, to release them from future obligations to the Earl Palatine.

Varlo arrived in Philadelphia on July 23, 1784, his bags bulging with documents to prove Plowden's claim, as well as a supply of the recently printed pamphlets. Among his papers was an assignment from Francis Plowden authorizing him to sue for back rents from his "tenants," the unsuspecting property owners in New Jersey. That Americans, who had fought and won their freedom from England in a bloody revolution, would pay any attention to a feudal grant made by a dead king to a deceased knight almost 150 years before was, of course, unrealistic and slightly fantastic.

This did not prevent Varlo from advertising in the *Pennsylvania Journal* under a Philadelphia dateline of July 30, 1785, to this effect:

> *And whereas the said Province was privately and wrongfully again chartered by King Charles the second to his brother the Duke of York, contrary to both law and equity, therefore his, the second usurped charter, having no foundation in right; every act or sale by deed and writing arising therefrom, must be null and void, and dead in the law, facts that cannot be denied by any person of sense.*

Francis Plowden also printed a broadside addressed to the people living in the Province of New Albion informing them of Varlo's mission and assuring them that he had no designs on their lands, but wanted to issue valid titles and releases to free them from lawsuits which would certainly arise from the defective titles under which they occupied their properties.

Varlo had no hesitancy about visiting the retired American President, George Washington, at Mt. Vernon, and giving him a copy of the 30-page tract published by Francis Plowden. In fact, he sought the ear of anyone who would give him audience, including Captain Edmund Plowden, an American patriot, grandson of Sir Edmund's grandson, George Plowden, who settled in Maryland in 1684, and the noted Philadelphia attorney, William Rawle, who advised him his claim was hopeless.

Varlo also published notices in the Philadelphia newspapers warning the residents of New Jersey that Francis Plowden was preparing to maintain his chartered rights and to cause residents of New Jersey to demand refunds from sellers who had conveyed lands to them under false titles. All this came as a sudden surprise to both the present owners and former owners. They had never heard of New Albion, Sir Edmund Plowden, nor of an English royal patent for lands that had been occupied by Swedes and Finns as far back as anyone could remember.

No one paid any serious attention to Varlo's threats and promises. He ultimately realized that he was the champion of a lost cause, and that the American courts would not be sympathetic to any efforts on his part to bring his claims to the bar of justice.

Charles Varlo returned to England, his mission unfulfilled. New Albion slipped away into oblivion, and the grant finally perished 125 years after the death of the eccentric grantee. Yet, in retrospect, it can readily be seen, from the point of vantage of more than 300 years after the New Albion charter was granted, that the Plowden heirs were shamefully denied their rightful inheritance. This was largely the result of arbitrary decisions made by Charles II when he granted the territory to his brother James, Duke of York.

There can be no doubt that Sir Edmund Plowden received his patent in good faith, after observing all prescribed procedures and legal technicalities. To deny him ownership rights is to deny the rights of Lord Baltimore, William Penn, Sir John Berkeley, Sir George Carteret, and others, whose patents were no more valid than his, but who also had to fight to maintain their territorial rights.

Plowden's charter contained no forfeiture or expiration clauses, and when Charles II presumed to grant the identical lands to his brother James, Duke of York, as part of his plot to seize the territory of his then Dutch ally, he impugned the integrity of his father, Charles I, as well as Parliament, who had officially recognized the Plowden grant. Moreover, he illegally confiscated privately-owned lands and abrogated individual property rights on which English common law is solidly based.

The two Stuarts were confirmed believers in the divine right of kings, as it applied to their attitudes and actions toward English possessions in the New World. "A king," said their father, Charles I, while on trial for his life, "cannot be tried by any superior jurisdiction on earth." The remarkable thing is that English customs, language, and political concepts became dominant in the Delaware Valley in spite of the Stuarts and their duplicity, inconsistency, and political immorality.

Notes

≋≋≋≋≋≋≋≋≋≋≋≋≋≋≋≋≋≋≋≋≋≋≋≋≋≋≋≋≋≋≋≋≋≋

NOTES TO CHAPTER 1

1 *Hakluytus Posthumus or Purchas His Pilgrims,* by Samuel Purchas, James Mac Lehose & Sons edition, Glasgow, 1906, 20 vols., 19:61; hereafter referred to as *Purchas.*
2 *Travels & Works of Captain John Smith,* Bradley-Arber edition, Edinburg, 1910, 1:172. The *Patience* was "by the keel nine and twentie foot; at the Beame fifteen foot and a halfe: at the Loof fourteen, at the Trausam [transom ?] nine, and she was eight foot deepe and drew sixe foote water." *Purchas,* 19:41.
3 *Purchas,* 19:73–84.
4 *Smith's Works,* 1:172.
5 *Purchas,* 19:83.
6 In his *New World* (1625), De Laet says that the bay "has two capes or headlands, of which the northern is named Cape May, and the southern Cape Cornelius, and these two capes lie east-north-east well to the north, and west-south-west, well to the south of one another, so far distant that one is scarcely able to see across with the eye, etc.," *Colls. N.Y. Hist. Soc.,* n.s. 1:303, 1841. Incidentally, Somers' voyage to Virginia, which was interrupted by storms which wrecked his vessel within sight of Bermuda, gave Shakespeare his theme for *The Tempest;* see *A Voyage to Virginia in 1609,* ed. Louis B. Wright, Univ. Press of Va., Charlottesville, Va., 1964.
7 *Purchas,* 19:91. I am not unmindful of Verazzano's trip along the North American coast in 1524 in behalf of France and the possibility that he may have seen Delaware Bay. A letter written by him describing his voyage appears in *Colls. N.Y. Hist. Soc., loc. cit.,* pp. 41–54. See

also A. R. Dunlap, "Names for Delaware," *Names*, v. 3, no. 4, Dec. 1955, pp. 230–235.

8 Heckewelder wrote, "The name 'Delawares,' which we give to these people is unknown in their language, and I well remember the time when they thought the whites had given it to them in derision; but they were reconciled to it, on being told it was the name of a great white chief, Lord de la War, which had been given to them and their river. As they are fond of being named after distinguished men, they were rather pleased, considering it as a compliment," John Heckewelder, *History, Manners and Customs of the Indian Nations, etc.*, Hist. Soc. of Penna., Phila., 1881, p. xli.

9 In his commission as governor he is referred to as "Lord La Warr," but the endorsement reads "Lord De la Ware," Alexander Brown, *The Genesis of the United States*, Cambridge, Mass., 1890, 1:375, 384. On June 22, 1611 he signed a letter "Tho: La Warr," *ibid.*, p. 477.

10 *Purchas*, 19:86–87.

11 "I have done all in my Power," wrote an early historian, "to inform myself whether any Map or Description was ever given of this Bay and River, by his Lordship [De la Warre] or any other Person, which are both called by his Lordship's Name, before the Dutch settled there; but cannot find any Account or Description of it, either of his Lordship's or any other Person's before the Dutch and Swedes had possessed it," *A Short Account of the First Settlement of the Province of Virginia, Maryland, New Jersey, New York and Pennsylvania by the English*, London, 1735, reprinted by the American Geographical Society, Condé Nast Press, Greenwich, Conn., 1922.

Actually, William Strachey, a contemporary of De la Warre, wrote that Argall "in the latitude of 39 discovered another goodly bay, into which fell many tayles of faire and large rivers, and which might make promise of some westerly passage; the cape whereof in 38½, he called Cape Lawar, from which, not far off lay a faier banck into the sea . . . ," *The Historie of Travaile into Virginia Britannia*, London, 1849 edition, pp. 42–43.

NOTES TO CHAPTER 2

1 *Brown, Genesis*, 1:457. Brown, who discovered the Velasco Map in the Archives of Simancas, thought it was drawn either by Robert Tyndall or Nathaniel Powell. I. N. P. Stokes, *The Iconography of Manhattan Island, N.Y., 1915–1928*, 6 vols., reproduces the full map in its original color in 2: C. Pl. 22, and suggests that it probably incorporated the results of Hudson's voyage. For a commentary on Spanish-English relations see Irene A. Wright, "Spanish Policy Toward Virginia," 1606–1612, *American Historical Review*, 25:448–479, 1920.

2 Wesley Frank Craven, *The Virginia Company of London*, The Virginia 350th Anniversary Celebration Corporation, Williamsburg, 1957, p. 10.

3 *Ibid.*

4 See Sir Ferdinando Gorges, Captain John Mason, the Laconia Company,

in *The New England Fur Trade in the 17th Century,* William I. Roberts III, a dissertation for the doctoral degree submitted to the University of Pennsylvania, Nov. 1959, pp. 113–114. I am indebted to Albright Zimmerman for bringing this fine work to my attention and lending me a copy. It will be referred to hereinafter simply as *Roberts.*

5 *Smith's Works,* 1:124.

6 *Purchas,* 19:151–152. In a tract published prior to Purchas' first edition entitled "A Declaration of the State of the Colony and Affaires in Virginia," London, 1622, p. 8, the author, Edward Waterhouse, refers to this episode and Parkinson's report that a people called *"Acanack-China"* lived 10 days journey west over the great hills.

7 *Brown, Genesis,* 1:584.

8 "On Hudson's Voyage, by Emanuel Van Meteren, 1610," *Narratives of New Netherland,* ed. J. F. Jameson, N.Y., 1909, p. 6; hereinafter referred to as *Narratives, Jameson.*

9 *Documents Relative to the Colonial History of the State of New York,* ed. E. B. O'Callaghan, Albany, 1856–1857, 15 vols. Vol. 12 was edited by B. Fernow. The map is reproduced opposite p. 11, v. 1. Hereafter this source will be referred to as *NYCD.* A 1614 map by Adriaen Block shows the Delaware River roughly sketched and Delaware Bay indicated by a river mouth, both nameless. The area had been only superficially examined at the time the map was made. The map is illustrated in *ibid.,* 1: opposite p. 13.

10 One author has questioned whether Smith actually made the drawings used by William Hole when he engraved the Smith map; see Worthington Chauncey Ford, "Captain John Smith's Map of Virginia, 1612," *The Geographical Review,* July 1924, pp. 433–443. He points out that Nathaniel Powell accompanied Smith during his explorations, and he argues that Powell was better qualified as a surveyor than Smith and may have made the initial drawings.

11 *Stokes, Iconography;* the Guèrard map appears in 2:127 as C. Pl. 43.

12 *NYCD,* 1:16.

13 *NYCD,* 3:6. Sir Ferdinando Gorges, Samuel Argall, and Captain Mason were signers of the remonstrance made to the King; cf. *NYCD,* 1:58.

14 The magnitude of Dutch trading was much greater than is generally realized; see Simon Hart, *The Prehistory of the New Netherland Company,* City of Amsterdam Press, 1959.

15 *Smith's Works,* 1:258,265.

16 *Loc. cit.,* 2:747.

17 Sir Ferdinando Gorges, "A briefe Relation of the Discovery and Plantation of New England: and of sundry Accidents therein occurring from the year of our Lord 1607, to the present, 1622," reprinted in *Sir Ferdinando Gorges and his Province of Maine,* ed. James Phinney Baxter, 3 vols., Prince Society, Boston, 1890, 1:203–240. This account is also reprinted in *Purchas,* 19:269–284.

18 Gorges gives additional details of Dermer's voyage in, "A Brief Narration of the Original Undertakings of the Advancement of Plantations into the parts of America, Especially Shewing the beginning, progress

and continuance of that of New-England," Sir Ferdinando Gorges, *loc. cit.*, 2:3–81. It is in this work, p. 28, that Gorges refers to Dermer having sent him a journal. Note that "A Brief Narration, etc." was published in 1658, whereas "A briefe Relation, etc." was dated 1622.

19 This information is taken from Dermer's first letter to Purchas quoted in full in *Purchas*, 19:129–134. The letter with editorial comment also appears in *Colls. N.Y. Hist. Soc.*, n.s., 1:350–354, 1841.

20 *Purchas, ibid.* Incidentally, Dermer learned that Rocraft was slain in a quarrel after his arrival in Virginia.

21 *Loc. cit.*, p. 133.

22 *Loc. cit.*, 14:413. *Stokes, Iconography*, 2:95 states that Dermer's missing letter was written to Henry Briggs. Stokes is definitely in error, confusing the preface to the Briggs' treatise written by Purchas with the treatise proper. It is in the preface that Purchas specifically refers to "my friend Master Dermer," having written to him. *Ibid.*

23 Gorges states that the journal Dermer sent him contained a description of the coast, "A Briefe Narration, etc.," p. 28, but he does not give a date when the journal was written. Perhaps it was the same "relation" dated June 30, 1620, a copy of which reposed in the papers of Governor William Bradford, also now missing; see *Colls. N.Y. Hist. Soc., loc. cit.*, 1:346. Nathaniel Morton apparently had access to this relation in 1669, quotes verbatim from it, and gives its date as June 30, 1620; see *New England Memorial*, 5th edition, ed. John Davis, Boston, 1826, pp. 56–58.

24 *The Records of the Virginia Company of London*, ed. Susan Myra Kingsbury, Washington, D.C., 1906, 1:504. *Cf.* J. R. Brodhead, *History of the State of New York, 1609–1664*, N.Y., 1853, pp. 92–95.

25 *Purchas*, 19:134.

26 *Purchas*, 14:422–426. The map accompanying this treatise in the 1906 edition of Purchas is identical with the one appearing in the 1625 edition. I am indebted to Clifford Lewis III for bringing the map to my attention in the first place, and to Robert O. Dougan, Librarian, Henry E. Huntington Library and Art Gallery, for the photocopy of the original following p. 852 in v. 3 of the 1625 edition, reproduced on the endpapers of this volume. There can be no doubt that Briggs was the author of the map, *cf. ibid.*, pp. 411, 414. Briggs' treatise was first published in 1622 by Edward Waterhouse in *A Declaration of the State, etc., loc. cit.*, but no map accompanied it.

27 *Stokes, Iconography*, 2:95 suggests that Briggs obtained information from Dermer's lost map which he incorporated in *"America Septentrionalis,"* but this is far from a certainty. There is as yet no evidence that Dermer and Briggs ever met; nor that Dermer sent a map back to England; nor that Briggs had access to such map if it ever existed.

28 *Stokes, Iconography*, 2:96, the Athanasius Inga Map is illustrated on C. Pl. 33. Francis Burke Brandt, *The Majestic Delaware*, Phila., 1929, has an illustration of part of this map on p. 67.

NOTES TO CHAPTER 3

1 *NYCD*, 1:10.
2 *Loc. cit.*, p. 13. The West India Company executives were familiar with the provisions of the Virginia charter and knew that separate grants were given the two companies, and that no English settlements were made between the 39th and 41st degrees, *loc. cit.*, p. 51.
3 *Pennsylvania Archives*, 2nd series, Harrisburg, 1890, 5:131. This source is referred to hereinafter as *Pa. Archives*.
4 These settlements are discussed in detail in *Weslager, 1961*.
5 There actually were three separate charters, 1606, 1609, and 1612; see Samuel M. Bemiss, *The Three Charters of the Virginia Company*, Williamsburg, 1957; *cf.* Alexander Brown, *English Politics in Early Virginia History*, N.Y., 1901.
6 David Petersen De Vries, *Voyages from Holland to America*, ed. and trans. H. C. Murphy, N.Y., 1853
7 *Loc. cit.*, pp. 50–51.
8 *Ibid.*

NOTES TO CHAPTER 4

1 Both letters appear in *The Evelyns in America, 1608–1805*, ed. and annotated by G. D. Scull, privately printed, Parker & Co., Oxford, 1881, pp. 55–59. Two additional letters written by Yong give further details about the voyage. *Colls. Mass. Hist. Soc.*, v. 9, 4th series (Aspinwall Papers), 1871, pp. 81–117.
2 The commission appears in full in Thomas Rymer's *Foedora*, 19:472–474.
3 "Relation of Captain Thomas Yong, 1634," *Narratives of Early Pennsylvania, West New Jersey, and Delaware, 1630–1707*, ed. A. C. Myers, N.Y., 1909, p. 37; hereinafter called *Myers, Narratives*.
4 *Loc. cit.*, pp. 44–45.
5 *Loc. cit.*, p. 49.
6 *Loc. cit.*, p. 47.
7 *Weslager, 1961;* the full letter is quoted in the Appendix, pp. 303–305.
8 The full deposition is quoted in *Weslager, 1961*, p. 300.
9 *De Vries, loc. cit.*, p. 111.
10 Yong left Delaware and went to New England in further search of the passage. Samuel Maverick in his description of New England, c. 1660, stated that in 1636 Yong went up the Kennebec River, where he was captured by the French and taken back to France. *Proceedings, Massachusetts Historical Society*, 2nd series (1884–1885), 1:231.
11 *Narratives, Jameson*, p. 375. Note also the reference to "Mr. Holmes" in Governor Berkeley's letter to Governor Printz appearing in the Appendix below.
12 C. A. Weslager, "Robert Evelyn's Indian Tribes & Place-Names of New Albion," Archeological Society of N.J., *Bulletin 9*, Nov. 1954, p. 1.
13 *Penna. Mag.* 80, No. 2, April 1956, p. 233.

14 Yong went from the Delaware to New England waters in further search of the passage, and in 1636 was reported in the Kennebec River from whence he portaged into Canada where he was taken captive by the French. *Proceedings,* Massachusetts Historical Society, 2nd series (1884–1885), 1:231.

15 Evelyn's complete letter appears in Weslager, "Robert Evelyn's Indian Tribes, etc.," *loc. cit.,* pp. 1–2.

16 The documents he carried back to England included a letter from Governor Harvey to Secretary Windebank dated December 16, 1634, an indication of the probable date Evelyn departed from Virginia; see *Maryland Archives* (Proceedings of the Council, 1636–1667), 3:30, published by the Baltimore Historical Society, 1885. Hereinafter this source will be referred to as *Md. Archives.*

17 The map is reproduced in *Stokes, Iconography,* 2: Pl. 34.

18 *Md. Archives,* 5:273.

NOTES TO CHAPTER 5

1 Hans Matsson, *250th Anniversary of the First Swedish Settlement in America,* Minneapolis, 1889.

2 *The Instruction for Johan Printz,* trans. Amandus Johnson, Swedish Colonial Society, Phila., 1930, p. 187; hereinafter referred to as *Inst. for Printz.*

3 A. R. Dunlap and C. A. Weslager, "More Missing Evidence: Two Depositions By Early Swedish Settlers," *Penna. Mag.,* Jan., 1967, pp. 35–45.

4 *Ibid.*

5 *NYCD,* 1:51.

6 *NYCD,* 12:19.

7 *Myers, Narratives,* p. 46.

8 *Weslager, 1961,* p. 65.

9 Daniel Denton, *A Brief Description of New York* (1670) reprinted in Gowan's *Bibliotheca Americana,* N.Y., 1845, p. 13. An excellent dissertation on the Indian trade by Dr. Albright Zimmerman entitled *The Indian Trade of Colonial Pennsylvania* (submitted to the faculty of the University of Delaware in partial fulfillment of the doctoral degree, 1966) discusses Dutch and Swedish trade contact with the Indians.

10 *Pa. Archives,* 2nd series, 5:59–60; *cf. NYCD,* 3:20.

11 John W. Wuorinen, *The Finns on the Delaware,* Columbia Univ. Press, 1938; see also A. R. Dunlap and E. J. Moyne, "The Finnish Language on the Delaware," *American Speech,* 27:2, May 1952, pp. 82–90.

NOTES TO CHAPTER 6

1 An excellent historical biography of Claiborne was written by Nathaniel C. Hale, *Virginia Venturer,* Richmond, 1951.

2 "The Commodities of the Island Called Manati Ore Long Isl Within the Continent of Virginia," *Colls. N.Y. Hist. Soc.*, 2:214–218, 1869. I also want to make reference to a source from which I borrowed considerable data; namely, Edward C. Carter II and Clifford Lewis III, "Sir Edmund Plowden and the New Albion Charter, 1632–1785," *Penna. Mag.*, April 1959, pp. 150–179. I am also grateful to Mr. Carter for lending me his thesis submitted in partial fulfillment of the M.A. degree, University of Pennsylvania, April 1956, entitled "Sir Edmund Plowden's New Albion Charter."

3 John E. Pomfret, *The Province of West New Jersey*, Princeton, 1956, p. 25. Clifford Lewis III, a descendant of Sir Edmund Plowden, and the best-informed living person on the subject, tells me that the whereabouts of the original charter is unknown although it was probably brought to America by members of the family at a later date. The enrollment copy in Dublin was destroyed in the fire that burnt the Four Courts, but a certified copy was made June 18, 1881, before the fire, and was reprinted in *Penna. Mag.*, 7:55–66 (April 1883). (The abbreviation, *Penna. Mag.* refers to the *Pennsylvania Magazine of History & Biography*, pub. by the Historical Society of Pennsylvania.)

4 Walter F. C. Chicheley Plowden, *Records of the Chicheley Plowdens 1590–1913*, privately printed, London, 1914, pp. 110–111.

5 This excerpt is from the Bankes Ms. 8, Folio 15, Bodleian Library which was microfilmed in September of 1958 by Clifford Lewis III who kindly permitted me to study the complete document. Plowden felt that if the Crown would affix the Great Seal of England (in addition to the Great Seal of Ireland) he would be entitled to certain support in his colonization effort otherwise not available to him.

The processing of a charter was a complicated procedure involving a number of successive steps which included engrossing the document in the Privy Signet Office, the signature of the Lord Privy Seal, and with the writ of Privy Seal as his warrant, the final affixing of the Great Seal by the Lord Chancellor; see Chas. M. Andrews, *Guide to the Materials for American History to 1783, in the Public Record Office of Great Britain*, vol. 1, The State Papers, Appendix A, Carnegie Institute of Washington, Washington, D.C., 1912; *cf.* Charles E. Dana, *The Great Seal of England and Some Others*, Phila., 1904.

6 Weslager, "Robert Evelyn's Indian Tribes, etc.," *loc. cit.*, 1954. The 1641 tract is now extremely rare, and only one copy is known to exist in America, now in possession of the Henry E. Huntington Library.

7 *Md. Archives*, 4:205, 210, 224. William Branthwaite of St. Mary's married Helenor Stephenson, one of the servants who accompanied Sir Edmund to Virginia, *ibid.*, p. 524. Humphrey Weiches was another, *Court Records, Northampton County*, 1642–1645, pp. 237, 313. William Audley was a servant to Lord Edmund in Virginia, Clifford Lewis III "Some Recently Discovered Extracts from the Lost Minutes of the Virginia Council and General Court," 1642–1645, *Wm. & Mary Quarterly*, 20:1, p. 64, Jan. 1940.

8 *Inst. for Printz*, pp. 114–115. Amandus Johnson, *Swedish Settlements on the Delaware*, Phila., 1911, I:382 says the instigators were shot as

traitors. This source hereinafter will be referred to as *Swedish Settlements.*

9 *Lewis, 1940*, p. 74.
10 *Md. Archives*, 5:454.
11 *Winthrop Journal*, ed. J. K. Hosmer, N.Y., 1908, 2 vols., 1:342.
12 "A Representation of New Netherland, 1650." *Narratives, Jameson*, p. 311.

NOTES TO CHAPTER 7

1 *Roberts*, pp. 18–19.
2 Isabel Calder, *The New Haven Colony*, New Haven, 1934.
3 *Records of the Colony & Plantation of New Haven, 1638–1649*, ed. Chas. J. Hoadley, Hartford, 1857, pp. 98–104. (These are the original court records, hereinafter referred to as *Hoadley*.)
4 *Loc. cit.*, p. 40.
5 This statement is made by Charles H. Levermore, *The Republic of New Haven*, Baltimore, 1886, and it is quite likely that Levermore had access to documents not now available.
6 Governor Johan Rising said of Eaton that "he contributed most to the English colony and plantation here in the river." *Myers Narratives*, p. 159.
7 These names all appear in Lamberton's protests, transcripts of which may be found in *Inst. for Printz*, pp. 231–232, fns. 14a, 14b.
8 The complete Waye deposition was published for the first time in *Weslager, 1961*, Appendix B, p. 300. The original ms. is part of the Hugh Hampton Young collections of documents in possession of the Enoch Pratt Free Library of Baltimore.
9 *Swedish Settlements*, 1:201.
10 *Swedish Settlements*, 1:211. Out of fairness to Johnson, a capable and thorough scholar, it must be said that he did not hastily come to the conclusion that both tracts were purchased in 1641, and he even went so far as to question the accuracy of copyists who mixed the dates of the English purchases; see fn. 17, *loc. cit.* The English record gives April 19, 1642 as the date of the purchase of land on the Schuylkill, which is evidently correct. *Inst. for Printz*, p. 231, fn. 14a.
11 *Winthrop Journal*, 2:56.
12 The three descriptions above are taken from Swedish copies of the protest preserved in the Royal Archives at Stockholm, which are unreadable in several places. The original English copies of the protest, as well as the deeds, are missing. The Swedish copies are reprinted in full in *Inst. for Printz*, p. 232, fns. 14a and 14b.
13 In *Indian Place-Names in Delaware*, Wilmington, 1950, p. 41, A. R. Dunlap and I discuss the meaning of *Tamecongh*, and on p. 44 we indicate that *Tomguncke* could be a variant. In view of the evidence presented above there is little question that both words refer to the same place.
14 *Swedish Settlements*, 1:211, 213. The fort was later destroyed by the

Indians, see Peter Lindeström, *Geographia Americae*, trans. Amandus Johnson, Swedish Colonial Society, Phila., 1925, p. 126.

15 *Hoadley*, 1:56.

16 *Swedish Settlements*, 1:213.

17 *NYCD*, 2:144.

18 *Winthrop Journal*, 2:70; *Inst. for Printz*, p. 68. Beauchamp Plantagenet in the 1648 *Description of New Albion* says there were 70 people at Watcessit. This, like other parts of the account, sounds like an exaggeration.

19 *Swedish Settlements*, 1:215–216.

20 *Inst. for Printz*, p. 84.

21 *NYCD*, 12:23.

22 *Loc. cit.*, p. 24.

23 *Colls. N.Y. Hist. Soc.*, 1:224, 1811. In the *History of New Netherland,* E. B. O'Callaghan (N.Y., 1846), it is incorrectly stated on pp. 253–254 that the Dutch also destroyed the English settlement on the Varkens Kill. They did not disturb the English seated in New Jersey.

24 Listed in *Swedish Settlements*, 2:709.

25 This is probably the "Mr. Spinage" who returned to New Haven in 1649, after living "at dillerway seven yeare." *Winthrop Papers*, Massachusetts Historical Society, 5:357–358; 361–362. He may be the "Goodman Spinnage" who was recorded as a resident of New Haven in 1639. *Hoadley*, 1:26.

26 Charles Andrews, *The Rise and Fall of the New Haven Colony*, published for the Tercentenary Commission of Connecticut, Yale U. Press, 1936.

NOTES TO CHAPTER 8

1 *Inst. for Printz*, pp. 70–72.

2 *Hoadley*, I:147.

3 *Inst. for Printz*, pp. 150–165.

4 *Loc. cit.*, p. 113.

5 *Loc. cit.*, p. 108.

6 *Loc. cit.*, p. 217. We can discount the statement made in "Representative of New Netherland" (1650), *Narratives, Jameson*, p. 314, that Kieft drove the English away from the Varkens Kill settlement with that on the Schuylkill. The English remained on the Varkens Kill throughout the Kieft administration.

7 The pamphlet was printed in London in 1648, and I am indebted to Clifford Lewis III for a photostatic copy. The reference to Master Miles is found on p. 23.

8 *Swedish Settlements*, 2:527.

9 *NYCD*, 12:24.

10 This account as related here is taken from the deposition made August 2, 1643 by John Thickpenny at the New Haven General Court. See Appendix, pp. 260–262.

11 A complete account of the trial is given in *Inst. for Printz*, pp. 229–243.

12 Frederic Kidder, "The Swedes on the Delaware and Their Intercourse with New England," paper read before the New England Historic, Genealogical Society, June 1873, pub. in the *New England Historical and Genealogical Register*, 28:42–50, Jan. 1874, contains a transcript and translation of Winthrop's letter of March 21, 1644; also an inaccurate transcript and a translation of Printz's letter of June 29, 1644. Revised translations of both letters were given by A. H. Hoyt, *Penna. Magazine*, 8:341–342. Amandus Johnson in *Inst. for Printz*, pp. 205–223, gives the Latin transcripts and new English translations of the full exchange of five letters, including the two cited above.

13 An account of the second hearing and a translation was first published by *Kidder*, pp. 45–46. A new translation may be found in *Inst. for Printz*, pp. 244–247.

14 *Winthrop Journal*, 1:160–161.

NOTES TO CHAPTER 9

1 *Inst. for Printz*, pp. 220–221.

2 *Winthrop Journal* (ed. Savage), 2:81–82. In this instance, I have used the revised Savage edition of 1853 because it contains pertinent footnotes not found in the Hosmer edition of 1908. Unless otherwise indicated, my references to the Winthrop journal are all from the Hosmer edition. An excellent account of the activities of Mason and Gorges is given by R. A. Preston, "The Laconia Company of 1629," *The Canadian Historical Review*, 31:2, pp. 125–144, June 1950.

3 *Kidder*, p. 47.

4 *Winthrop Journal*, 1:164.

5 *Ibid.*

6 *Inst. for Printz*, p. 222.

7 *Loc. cit.*, p. 223.

8 *Winthrop Journal*, 1:190.

9 Ebenezer Hazard, *Historical Collections*, Phila., 1839, 2:214–215. This source also contains a number of citations from the records of the General Court. See also Samuel Hazard, *Annals of Penna.*, Phila., 1850, p. 80.

10 *Swedish Settlements*, 1:314.

11 *Loc. cit.*, pp. 316, 318.

12 *Winthrop Journal* (ed. Savage), pp. 250, 289. Note Savage's footnotes, and his reference to a marginal note in the original manuscript identifying Luter as one of the men slain by the Indians.

13 The existence of this document was first brought to my attention by Dr. Albright Zimmerman.

NOTES TO CHAPTER 10

1 The first translation appears in *Myers Narratives*, p. 124; the second in *Inst. for Printz*, pp. 134–135. At least one New Havener, Thomas Pell,

traded along the Delaware in 1647, and the records state that on his return from the Delaware the Dutch authorities stopped his vessel at Manhattan and made him pay duty on the furs he had obtained from the Indians, *Colls. N.Y. Hist. Soc.*, 2:5, 1869.

2 *Lewis & Carter*, p. 174.

3 *Inst. for Printz*, p. 178.

4 Why the New Haveners never attempted a settlement in Maryland is puzzling. In 1643, Lord Baltimore extended an invitation to the people of Massachusetts to come to his province and settle where liberty of religion and other privileges would be guaranteed, but there was no response. *Winthrop Journal*, 2:150.

5 *Ancient Town Records* (New Haven Town Records, 1649–1662), ed. Franklin B. Dexter, New Haven, 1917 1:54. I have normalized the spelling and punctuation in this and other citations from the above volume hereinafter referred to as *Dexter.*

6 Lindeström, *Geographia Americae, loc. cit.*, pp. 132–133.

7 *Myers Narratives*, p. 149.

8 *Hoadley*, 2:112.

9 *Hazards Annals*, pp. 156–157 for the complete letter. See also *Hoadley,* fn. 1:128.

10 *Myers Narratives*, p. 162.

11 *Hoadley*, 2:128, fn.

12 *Dexter*, 1:226–227.

13 *NYCD*, 12:39–40.

14 *NYCD*, 12:50–51.

15 *Loc. cit.*, p. 52.

16 *Hazards Annals*, p. 122.

17 The General Court, upon receipt of a letter from New Haven requesting aid in their settlement efforts, decided "we will have no hand in any such controversy about the same," *Records of the Colony of New Plymouth in New England*, ed. N. B. Shurtleff, Boston, 1855, 1:169. The second volume of this series, ed. David Pulsifer, Boston, 1859, also contains references to the Delaware, most of which appear in *Hoadley, loc cit.*

18 *Hazards Annals*, pp. 128–129; *NYCD*, 12:69.

19 *Ibid.*, p. 129.

20 *Loc. cit.*, pp. 130–131.

21 *Loc. cit.*, p. 132.

22 *Hoadley*, 2:128–131.

23 *Ibid.*

24 *Dexter*, 1:236–237.

25 Eva L. Butler & C. A. Weslager, "Thomas Doxey's Letter from the Delaware," *Delaware History*, 8:1, pp. 51–53, March 1958.

26 *Hoadley*, 1:131 fn. Goodyear held a number of political offices in New Haven. He aided in building the "Great Ship" in 1646–1647 on which he and his wife and others (including Lamberton, Turner, etc.) were lost. See "Historical Sketch of Stephen Goodyear," v. 2, pp. 155–172, *Papers of the New Haven Colonial Historical Society*, New Haven, 1877.

27 *Myers Narratives*, p. 158.
28 *Swedish Settlements*, 2:510.
29 Amandus Johnson says that the English settlers left the Varkens Kill before 1647. *Swedish Settlements*, 1:399. But this is doubtful because "Mr. Spinnage" returned to New Haven in 1649 after seven years on the Delaware; see fn. 24 Chapter 7 above.

NOTES TO CHAPTER 11

1 Excerpts from the will are quoted in "Sir Edmund Plowden's Patent for New Albion," *Penna. Mag.*, 7:51–52, 1883.
2 *NYCD*, 12:278.
3 *Loc. cit.*, pp. 201, 215.
4 *Narratives, Jameson*, p. 316. During the administration on the Delaware of the City of Amsterdam, it was reported that English from Maryland were trading at the Whorekill and were beginning to settle there. Van Sweringen wrote that the city of Amsterdam "did send us express orders to protest against the said Englishmen, and in case they would not remove then to compell them by force of arms. All this while we stood upon or defence against Maryland. A Commander and sixtene men were sent to the Whorekill to take possession againe, but another resolucon was taken a short time after to call the said soldiers back, and soe the Whorekill was left againe . . ." *NYCD*, 3:345.
5 *Narratives, Jameson*, p. 248.
6 *Md. Archives (Proceedings of the Council 1636–1667)*, 3:365.
7 *Ibid.*
8 *NYCD*, 12:251.
9 The names of some of the soldiers who deserted New Amstel and fled to Maryland have been recorded, e.g., Hans Roeloff (from Stockholm), Andries Thomasen (from Jutland in Denmark), Jacob Jansen (from Antwerp), Jan Hinger (from Utrecht), Evert Brands (from Amersfort), *Pa. Archives, loc. cit.*, p. 317; also Abraham, the Finn, and a Dutch woman who ran away with him. *Narratives, Hall*, p. 363. (Abbreviation refers to *Narratives of Early Maryland*, ed. C. C. Hall, N.Y., 1910.)
10 *NYCD*, 12:259.
11 *NYCD*, 12:262.
12 *Narratives, Hall*, pp. 314–333.
13 *Loc. cit.*, p. 324. Herrman later wrote that the maps in the possession of the English in Maryland were "utterly imperfect," and he advised Stuyvesant of the need for making a map accurate as to latitude and longitude on which all the land and streams were shown. *Pa. Archives*, 2nd series, 5:378. Smith's map of Virginia was the principal one used in laying out the bounds of Maryland. *Loc. cit.*, 16:4.
14 *Md. Archives, loc. cit.*, p. 370.
15 *Ibid.*
16 *Narratives, Hall*, p. 322.

17 *Md. Archives, loc. cit.,* p. 370.
18 *Narratives, Hall,* pp. 329–330.
19 *Pa. Archives, loc. cit.,* 5:400–401.
20 *Loc. cit.,* p. 402.
21 *Loc. cit.,* p. 410.
22 *Loc. cit.,* pp. 403–404.
23 *Loc. cit.,* p. 406.
24 *Loc. cit.,* p. 411.
25 *Loc. cit.,* pp. 401–402.
26 *Md. Archives, loc. cit.,* pp. 426–427.
27 *Loc. cit.,* pp. 427–428.
28 *Pa. Archives, loc. cit.,* p. 473.
29 *Loc. cit.,* p. 476.
30 *Md. Archives, loc. cit.,* p. 428.
31 *Ibid.*

NOTES TO CHAPTER 12

1 *Pa. Archives,* 2nd series, 5:529.
2 *Loc. cit.,* p. 553.
3 Mrs. Schuyler Van Rensselaer, *History of the City of New York,* N.Y., 1909, 1:528–529.
4 *Pa. Archives, loc. cit.,* p. 564.
5 *Loc. cit.,* p. 565.
6 *Loc. cit.,* p. 530.
7 *Loc. cit.,* p. 571.
8 For an account of the battle by Dutch eyewitnesses, see *Weslager,* 1961, pp. 240–245.
9 *Pa. Archives, loc. cit.,* pp. 577–578.
10 *The Duke of York Record, 1646 to 1679,* Sunday Star Print, Wilmington, 1903, p. 25.
11 Stocke later returned the Negroes to Alricks, *Pa. Archives, loc. cit.,* p. 602.
12 *Pa. Archives, loc. cit.,* pp. 575–576.
13 The prefix "Mr." was usually applied to William Tom's name, suggesting he was a man of substance and literate. He later became one of the commissaries in the Duke of York's government on the Delaware and also held other official positions. On August 27, 1668, he was discharged from military service and remained on the Delaware as a prominent and influential resident. *Pa. Archives, loc. cit.,* p. 603.
14 Francis H. Hibbard, a descendant of John Ogle, has spent years compiling an Ogle genealogy, including those persons directly descended from the English soldier, John Ogle, who remained on the Delaware and had 1,000 acres at his death. He was survived by two sons, Thomas and John, who were large landholders.
15 *Pa. Archives, loc. cit.,* pp. 569–570.
16 *Loc. cit.,* p. 249.
17 *Colls. N.Y. Hist. Soc.,* 2:81 (1869).

18 *NYCD*, 3:110.
19 *NYCD*, 12:460.
20 *Md. Archives*, 5:587.
21 *Pa. Archives, loc. cit.*, pp. 603–604.
22 *Loc. cit.*, pp. 586–587. Possibly Jones' letter resulted from court action in 1663 when it was agreed the committee should treat with a Captain Scott about getting a patent for Delaware. *Hoadley*, 2:515.
23 *Dexter*, 2:176.
24 *Md. Archives*, 5:56. "Hoerenkil" was the Dutch equivalent to "Whorekill."
25 *Loc. cit.*, p. 58.
26 *NYCD*, 12:497. An entry in the *Md. Archives*, 5:81, indicates that on Dec. 24, 1670, James Weedon was commissioned deputy-surveyor, and among other assignments was instructed to lay out land at the Hoerenkil.
27 Leon de Valinger, Jr., "The Burning of the Whorekill, 1673," *Penna. Mag.*, Oct., 1950, pp. 473–487.
28 *Md. Archives*, 5:111.
29 *Loc. cit.*, p. 111.
30 *NYCD*, 12:500.
31 *De Valinger, loc. cit.*, p. 478.
32 *NYCD*, 12:504.

NOTES TO CHAPTER 13

1 E. B. O'Callaghan, *The Documentary History of the State of N.Y.*, 3:87, Albany 1850.
2 *Loc. cit.*, p. 92.
3 *Loc. cit.*, p. 95.
4 *NYCD*, 12:509.
5 "Extract from the Register of Secret Resolutions—States-General, Oct. 25, 1673," one of the documents in the collection of New Netherland Papers, Manuscript Room, New York Public Library. These documents, also known as the "Hans Bontemantel Papers," were sold at auction in 1869 by Frederick Muller, and part of the original collection is owned by the Penna. Historical Society; see *Stokes, Iconography*, 6:233. They are referred to by Evarts B. Green & Richard B. Morris, compilers of *A Guide to the Principal Sources for Early American History (1600–1800) in the City of N.Y.*, Columbia Univ., 1930, p. 104, under the caption "1636–60 30 copies New Netherland Papers in course of publication by V. H. Paltsits."
6 *Colls. N. Y. Hist. Soc.*, 2nd series, 1:115, N.Y., 1841.
7 N. C. Lambrechten's, "A History of the New Netherlands," trans. van der Kemp, *Colls. N.Y. Hist. Soc., loc. cit.*, p. 114.
8 O'Callaghan, *loc. cit.*, pp. 80–91.
9 *Md. Archives*, 15:27–29.
10 Details of the attack are given in the depositions cited by *de Valinger*,

loc. cit. See also Philemon Lloyd's deposition in *Weslager*, 1961, Appendix, pp. 295–297.

11 *Md. Archives*, 2:416.

12 *NYCD*, 12:511.

13 See their depositions in *de Valinger, loc. cit.*, pp. 475–478.

14 O'Callaghan, *loc. cit.*, pp. 67–68.

15 *Ibid.*

16 *NYCD*, 12:513. It didn't take Peter Alricks very long to ingratiate himself with the Andros government, and in 1680 Andros appointed him a justice.

17 I have chosen not to discuss these laws because this subject is worthy of a treatise itself. The original laws and amendments appear in *Charter to William Penn and Laws of the Province of Pennsylvania*, compiled and edited by George, Nead, and McCamant, Harrisburg, 1879. See also H. Clay Reed, "The Court Records of the Delaware Valley," *Wm. & Mary Quarterly*, 3rd series, 4:2, pp. 192–202, April 1947.

18 *NYCD*, 12:513–514.

19 *NYCD*, 12:545–546.

20 *Loc. cit.*, pp. 571, 576.

21 *Md. Archives*, 15:153.

22 *NYCD*, 12:659.

23 *Loc. cit.*, p. 662.

NOTES TO CHAPTER 14

1 A reproduction of a manuscript draft of the bounds with Sir John Werder's alterations appears opposite p. 32 in Dudley Lunt, *The Bounds of Delaware*, Wilmington, 1947.

2 A facsimile of this map appears as a frontispiece in *Narratives, Hall.*

3 *Hazards Annals*, p. 521.

4 Richard S. Rodney, *Early Relations of Delaware and Pennsylvania*, Hist. Soc. of Del., 1930.

5 *Pa. Archives, loc. cit.*, 16:394–395.

6 *Loc. cit.*, p. 403.

7 Nicholas B. Wainwright, "The Missing Evidence: Penn v. Baltimore," *Penna. Mag.*, 80: No. 2; 227–235, April 1956.

8 *Pa. Archives, loc. cit.*, p. 403.

9 *Loc. cit.*, p. 405.

10 *Loc. cit.*, p. 406.

11 *Loc. cit.*, pp. 425–429.

12 *Loc. cit.*, p. 155.

13 *George Fox's Journal, etc.*, 4th edition, printed by Isaac Collins, N.Y., 1800, 1:147.

14 John E. Pomfret, *The Province of West Jersey, 1609–1702*, Princeton Univ. Press, Princeton, N.J., 1956. The most recent contribution is Wesley Frank Craven's *New Jersey and the English Colonization of North America*, D. Van Nostrand Co., Princeton, N.J., 1964.

Appendixes

〰〰〰〰〰〰〰〰〰〰〰〰〰〰〰〰〰

1. Document Relating to New Albion Sent by Charles I to Jamestown, c.1642

(Transcribed by Clifford Lewis III from a defective copy in the Royal Archives, Stockholm, Sweden, whose permission to reprint is gratefully acknowledged. Footnotes are by the present writer.)

[Charles] by the grace of God Kinge of England Scotland ffrance . . . defender of the faith Ec to all our loving subjects [in]habitants and other christians Aliens & Indians within the [Province of New] Albion betweene delaware bay or South River [and] Hudsons Riv[er] beinge and dwellinge or within the Isles of the Province health.

Whereas wee are informed that within these five . . . yeares since the departure of one Captaine Younge[,] Ro[bert] Evelin and others our good Subjects from the fort or factor . . . Erewomicke [1] diverse Alyens both Sweads and Duch and alsoe s[ome] of our Native English Subjects Comminge from our Province of New England have intruded themselves and without our warrant and Comission have unlawfully entred builded and Setled them within [De]laware Bay or Charles River being within the bounds of that our [Pr]ovince of new Albion wch Province wee have formerly graunted [un]der our greate Seale unto our loving Cozen Sr Edmund [P]lowden Kn[igh]t by us therein created and made Lord Earle Palatine a[nd] Governor of the said Province.

And whereas wee are further informed that some of our . . . English Subjects within Delaware bay beinge, have without . . . said Comission or warrant taken upon them[selves] our Royall Power . . . & Soveraignty within that our Province and Dominion as in making [a]nd swearing of officers doeinge Justice imprisoninge[,] fyninge & . . . [?]ige of orders against and betweene other of our Lovinge [subjects] and inhabitants all wch have both by the Common Law of [England] and the Severall Statutes of our Royall Progenitors Kinge [Richard] the 3d and Richard the 2d[,] Kings of England the doers hereof . . . declared and Judged the highest Delinquents and to have . . . the penalty of their said Statutes of Provision and . . . have been therefore put out of the said Kinges [domin]ion and declared as enemies.

Whereas we are further informed that some of o[u]r said [subjects] within Delaware bay Residinge have in contempt of our . . . soveraignity and Dominion and indoubted title there doe[live] [a]nd maintaine the title and right of inheritage of the said . . . [coun]trey to be incertaine[,] poore heathen Pagan Indian Captaines [the]re residinge[,] have by way of purchase for 20 lb or wares to that [val]lew bought the title of Some of the said Pagans and live [und]er their protection and defence.[2]

Whereas wee our Royal Progenitors Kings and Queenes of [E]ngland above this hundred yeares have been in actual and Reall [p]ossession of the said Country and territories and have had homag . . . and attournemt (attornment) of the said Indians Captaines insomuch as [our Royal] Progenitors Kinge Henry the 7th made a graunte and . . . [pa]ttents of the said Countries to one Gobott[3] of Bristoll his . . . [sub]ject who had actuall possession and homage of the said Indian captaines and King Henry the eight another of our Progenitors . . . Commission to one Hore[4] haveing taken the like possession & homage [brou]ght some of the Indian Captaines into England who therein . . . did the same and our late deare sister Queene Elizabeth have[ing] . . . made the like graunte under her greate Seale to one Sr [Wal]ter Raleigh Kn[igh]t he and his deputy took possession & homage . . . said Indians by whose Attaindour the said Provinces and . . . territories fallinge into our late deere & Renowned . . . King James of blessed memory and Lord Delaware by him [made] [gove]rnor thereof under whom Sr Thomas Dale[,] Sr Samuell [Argall] havinge made discovery in the said Bay and taken possession and homage of the said Indians there . . . said bay by the name of the said Governor Delaw[are] [of] lawful descent in right of our Crowne haveinge . . . wee haveinge made both Comissions and graunts as afore[said] taken by Divers of our Subjects as by the said Younge [and others] aforesaid.

[Here the manuscript ends]

2. Governor William Berkeley's Letter to Governor Printz and Others, March 18, 1643 [5]

Whereas his Maties Governr of Ne . . . as follo . . . as about . . .
Since Kinge Hen: the 7th one of our . . . Lord Charles famous
[progen]itors then Ki[ng] . . . upon his then discoverie and acknowl-
[edged] . . . supreme and direct Superioritie to his Mat[ies] Indian
Kings in these Westerne partes of America from the degrees of thirty
Six unto the degrees fifty or thereaboute northward, did by [letters]
pattents under his greate Seale of England grant all this said Country
and Territory unto one Cabott of the Citty of Bristoll his Subject to
be possessed and planted[,] who entered and was received accordingly
And whereas King Henry the 8th sonne of King Henry the 7th
brought some of the said Indian Kings into England whoe did theire
due obedience unto his Royal Matie. Insomuch as Kinge Edward the
6th Sonne of the said King Henry the 8th in full and open parliament
in a full assembly of his peares and States of his said Realme, made
Lawes concerning his said new Land and in pursuance thereof[,]
Queene Elizabeth of happy memory under the name of Virginea
granted under her greate Seale unto Sr Walter Raleigh Knt her Subject
all his parte now called Virginea and these Land[s] called Maryland[,]
New Albion, and New England and begann and planted Colonies and
one with 30 men and some "greate peeces of ordinances in that River
and Bay called by us Delaware Bay and by you called South River [6],
wch said plantacon then and there begunn was againe continued by
Gv Samuell Argoll and Gv Thomas Deale of Virginea[,] Knights[,] and
by the direction of the Barron of Delaware the then Governor of Virginea [Lord de la Warr] and by his name called Delaware Bay aboute
thirty seaven yeares since in ye time and raigne of the most renowned
King James of England [7] and the same River and Bay possessed
planted and traded nyne yeare since by Capt Young[,] Leift Evelin[,]
Mr. Holmes and others insomuch as the Mighty Lord and Lords of
the Low Countries by their instrumt as well as one of their Governors

in Hudsons River by his lre (letter) directed to Gv John Harvey Knt[,] the late Governor of Virginea[,] have acknowledged of our Soveraigne Lord the King his undoubted title & dominion of both the said Rivers and Countries and generall orders aboute the same made at his now Maties councell table. And his now Matie haveing made and Created Gv Edmund Plowden Knt both Lord and Governor of parte of the same Land and Countrys called by the name of the Province of New Albion from Delaware bay or South River unto Hudsons River or Monatoes. And he the said Governor haveing acquainted the Lords and Peeres of his now Maties great and high Parliamt in England of the entrie and intrusion on certaine aliens on his Maties said dominion and Province in Delaware bay or South River they by their lres (letters) have required us the Governor and Councell of Virgeina to give speedy and reall assistance to his Maties said Governor there, wee therefore being informed by his Maties said Governor there of his intended friendship good and peaceable correspondency with you there now seated and tradding with the Native. He desireinge that you contrary to the lawes of Nations doe not sell or give to the Native Indians there any armes or amunition nor hinder the free tradde[,] passage[,] residence or Commerce of his Maties said Subjects in the said South River and Province[,] and that you will recognize our said Soveraigne Lord his title and dominion and his said Governor there. Wee do hartely and earnestly persuade you to doe and Submitt to the same, that his Maties said Subjects of this Province and New England that both trade and Supply you with victualls and necessaries may be still encouraged to Continue their Commerce and friendshipp with you. And by the ayd of his Maties said Governor there you may be incouraged and defended from all Indians and enimies of wch wee desire your answere and resolution[,] resting

Yor Loving friend
William Berkley Governor

James Citty the
18th of March
1642.

To the right worthy the Governor of Manatas and to Jno Jackson (Jan Jansen at Fort Nassau) his Commaunder in th: River and to the righte worthy the Governr of the Sweads and to Henrich Hugo (Hendrick Huygen) in Charles or South River 8

3. John Thickpenny's Deposition Before the New Haven Court, August 2, 1643 [9]

(For purposes of clarity, I have normalized all spelling and supplied punctuation and paragraphs in this transcript.)

John Thickpenny, about the age of 25 years, mariner, in the *Cock* with George Lamberton in his last voyage to Delaware Bay, being duly sworn and examined, deposeth:

That he was present in the pinnace called the *Cock* whereof George Lamberton was master, riding at anchor about three miles above the Swedes' fort in Delaware River, when a letter was brought [from] the Swedes' governor by Tim. the barber [Tymen Stidham] and Godfrey [Harmer], the merchant's man, coming with him. They told him, this deponent, in Dutch, a language which he understood, that the contents of the letter was that the Indians, being at the fort [Fort Christina] the day before, had stolen a gold chain from the governor's wife, and that the governor did entreat Mr. Lamberton to use means to get it again of the Indians, who were then come to trade with the said Mr. Lamberton, desiring that they might stay aboard till the next morning, that he might discover the Indian to him, affirming that he could know the Indian that had stolen it, by a mark which he had in his face, but, though many Indians came aboard while he was there, yet he went away and never made more words of it.

This deponent further saith that he was aboard when a second letter was brought aboard the *Cock* to Mr. Lamberton from the Swedes' governor, the contents whereof he knows not, but a while after, the same day, he with Isaac going to carry Mr. Lamberton ashore to the Swedes' fort, into which being entered, before they spoke with the governor, the said Mr. Lamberton, this deponent, and the said Isaac were all cast into prison together (but a while the said Mr. Lamberton was taken forth of that room, but as he understood, was kept in another prison) where he, this deponent, continued three days, in which time John Woollen, servant to Mr. Lamberton (and his interpreter between him and the Indians) was committed to the same prison in irons, which he himself said, the governor had put upon him with his own hands.

And further this deponent saith that the said John Woollen told him that at his, the said John Woollen's first coming into the Swedes' fort, he was brought into a room which the governor's wife, Tymothy, the barber, and the watch master came to him and brought wine and strong beer and gave him, with a purpose, as he conceived to have made him drunk, and after he had largely drunk there, the governor sent for him unto his own chamber [10] and gave him more strong beer and wine, and drunk freely with him, entertaining of him with much respect seemingly, and with profession of a great deal of love to him, making many large promises to do very much good for him if he would but say that George Lamberton had hired the Indians to cut off the Swedes, but the said John Woollen denied it, then the governor drunk to him again, and said he would make him a man,[11] give him a plantation, and build him a house, and he should not want for gold nor silver, if he would but say as is said before. He would do more for him than the English could, for he loved him as his own child, but the said John answered that there was no such thing, and if he would give him his house full of gold, he would not say so, and then the governor seemed to be exceeding angry, and threatened him very much, and after that drunk to him again, and pressed him to confess as before, which the said John Woollen refusing, the governor was much enraged, and stomped with his feet (which this deponent himself heard being in the room under him) and calling for irons, he put them upon the said John Woollen with his own hands, and sent him down to prison as before is expressed.[12]

And this deponent saith, that the aforesaid Swedes' watchman came into the prison, and brought strong beer, and drunk with them about two hours in the night, and pressed the said John Woollen to say that the said George Lamberton had hired the Indians to cut off the Swedes, and he should be loosed from his irons presently, but John Woollen said he would not say it is he should be hanged, drawn, and quartered, because he would not take away the life of a man that was innocent. Then he pressed him further, that he would speak anything to that purpose, be it ever so little, and he should be free presently, but John Woollen said he could not say it, nor he would not say it.

And he further saith that the said watchmaker pressed him, this deponent, to the same purpose, and he should have his liberty, which he also refused, knowing no such thing.

This deponent, that at another time while he was in prison, Gregory, the merchant's man [he means the aforesaid Godfrey Harmer] came to him and told him they were sent by the governor to charge him with treason which he had spoken against the Queen and Lords of Sweden, namely, that he had wished them burned and hanged, which he, this deponent, utterly denied, and then the said [Godfrey Harmer] fetched a flagon of strong beer and drunk it with him, and after that fetched the said flagon full of sack and drunk that with him also, and bid him call for wine and strong beer what he listed, and questioned with him about George Lamberton's hiring the Indians as aforesaid. His answer was, he knew no such thing.

Then the watchmaker affirmed that it was so, and that George Lamberton had given cloth, wampum, hatchets, and knives for that purpose, pressing him to say so and he should be free, and he would take up and clear him of the treason that was charged upon him, and if he feared to say so because of Mr. Lamberton, he should not need to fear him, for he should pay him his wages before the vessel went, and he should choose whether he would go back, or stay with them, but he answered, let them do what they pleased with him, for he could not say any such thing, and further he saith not.

4. Elizabeth Luter's Letter to the Governor of Massachusetts [13]

To the Right Wor[shi]pp the Governor the Deputie Governor with the rest of the Honoured Magistrates together with the Deputies of the freemen of the Country now assembled and sitting in the Generall Court the Humble petition of Elizabeth Luter a poor distressed widdow Humbly sheweth that

Whereas yor poore petitioner hath lately lost her deare husband at the De la Ware Bay where he was most barborously and Cruellie slaine in his Pynnace by the Indians while he was imployed in service & traddinge for some Marchants of this Country by whom he was sent thyther & that by this meanes she is now left helplesse & desolate with a Company of poore fatherless Children upon her hand which she is unable to maintaine & pvide for, yet unto this her great affliction & losse there is another added withall, that such wages as was due unto her sayd husband for the time of his service afore his death (beinge twenty & foure pound) is detained & withholden from her by the Marchants or some of them who ought in Justice as yor petitioner Conceiveth to pay the same accordinge to there engagment to her sayd husband, Wherin her greife is the more and her condition the more distressed in that being forced to sue at the Lawe for the recoveringe and obtayninge of her husbands wages aforementoned which (specially in such a land as this is) should have bene payd to a poore widdow without suite. And haveinge obtained from the Justice of the Court a Judgmt & verdict one her behalfe and an Execution uppon that Judgment, yet the good soe awarded to her for her satisfaction were taken away againe uppon a reveiwe soe that shee could have noe releife nor benifitt by the Judgment & Just sentence of that Court & when the matter upon that reveiwe was brought unto an heareinge a second tyme at another court & soe uppon that second hearinge had obtayned a second verdict which passed one her side like as the former had done yet for all this by one meanes or other Justice is now soe stopped or Delayed that she can get noe Executon uppom the Judgement & two verdicts aforementoned nor any releife at all in her distressed Condition but notwithstandinge the Judgment of the Court & the aforementoned verdicts she is like (beside the losse of her husband) to have the wages soe dulie deserved to be utterly detayned & kept from her (and this by them that ought & are able enough to pay it she a poor aflicted & desolate wydow beinge unable to beare the want of it) unless the lord in mercie shall move the heartes of this Honorable Court to take some efectuall course for her speedy succour & releife

May it therefore please this Honorable Court to take her distressed condition into yor wise & Mercifull consideration & to take some course such as to yor wisdome shall seeme meete that Justice and the Execution thereof may be noe longer stopped & delayed as hitherto it hath bene but that the wages due to yor petitioners husband afore his decease may be dulie satisfied & payd to yor petitioner accordinge to the Judgmt already passed and the verdict forementioned and also some recompence unto her & others which have travelled in & about the same for the recoverie of it

And soe yor poore petitioner & her fatherlesse Children shal be for ever bound to pray for yor health & happiness and that a mercifull & plentifull reward may be given unto yor Bosomes from the god of heaven who hath been ever wont to take that wch is done to the widdowed & fatherlesse as if it were done unto himself

Yor wor[shi]pps poore petitioner
Elizabeth Luter

5. Letter From Governor Theophilus Eaton to Governor Johan Rising June 6, 1654 [14]

Honoured S[i]r

Upon a due Consideration of the long continued peace betwixt [these] Nations to which we belong and upon information of a treaty lately [&] hopefully carryed on, and we hope before this confortably finished [between] the Ambassador for England and the Qu.[een] of Sweden to [?] . . . [for]mer Neighbourly correspondence or the settl[?] . . . We thought fit to write these few lines to prevent offences & [mis] understandingh betwixt the English of Newhaven colonie & yourse [lves at De]laware, we suppose it is sufficiently known to some, at least, of the Sw[edes &] the Dutch & to the Indians in those parts that about or above twelve [ye]ars since by our Agents Capt. Turner Mr. Lamberton &c we purchased [of the In]dian Sagamores & their companyes, who were then the true owners thereof, several large tracts & pcells of land on both sides De[laware Bay] & River unto or somewhat above the Dutch house, or ffort [?] . . . the Originall deeds of purchase expressing the limitts & the consid[eration] given for the same, acknowledged by the han[d]s of the said India[ns & testi]fyed by many witnesses, may sufficiently appeare [?] what [?] . . . yet met with & in what injurious & hostile way [?] . . . sieur W[illia]m Kieft the form[er] Dutch Govern[or] (though herein [the Swe]dish Govern[or] Mr. Prence [Johann Printz] did then to[o] much comply w[i]th him) we [?] . . . disturbed & stopped both in o[u]r planting & trading there, is also [well kno]ne to many in these parts & to some in Europe, but we inte[nd not to] revive former differences and grievances in reference to yo[u]rselves [?] . . . o[u]r ayme & desire rather is to declare & reminde you of the [English] interest & rights there, & to provide that for the time to come [we may] peaceably & w[i]thout further disturbance enjoy the same both in [?] . . . & tradings, w[hi]ch we hope you wil[l] readily Grant, & upon due [notice] there of we

shal[l] as freely ingage not to disturb eyther yo[u]rse[lves or any] other Nation in any of their just rights, but to live [?] . . . in all Neighbourly Love & Correspondency. We there[fore ask] yo[u]r full & cleare Answer by the Master or Merchant of this ve[ssel] that we may both acquaint His Highness the Lord Protecto[r of] England, Scotland, & Ireland [15] with yo[u]r resolution & may accordingly consider & order [?] occasions & upon yo[u]r just compliance & desyre (if there be cause) we shall w[i]th o[u]r first fit opportunity find a messenger or Agent to cleare o[u]r purchases and limits. In the meantime we have both licensed & recommended Henery Rutherford Master of the pin[n]ace called the Swallow of Newhaven, that we may show o[u]r Neighborly Intentions & may open and settle a free trade betwixt yo[u]rselves & us. W[i]th o[u]r due respects we rest—
> Your loving friend
> *Theoph: Eaton Governor of Novohaven*
> Colonye and by order of thi[s] Court.

Novohaven Juni 6ⁿ 1654.

6. Patent for Land Granted Mr. William Tom for His Services in Reducing Fort Amstel, June 20, 1665 [16]

Richard Nicolls Esquire Principal Commissoner from his Majesty to New England Governor General under his Royal Highness James Duke of York and Albany and of all his Territories in America Commander in Chief over all the forces Employed by his Majesty to Reduce the Dutch Nation and all Their Usurped Lands and Plantations Under his Majesty's Obedience Makes Known unto all men by These Presents That—

In Consideration of the Good Service Performed by Mr. William Tom at Dellaware I have Thought fit to Give and Grant and by These Presents do give and Grant and by These Presents do give Grant, Ratify and Confirm unto the said William Tom his heirs and assigns a Certain Island with A Plantation There Upon Belonging to Peter Allricks Lying about seven miles below New Castle towards the mouth of the River the said Island standing Confiscated upon the account of the said Peter Allricks who was in Hostility against his Majesty at the Reducing of the fort at Dellaware and I do likewise hereby give and Grant unto the said William Tom a Certain Piece of Meadow Ground or valley lying at the Mouth of the said river at Dellaware, between Christina Creek or Kill and verdrechts hook, being bounded on the Back side with the creek Commonly Called Brandywine Kill Containing by Estimation five Hundred acres be they more or less. As also a small Parcell of Land in the Town Containing about half an acre of Ground bounded on the south with the mill on the north by the Highway on the East the Strand on the west the Mart: To have and to hold said Island piece of Meadow and small parcel of Land and Premises unto the said William Tom his heirs and assigns unto the Proper use and behoof to him the said William Tom his heirs and assigns forever yielding and Paying yearly and every year unto his Majesty's use for and in Consideration of the said Island and Premises Eight Bushels of wheat as quit Rent when it shall be Demanded by Those Persons In Authority which his Majesty shall be pleased hereafter to Empower and Establish on Dellaware River and in the Parts and Plantations Adjacent In Confirmation and Testimony whereof I have hereunto Setting hand and Seal at Fort James In New York the 20th day of June in the 17th Year of his Majesty's Reign Anno Dominno 1665.

Rich. Nicolls

7. Patent for Land Granted Captain John Carr for His Services in Reducing Fort Amstel, January 1, 1667 [17]

Richard Nicolls Esqr. principal commissioner from his majesty in New England Governor General under his Royal Highness James Duke of York of Albany & of all his Territorys in America Commander Chief of all the forces Employed by his Maty to reduce the Dutch Nation [and] all their usurped Land and Plantacons under his Matyy's Obedience & all to whom these presents shall come sendeth Greeting Whereas there is a certain piece or parcel of Meadow Valley or Marsh Ground Scituate lyinge [and] being in Delaware River near the fort containing by Estimacon One hundred [and] fifty acres or there about be they more or less not long since in the [possession] or occupacon of Alexander D'Hinosa butted and bounded upon the South [by] the River upon the North and Nor: East by the Land & meadow or Valley in the possession of Gart Vanswering upon the Northwest by the Place commonly called the Landery [18] and upon the south and southwest by [the] Land lately belonging to John Webber now it being Sufficiently known that the said Alexander D'Hinosa then Governor was in Hostility against his M[ajesty] for which reason all his Estate Stands confiscated Know yee that by virtue of the comission & Authority to me given and in consideration of the Service performed by Captain John Carr in storming and reducing the fort at Delaware I have thought fitt to give and grant & by these presents do give ratyfie confirm and grant unto Captain John Carr the afore recited piece or [parcel] of Meadow Valley or Marsh Ground unto the sd Captain John Carr his Heirs & Assigns unto the proper use and Behoof of the sd Captain John Carr his heirs and Assigns forever [yield]ing and paying therefore yearly & every yeare unto his Maties use one and a half [bushels] of Wheat as Quitt rent when it shall be demanded by such [person] or persons in Authority as his Maty shall please to Establish and Empower in [the] Delaware river & the parts & plantations adja-

cent given under my hand at Fort James in Newyork on the Island
of Manhatans the 1st Day of J[anuary] in the 19th year of his Matys
Reign Annoq. Dom. 1667

Richard Nicolls

recorded by order of the Governor
the day and year above written—
Examined by me, Matthias Nicholls

8. Instructions for the Dutch Squadron that Recaptured the New Netherland, October 12, 1672 [19]

(Translation) Secret Instruction for the Squadron to be dispatched conform to the Secret Resolution of the Hon. Mighty Lords States of Zeeland, adopted October 12, 1672.

1

When the said Squadron shall have sailed from the Cape Verde Islands, and in the manner as has been designated in the previous instruction,[20] the Secret Council of war shall issue orders to set course for the equinox, and further use all dutiful diligence, as far as lies in their power, to pass the same as soon as possible, for this purpose also continually causing the pilots to exert and busy themselves, for the sake of duly taking care that on the one hand the Squadron shall not happen to turn upon the Bight of Guinea, or on the other hand land on the coast of Brasil, whose jutting bars it is very necessary to avoid.

2

For this purpose the pilots shall regulate themselves according to the common run and course generally followed by the Ships sailing to the East Indies; for this purpose each ship shall be provided with a passage map, on which it is noted down in writing how and where the Equinox can be most easily passed; for further information there shall be added an instruction, such as all ships going to the East Indies are supplied with, in order to pass said Equinox in the shortest time; and further to set Course to the Tropic of Capricorn which can be performed quicker in the months of December, January and February than during the summer months, as has been shown by experience.

3

Therefore continual care must be taken that all favorable opportunities be speedily taken advantage of, to which end the first and other officers of the Secret Council of War shall continually admonish, stir up, and if need be oblige the pilots, always calling their attention to the fact that the exploit be performed at and near the Island of St. Helena has for its chief purpose the observing and capture of the English East India return ships which cannot well succeed unless the Squadron arrive in time at the said Island, and conquer the same; on account hereof daily and nightly the speedy termination of this voyage must be attempted, to which end the pilots who before this have sailed to the Cape of Good Hope, will be able to be of service with their experience and knowledge.

4

The Squadron will run so far through the Tropic of Capricorn, until it meets the West winds, then to run sixty miles eastward of the Island of St. Helena, which is to be taken in a broad sense, in order not to fail said Island; and being assured hereof shall then keep their course without any alteration to the said Island, and land where it is widest, on the North side where the little church stands and the small fort is built: And when the course to the said Island shall have been fixed, and the Squadron subsequently will also arrive in the course also passed by the English East Indian return ships, it will be necessary diligently to be on the lookout for sails, in order, subsequently, to attack and capture them.

5

But before coming within sight of the said Island, everything will be first made ready in the Squadron, in order to be able immediately to land there in good order, and subsequently with God's blessing to conquer said little fort and Island. But whereas it is very important that previous information be had concerning the number of people and other strength on the said Island, the Squadron, on arriving before it shall pretend to be English and french, for this purpose displaying English flags from the ships *Swanenburgh*,[21] *Surinam,* and *St. Joris* [St George], and French flags from the ship *Schakerloo* and the *Snauwe* [brig] and, benefitting before acting in a hostile manner, by this display try to entice some people away from the land, and subsequently to detain them, in order to learn from them the entire situation; but should this not be successful, a landing shall be immediately undertaken in proper order, with as many soldiers and sailors, and in such manner and fashion, either at one or more places, as the Secret

Councill of War, according to the condition of affairs and after due consultation with all the Chiefs shall deem necessary. Trying also to take the little fort or stronghold from the enemy; for that purpose employing all possible means, either by approaching closely under and in front of said stronghold, in order to be able effectually to bombard the same from the ships or to attack in such other manner as to be able to capture said fortress in the easiest and speediest manner.

6

For the better information and instruction in this matter will be of service the description of the Island of St. Helena during the voyage thither by Admiral W. Verhoeven in the year 1608 from page 8 to page 12, besides the one in the year 1624 by W. J. Bontekoe pages 54, 55 and 56. And in the year 1632 by Seygert Van Rechteren pages 80, 81, 82. And further certain declaration deposed in this current year concerning the said Island by a Skipper and Pilot. It is also said that it is not only well possible to land in the Church Valley, but also in the Apple Valley situated on the South side where it is also said that good water is to be had. That even the little fort is so situated at or in the Church Valley that it is not only possible to bombard and attack the same from the Seaside, but also in the rear from the Land side, across some high Mountains, because, as is averred, the same is absolutely exposed and open on that side and that subsequently it would be feasible by one or two small pieces of artillery and a sufficient number of musketeers, to chase everybody out of it.[22]

7

Should it happen that on the Squadron's arrival at the Island of St. Helena any French or English ships should be found there, this country's ships will also act as if they were English and French ships, but nevertheless, must immediately attack the enemy ships and try to overpower them, without granting them any opportunity to get close to the shore or to construct there any batteries for their defence. For the sake of this attack the Squadron will previously have fitted out and ready a good fire-ship, either using for this the Ship the *St. Joris,* or any other ship or a fit vessel captured from the enemy. But since their Noble Mightinesses expect to find here richly laden merchant vessels rather than men of war therefore no fire ships shall be used unless it is highly necessary, and the hostile Ships could not be captured in any other way.

8

Their Noble Mightinesses deem it necessary here to remind their Chiefs of the seventienth article of the first Instruction concerning the improper ransacking of the hostile ships, and the breaking open and embezzlement of goods, merchandise, gold, silver, pearls, diamonds and in general everything that might be found in the hostile ships outside the seamen's perquisites, nothing excepted; also concerning the bounden duty of the Chiefs in saving the books, bills of lading, Charter parties, lists of the cargoes and other similar important documents; who [said Chiefs] are, by these presents, not only ordered on their Oath and loyalty, as far as they are personally concerned, faithfully to observe all that has been mentioned before, but likewise to take care that the same is also observed and obeyed by the other officers, sailors and soldiers or that the transgressors shall be vigorously punished as the case requires; concerning which their Noble Mightinesses will demand a very exact accounting; they will also show their indignation against, and will punish those who shall be found to have connived at similar transgressions, or who themselves have committed any faithlessness or fraud. The merchants and Skippers of the captured ships shall also be conveyed to the Fatherland, at least of each a merchant and a skipper or another first officer; further the valuable pearls, diamonds and whatever else occupies little space shall be taken to the ship *Swanenburgh,* and put in the custody of the Secret Council of War: All which their Noble Mightinesses think can be done so much better and easier, because it is not apparent that these hoped for hostile ships shall be captured after any hard fighting, but just through a simple surrender.

9

The Chiefs of this Squadron must keep in mind that at the time of their arrival at the Island of St. Helena the water in the ships shall be very much diminished, and that it will be difficult or may be impossible always to get water at the said Island, unless they conquered the same; on account whereof, for the sake of sustaining the Squadron, this capture will be necessary even though the enemy should be more numerous there, then is now supposed.

10

Their Noble Mightinesses, however, moreover leave it to the pleasure of the Secret Council of War after the Squadron shall have proceeded so far [alone] through the Tropic of Capricorn that the West winds have been encountered, then to send one of the captured vessels to the Cape of Good Hope with a goodly number of water casks, and to have these filled there in the most speedy manner with water; and further having acquired some refreshment of cattle and fruit, shall without any loss of time set course therewith for the Island of St. Helena and refresh the Squadron with the same. The vessel is to have a crew of ten or twelve under a good Commander and one or two pilots, as the Squadron shall be able to spare, who subsequently shall also deliver there at the Cape this accompanying missive of their Noble Mightinesses.

11

After the Island of St. Helena shall have been captured special inquiry shall be made whether the English are in the habit of signalling from the land, to the arriving ships, or also to receive any signs or signals from said ships. If so, what said signs and signals consist of; subsequently to issue orders that our people shall make similar signs and signals to all ships which after the capture of the Island should approach it, that the English and French should not perceive too soon that the Island had been captured, which is to be kept clearly in mind; care must also be taken, in this respect, not to be fooled by the English of the Island. Meanwhile, on the Island's high places continual watch shall be kept so as to be able to discover all ships from a distance, and give timely warning of the same to our people.

12

It is also necessary thoroughly to consider the best way of attacking with greatest success, and capturing the ships arriving there at or near the Island; whether the Squadron remains united in the bay, as if they were English ships taking in refreshments there; but nevertheless stationing one or two of the smaller vessels a little distance further from the land, in order should the arriving ships perceive any danger, and consequently attempt to run past, to be able to attack and capture them, or at least to stay them in their course until further assistance arrives; or otherwise that the Squadron station itself and take up an advantageous position at sea at some distance from the Island, thus to be able to intercept and capture the arriving ships at sea; this must be decided on after proper deliberation and with naval skill, after duly consulting the pilots, taking account of the prevailing winds at and about the Island of St. Helena, as also the Currents and direction of the tides, in order, on account of any battle or the pursuit of the hostile ships not to float so far below the Island, that the ships could not again reach the Roadstead, which might cause great inconvenience, on account whereas it is very necessary to pay close attention to this matter.

13

When any hostile ships shall have been captured orders shall be given to unload the least valuable one, and to reload the goods and merchandise, at the same time making a good and reliable inventory into the ship *Surinam;* and the members of the Secret Council of War shall take the utmost care that at this discharging and loading no fraud or theft take place, nor that any goods be alienated or otherwise embezzled, in what manner soever the same might be accomplished directly or indirectly, under penalty as has been mentioned in the 8th article.

14

After the discharge of said ship all the English and French of the captured vessels (some merchants and skippers excepted) also as many from the Island as the Secret Council of War shall deem proper shall embark as speedily as possible in the said discharged vessel, and be furnished with the necessary victuals and water to reach Brasil along the shortest course, unless the coast of Angola or some other inhabited country could be reached easier and in a shorter time. Furthere the remaining victuals of the captured ships shall be distributed among the Squadron so as to make the others last longer. Good care shall also be taken that the prisoner be not abused but treated decently according to the usage of war. Nor shall it be forgotten properly to secure the captured ships by good watch and care, and continually to keep them well guarded among the Squadron.

15

The entire Squadron shall remain at the Island of St. Helena till the first of June of next year 1673, unless it should be evident from intelligence received of the Cape of Good Hope by the vessel that might have been sent thither, or from documents and papers of the captured ships, or from the examination of the prisoners, that after said time some richly loaded vessels from the East Indies were still about to arrive at said Island, which must be most carefully enquired into, in order to regulate the earlier or later departure of said Squadron according to the [received information]. However it is their Noble Mightinesses' intention and desire that the Squadron be not permitted to remain at said Island any longer than the tenth of said month of June 1673, unless the Secret Council of War, for some evident reasons and impelling cause, should deem fit to extend or shorten with some days [the time of departure] which by these presents is left to their thorough and faithful deliberations.

16

As soon as the Island of St. Helena as is hoped for under God's blessing shall have been captured, proper care shall be taken immediately to disembark the sick, and be refreshed and thus restored to their previous health, by fresh meat, fish, green herbs, oranges and lemons, which shall be accomplished in good order, and consequently care be taken that the oranges, lemons and other herbs shall not be ruined, spoiled or immediately squandered. Good order shall also be observed and kept regarding the hunting and capturing of game in order that all may be the better distributed for the use of the ships.

17

The Secret Council of War, during their stay at the Island of St. Helena, will take good care that the ships of the Squadron as well as those to be captured from the enemy shall continually be properly occupied by a sufficient number of sailors and marines, and subsequently be commonly held in readiness, not only for the sake of promptly meeting the hostile ships arriving from the Indies, but also to be able to resist a greater force, because it might happen that the enemies might also intend to dispatch thither some ships for the protection of the Island and the expected return-ships. On account hereof the Squadron together with the ships which are hoped that shall be captured by the same, must always be kept in perfect shape, not only to be able to take the arriving return-ships, but also to encounter a strong and equal enemy, or even to be able to evade the same should his power be too great through fresh arrivals from England, so much so that the Squadron should not be able to resist the same and defend the captured vessels, In this case they shall be at liberty to evacuate the Island which, however, shall be only resorted to in the last extremity, in order through this to prevent not only that the captured ships but even the Squadron itself might fall into the hands of the enemies. For this reason it will be the more necessary ordinarily properly to keep the crews on board, not permitting them unlimited shore-leave, because on the arrival of the enemy it might often not be possible to get the crews aboard. On account hereof the Secret Council of War, in like and similar cases, shall always be prepared and guard against surprises through wise and quick measures.

18

When the Squadron shall again leave the Island of St. Helena all the slaves which shall have been found there at the time of the capture shall be taken along. On said Island will be left only six of those English that shall have been first found there, and who by their outward appearance, would be able to cause the least damage, and further ten or twelve of our people who should voluntarily offer themselves or be secured in some other way, among whom there will be one fit to exercise supreme command at the Island; also a second person to assist him, in order thus to keep possession of the Island. Subsequently they will all take the oath of allegiance, the remaining English as well as the Netherlanders, and also be promised a little more pay, until they shall be fetched to the Cape or to the Fatherland. For the use of these remaining people some slaves, if needed, may also be left behind; also one or two of the English vessels which should have been found there at the capture of the Island, with as great a quantity of arms, ammunition of war and victuals as the Secret Council of War shall deem necessary and reasonable to the greatest satisfaction of those remaining behind. They will also leave them one or two flags, in order, on occasion and when they see fit to have these displayed from the land.

19

After the Squadron, with the captured ships, shall have left the Island of St. Helena, those of the Secret Council of War shall open the second secret Instruction, which sealed, has been joined to the present one in order further to regulate themselves according to its contents.[23]

Thus adopted and decreed by the Commissioned Councillors of the Noble Mighty Lords States of Zeeland in the Court of Zeeland at Middelburgh, November 21, 1672.

In my presence

Justus De Huÿbert

9. Further Instructions for the Dutch Squadron that Recaptured the New Netherland, October 12, 1672

(Translation) Second Secret Instruction for the Squadron to be sent out, conform to the Secret Resolution of the Noble Mighty Lords States of Zeeland, adopted October 12, 1672.

1

Further their Noble Mightinesses give orders that the Squadron, on their return from St. Helena, shall set course for Cape Orange, situated to the Eastward of Cajana, on the wild coast, otherwise named Guyana, about which time their Noble Mightinesses shall take care that a dispatch yacht with further orders shall be found there, and perhaps some reinforcements, depending on the course of affairs in the fatherland.

2

Upon arriving at said Cape Orange the Secret Council of War shall take care that the Squadron and the captured ships shall there or thereabout be provided with every refreshment, and thus be rendered the more fit for the further voyage.

3

If the Lord God should have blessed the attempt against and about the Island of St. Helena, and subsequently have caused the Squadron to capture some English or French East Indian return ships, which together should form a rich booty, it is their Noble Mightinesses' intention and desire, in this case not to undertake anything further with the Squadron or to look for any more booty or captures, but that all proper care and vigilance shall be used sufficiently to safeguard the captured ships, and thus to order and regulate matters as to be able after ten or twelve days of rest again to quit Cape Orange, and on the way to enquire at the mouth or in the River of Surinam, how matters are going there, because their Noble Mightinesses intend and desire, should the fort and Colony not have been captured by the enemy, to have some ammunitions of war delivered at said fort, and as many other necessaries as the Squadron shall be able to spare, without on account hereof, causing itself any scarcity. In the meantime and by the way a small vessel may also be sent to enquire after conditions at the Colony of Essequibo, in order to find out whether the same can be assisted with some small things.

4

But if, which God forbid, the enemy should be found to have conquered the fort and Colony of Surinam, attempts shall, even then, be made to capture or to ruin in the river some hostile ships, should the opportunity be favorable, and not otherwise, because it must be the chief concern adequately to preserve and defend with the power of the Squadron, and, under God's further blessing to bring to safety the rich booty which it is hoped shall have been captured at the Island of St. Helena. On account here of the Caribbean Islands shall also be avoided, owing to the hurricanes to which they are often subject during that time of the year.

5

But if it should happen that the design and intention against the Island of St. Helena should not succeed as well as is hoped for, or that only a middling booty were taken, their Noble Mightinesses desire that in this case it shall be seen what advantages there may be obtained at the French colony Guiana. Also whether it might be possible to reconquer the fort and Colony of Surinam, should the enemies have conquered the same, for which purpose all the force, as well on land as in the water, shall be utilized. But in case it should be found impossible to accomplish this object, then to ruin the Colony, and to take away from there whatever it shall be possible to do so, and subsequently to dispose, to the greatest advantage, somewhere else of the captured slaves. And further they will see what advantages may be gained against any hostile ships about the Barbadoes and the other French and English Islands.

6

Their Noble Mightinesses are further considering the Island of the Bermudas, in order, as has been mentioned in the previous article, should the attempt against the Island of St. Helena fail, then to attack, to ransack or even occupy the said Island of Bermuda, as shall be considered best and also feasible. And further that a Cruise shall be undertaken before and along the coasts of Virginia, New Netherland, without forgetting New Foundland, subsequently capturing and ruining there whatever shall be possible; so that, should the design against the Island of St. Helena have miscarried, which is not surmised, to acquire through this [cruise] so much booty, that the expenses of this equipment shall be generously defrayed through the same.

NOTE

After maturer deliberation it was resolved not to call at the Bermudas but in case of no sufficient success at the Island of St. Helena, to endeavor most strenuously to capture and ruin everything possible at New Foundland and to dispatch most prizes from there to Spain, in order to be sold there for the benefit of the country.

7

Should the Squadron not meet with a dispatch boat at Cape Orange or there about, then the same shall call at the Island of Fayal, one of the Flemish Islands,[24] and neither finding there a dispatch boat with further orders, the squadron shall immediately quit said Island and set Course for Hitland, to the North of England, to find out whether any further orders from the fatherland should have arrived there. But if, unfortunately, it should happen, that here also nothing was found, and that, consequently, all the dispatch boats should have foundered or been taken by the enemy, the Squadron shall in no case tarry at Hitland but from there immediately make straight for the fatherland and the harbors of Zeeland, without landing in Norway, whether the course be directed along the Scottish coast and the North of England, or otherwise, as shall be deemed best and safest, either owing to information or for other reasons, which after having heard the advice of all the naval officers, and after proper and thorough consideration by the Council of War, is entirely left to their discretion and knowledge continually employing and maintaining proper military caution and skill in navigation.

8

And that the supplementary orders, unfortunately falling into the enemy's hands, should not become known, the same shall be written in cipher, the key to which is here added, in order, having received said orders, to be able to decipher the same with its aid.[25]

Thus adopted and resolved by the Commissioned Councillors of the Noble Lords States of Zeeland in the Court there at Middelburgh, November 21, 1672.

In my Presence,

Justus De Huÿbert

NOTES TO APPENDIXES

1 A place in New Jersey where Captain Thomas Yong temporarily seated in 1634, also known as *Armewamex, Ermewamex, Eriwomeck*, etc., depending upon the ear conditioning of the scribe recording the name. It was probably the site of the Dutch Fort Nassau. The name was possibly derived from the Algonkian *all-maa-wampk* (see Murray vocabulary in Frank G. Speck, *The Nanticoke and Conoy Indians*, Wilmington, 1927), meaning "point of land."

2 This evidently refers to the amount Lamberton and Turner paid the Indians for the lands on the Varkens Kill.

3 In 1496, Henry VII granted John Cabot and his three sons a patent to discover unknown lands in the eastern, western, or northern seas with the right to occupy and have exclusive commerce, paying the Crown one-fifth of the profit. John and Sebastian Cabot left England in May of 1497 and reached North America in June. They landed in Nova Scotia, giving England its claim to the mainland of North America and prepared the way for the founding of the English colonies in the New World. Although the Cabots were Italians, they were residents of Bristol when Columbus made his voyage.

4 Master Robert Hore of London sailed to Newfoundland from April to October, 1536, in two vessels, during the reign of Henry VIII. He was described as a "man of goodly stature, of great courage and given to the study of cosmography." *Brown, Genesis, loc. cit.*, 1:2; 2:926. On p. 16 of the 1648 edition of Beauchamp Plantagenet's *A Description of New Albion* it is stated: "Shortly after one Master Hore in the Reign of King Henry 8th renued this actuall possession, atturnment of the Indian Kings, brought home divers of the chief Indian Kings to England, who gave their Homage and Oath of fidelity for these countries to King Henry the eighth in person sitting on his Throne in State in his Palace at Westminster."

5 Transcribed from a slightly defective original document in the possession of the Royal Archives, Stockholm, Sweden, whose permission to reprint is gratefully acknowledged. Johnson in *Swedish Settlements*, I:216, illustrates a facsimile of the document, but the reproduction is too small to be read without the aid of a magnifying glass.

6 The above reference to Sir Walter Raleigh planting a colony on Delaware Bay was reiterated in the 1648 edition of Beauchamp Plantage-

net's *A Description of the Province of New Albion,* wherein it is stated that "Sir Walter Raleigh left there thirty men and four guns, etc." There is absolutely no documentary evidence to support this contention obviously made to consolidate English claims to the lands along the Delaware.

7   Neither Argall (see Chapter 1 above), nor Thomas Dale, ever seated English colonists on the Delaware River, nor was there an English settlement established there by anyone prior to Captain Thomas Yong's voyage. This unsupported statement was also made by Berkeley for the purpose of persuading Printz that England had prior settlement rights to lands along the Delaware. The reader will recall that under international law, the right of a nation to unclaimed lands depended upon both exploration and possession by settlement.

8   Since Berkeley does not name either Peter Stuyvesant or Johan Printz in this letter it would appear that he did not know the names of the ranking officials in New Netherland and New Sweden, which is further evidence of how ill-informed the English were about their Dutch and Swedish neighbors. Furthermore, the names of the two lesser officials given above are badly garbled.

9   Taken from *Hoadley, loc. cit.* (New Haven Court Records), pp. 106–108. In *Hazards Annals,* pp. 74–76, there is another transcript of the same deposition. Hazard has also taken certain permissible liberties in normalizing words and punctuation although he does not state that he has done so. Hoadley's version is a more faithful transcript.

10 It seems clear from these details that Governor Johan Printz and his wife lived at Fort Christina prior to moving to the new mansion, which he built on Tinicum Island. In *Inst. for Printz,* p. 25, Johnson says that Printz began the erection of his residence and stronghold, New Gothenburg, in April of 1643. It was evidently not completed at the time of the incident described by Thickpenny.

11 What this appears to mean is that Printz promised to give Woollen, a servant and doubtless indentured, the status of a freeman if he would bear witness against his master, Lamberton.

12 Since descriptions of Fort Christina are very meager it is of interest that a jail was located below the rooms, probably in a cellar.

13 A transcript of the photostat of an original manuscript in the collections of the Massachusetts Historical Society whose kind cooperation is acknowledged with thanks. Although it is undated it was probably written in 1646. I also want to acknowledge the assistance of Dr. A. R. Dunlap of the University of Delaware in making the transcript for me from the photostat.

14 Transcribed, with the assistance of Dr. A. R. Dunlap, from a defective original, unpublished document in the Royal Archives, Stockholm, Sweden. Johnson notes the existence of this document in *Swedish Settlements,* 2:574, fn. 11.

15 This refers not to the King, but to Cromwell.

16 Transcribed from the manuscript appearing on folio 15, v. 15, *Penn Mss Relating to the Three Lower Counties,* Historical Society of Pennsylvania, whose permission to reprint is gratefully acknowledged

I have normalized all the spellings except those of persons and places, and I have followed the capitalization and punctuation of the original. A slightly different version of this same document was published in *Duke of York Records, loc. cit.,* p. 26.

17 Transcribed from a document owned by the Historical Society of Delaware, whose permission to reprint it is hereby acknowledged. A slightly different version of the same document may be found in the printed *Duke of York Records,* p. 129.

18 The English rendition of a Dutch word *Landerijen* meaning "landed property," but herein used as the name of a tract of land. It appears elsewhere as "landey" and "landrey." See A. R. Dunlap, *Dutch & Swedish Place-Names in Delaware,* Univ. of Del. Press, 1956, p. 39.

19 These instructions and the second set that follows are transcribed from a longhand translation from the original Dutch made by the late Victor Paltsits, and are now published for the first time. They are reprinted by courtesy of the Manuscript Division, the New York Public Library; Astor, Lenox and Tilden Foundations. Both the original Dutch manuscript and Paltsits' translations are in possession of the Library.

20 Evidently there was also a previous set of instructions whose whereabouts is unknown.

21 Note in chapter 13 above that the vessel *Swanenburgh* was anchored off New York in the attack of 1673. Doubtless the other ships named here were also part of the squadron that captured New York.

22 St. Helena lies about 1200 miles off the west coast of Africa, and, as pointed out in the above instructions, English ships returning from the East Indies could be intercepted there. The island is rough and mountainous and covers an area of only 47 square miles. The island has belonged to Great Britain for more than 300 years, and is best known as the place of exile of Napoleon Bonaparte from 1815 until his death May 5, 1821.

23 The second set of secret instructions follows on the next page and within it may be found the specific orders in Article 6 relative to the course of action to be followed off the coasts of Virginia, New Netherland, and Newfoundland, primarily intended as a raiding mission. One cannot help but be impressed by the remarkable amount of detail given in the instructions and how every eventuality was anticipated with a thoroughness characteristic of the Dutch.

24 The present name of the Flemish Islands is the Azores. [This is Paltsits' footnote.]

25 See page 209 in the above text for further reference to this cipher.

Index